Inventing Ad

KE308 Youth: Perspectives and Practice

This book, *Inventing Adulthoods*, has been adopted as the set book for the Open University course KE308 Youth: Perspectives and Practice. See www.open.ac.uk.

Inventing Adulthoods

A Biographical Approach to Youth Transitions

Sheila Henderson,
Janet Holland,
Sheena McGrellis,
Sue Sharpe
and
Rachel Thomson
with Tina Grigoriou

Los Angeles | London | New Delhi
Singapore | Washington DC

Sheila Henderson, Janet Holland, Sheena McGrellis, Sue Sharpe and Rachel Thomson 2007

First edition published 2007

Reprinted 2009 (twice)

SAGE Publications Ltd
1 Oliver's Yard
55 City Road
London EC1Y 1SP

SAGE Publications Inc.
2455 Teller Road
Thousand Oaks, California 91320

SAGE Publications India Pvt Ltd
B 1/I 1 Mohan Cooperative Industrial Area
Mathura Road
New Delhi 110 044

SAGE Publications Asia-Pacific Pte Ltd
33 Pekin Street #02-01
Far East Square
Singapore 048763

British Library Cataloguing in Publication data

A catalogue record for this book is available from the British Library

ISBN-13 978-1-4129-3068-0
ISBN 13 978-1-4129-3069-7 (pbk)

Library of Congress control number: 2006924792

Typeset by C&M Digitals (P) Ltd., Chennai, India
Printed and bound in Great Britain by CPI Antony Rowe, Chippenham, Wiltshire
Printed on paper from sustainable resources

FSC
Mixed Sources
Product group from well-managed forests and other controlled sources
Cert no. SGS-COC-2953
www.fsc.org
© 1996 Forest Stewardship Council

Contents

Acknowledgements

In addition to the team of authors, this book draws on the labour and intellectual input of others, including Robert Bell (chapters on Work and Education), Tina Grigoriou (Intimacy and Well-being) and Rebecca Taylor (Mobility and Sociality). We are indebted to the contribution that they and other researchers made to the study, including: Sean Arnold, Emerson Jackson, Amy Lenderyou, Helen Membry, Matthew Waites, and Isabel Walter. Fergal Barr, Ian Draper and Stephen Maynard helped us with focus groups. Deborah Holder edited a full draft of the book. We valued being part of the Families and Social Capital ESRC Research Group at London South Bank University between 2002 and 2006, and the support for our project through the years from Jeffrey Weeks. The University of Ulster at Magee housed Sheena McGrellis from 1999. The Economic and Social Research Council funded the study throughout, and we are also grateful for additional support from London South Bank University. We thank the schools and other organisations, and the teachers who supported our research and gave us access to the young people. We are most indebted to the individuals who shared their lives and stories with us over the course of the study.

Part 1
Theorising transitions to adulthood

Chapter 1

Introduction: Time, place and method

This book provides a unique window on the lives of around 100 young people growing up during an important period of social change in the decade 1996–2006. A period which saw, among many other things, the Millennium, the mobile phone revolution, the Northern Irish peace process, the devolution of government and prolonged anxieties about a seeming 'disconnection' from mainstream society amongst young people.

The research on which it is based involved many, but at the heart of the study was a core group of researchers: Sheila Henderson, Janet Holland, Sheena McGrellis, Sue Sharpe and Rachel Thomson. We came together in 1996 for a study that sought to capture, describe and compare the moral landscapes of young people in five contrasting areas of the UK. In 1999 we identified a sub-group of 118 young people from this study and decided to follow them over a further 3 years. In 2001 we managed to secure funding to follow them for a further 5 years. In the most recent set of interviews over 70 were still involved. Overall then, this group of researchers have met with, talked to and sought to understand the ways in which this diverse group of young people have changed and developed over a 10-year period. This book is the result of these labours (for more on methodology see Appendix 1 at the end of the book).

During these 10 years the young people in the study followed a variety of routes to young adulthood: some, predominantly middle class, eased their way through to a university education only to find difficulty in getting a job afterwards; others left school at 16 and 'yo-yo'd their way in and out of work, training and/or unemployment; others are still in the process of making their way back into education after working for a few years. The majority are single and living with their parents, often having previously been in long-term relationship. Eight have become parents themselves. As the study progressed we also found our group of young people changing. The sample began as predominantly working class. Over time we lost young people, for whom the benefits of being in the study were outweighed by the demands. Some have dropped back into the study, others we hear of from time to time from friends who have stayed in. Predictably, the sample has become more middle class and more female over time, reflecting something about the young people themselves and something about the research team.

Time and place

The UK is a diverse and unequal society relative to many of its European neighbours and it is not possible to talk of standard 'youth transitions' in a society in which young people's lives are shaped by such uneven material, social, cultural and symbolic resources. Over the course of the book you will get a sense of the significance of locality in young people's lives, and the extent to which these places shape the kinds of youths and adulthoods that young people are able to create. The places where this research was conducted reflect the very different kinds of environments in which young people in the UK grow up: north and south, urban as well as rural, diverse as well as homogeneous, affluent as well as disadvantaged, 'local' as well as 'cosmopolitan'.

Before discussing the book itself and outlining its structure and content, we want to introduce the five places in which the research was conducted. The study was designed to maximise continuity of contact between researchers and young people, and as far as possible it has been the same researcher working with the same young person over the course of the study. As a result they have got to know each other well and formed trusting relationships. These relationships have in turn enriched the interviews and analytic process and become part of the lives of both the young people and the researchers. The researchers who worked in these localities throughout the study will make the introduction. First, Sheila Henderson takes you to two very different sites.

The isolated rural area

We wanted to explore the lives of young people growing up in a remote rural landscape and the area we found fits this bill very well. The high school that was our first point of contact was one of the smallest in England, serving an area predominantly comprised of small villages and remote farmland spanning two counties. When the research team drove in convoy for a first meeting at the school through country lanes that seemed to go on forever (with the map suggesting just a few miles' distance), we gained a first-hand experience of the necessity of long hours of travel to maintaining everyday life. For these young people, living up to 20 miles away from school, considerable physical mobility was the norm. In the absence of good public transport links, getting about under your own steam was a key marker of young adulthood.

Through the urbanite lens of the research team, it was tempting to view this area as a rural idyll: the intimacy and familiarity of the school culture, the close social networks, the slower pace, the peace and quiet, the safety of public space, the low crime rate, the centuries old houses some of the young people lived in, the extensive family networks, the relative lack of disruption in young people's lives and their healthy appearance all added to this. The same urban lens simultaneously assumed inevitable constraints on the lives of teenagers and young adults, particularly the lack of access to the leisure facilities and cultural and ethnic diversity of the city. Yet, high levels of sociality through pubs, community discos and, later, parties and clubs were evident here, as was inventiveness in accessing these leisure and pleasure zones. Meanwhile, black, urban music and club culture was a key resource for those who wanted to stand out from the crowd. The emergence over time of stories of domestic violence, parental and family conflict, rural drug use, deprivation and ill-health added further to this contradictory picture of late modern rural young life: inclusive and caring but also intrusive and constraining, especially during the teenage years.

We began with an interview sample of 18 young people in this site (10 female, 8 male) and are still in contact with 11 at the time of writing – the majority of whom are female (8 female, 3 male). We first interviewed the young people at school, but moved on to interviewing them at home at an early stage in the study. Telephone relationships with parents were transformed into invitations to dinner, previews of wedding dresses, a guided tour of the new extension. Ten years on, a drive through the small villages and farmland of the area brings a strong sense of the changes that have taken place during the course of the study. We expected this area to reflect wider trends in rural communities, where economic restructuring within the context of globalisation has involved the loss of local services and jobs in agriculture as well as other traditional industries, and increased mobility, especially for young people (Countryside Agency, 2003). At the beginning, young people tended to assume they would have to leave the area in order to access quality employment, university and/or a more cosmopolitan lifestyle. However, their attachment to this area and perceptions of the need to 'get out' to 'get on' varied and changed over time. Educational aspiration was not a key feature: although young people initially 'talked the talk' of education as the route to a secure future, few actually 'walked the walk' and although faltering flirtations with post-16 education were common, only one working-class and three middle-class (one male) young people have been to university to date. Young working-class men from 'local' families who assumed that they would stay and work in the area, did find it necessary to leave to get work a few years after leaving school. In contrast, middle-class young men and women who previously felt leaving was essential, have either stayed or returned to the wider locality. Full-time work in the wider area has been in manual and retail jobs, rather than agriculture. A counter-urbanisation trend that currently sees 90–100,000 people per year migrating to rural England was evident in young people's stories of 'cosmopolitans' and 'locals'. A third of the original sample here had moved into the area within their own lifetime, whilst around a half came from more longstanding 'local' families. The university attenders have, to date, all been from 'incomer' families. The area clearly has a strong pull for young people and is widely viewed as a good place to return to raise a family, by incomers and locals alike.

The disadvantaged estate, situated in the north of England

We were keen to include the lives of disadvantaged young people in the study and the estate we selected has many of the markers of 'social exclusion' together with a long history of targeted policy initiatives. In the city it edges, the estate has long had a reputation as a violent place dominated by gang turf wars and drug use – a reputation against which local young people are forced to measure their identities and sense of place. High crime and unemployment, poor local job opportunities and poor health are hallmarks of the area and, despite the obvious dedication of the teaching staff, the research period saw the high school where we first made contact officially named as one of the UK's 500 'failing schools'. This said, the estate is very large and by no means homogeneous. New build and the rise of private ownership have provided an increasing contrast to older, 'no-go' areas, sharpening the distinction between 'respectable' and 'unrespectable' neighbourhoods, while certain areas are located much closer to transport links, affording easier access to surrounding towns and the city.

The contrast between this site and the rural area where I was also conducting interviews was stark. The 7-mile journey from the estate to the city, for example, a seemingly short drive for a researcher (and by the standards of a young person from the rural area) was a very different spatial experience for young people living here. A strong inward-looking culture and a lack of access to affordable transport limited young people's options here (public transport involved lengthy travel times and car ownership was low), with the result that, for example, the leisure facilities of the city centre were rarely considered an option (at least until they reached young adulthood).

The spatial confines of the research were also more restricted: young people here were less keen to invite researchers into their homes. Home in this site bore the physical signs of poverty and functioned much more obviously as a place of refuge from the dangers of the outside world – even if shifting parental relationships and arrangements frequently meant that the domestic arena was an emotionally volatile space demanding considerable input of young resources. Complex, reconstituted families sustained primarily by women were the norm.

The harshness of growing up in the area was obvious from the outset: conformity was the name of the game, being different was dangerous. In adolescence, this involved wearing particular designer labels at school ('snide' or 'fake' labels invited bullying), and 'hanging out' on the streets and drinking. 'Hardness' was a requirement for young masculinities, a trait often admired by young women. Policed gendered identities continued into young adulthood: young women who adopted what they felt was a more 'feminine' appearance by avoiding standard issue track suit bottoms were given a hard time; armed gangsters wearing bullet-proof vests (the perpetrators of regular shootings in the local pubs) held a strong appeal for some young women.

Perhaps predictably given the resources available, aspirations were either pretty unrealistic (becoming a spaceman) or low, and 'getting on' was more likely to translate as skilled manual trades or office jobs for young women and more nebulous 'good jobs' for young men. Those who wanted to 'get on' through education assumed this would inevitably mean 'getting out' of the area. Although their educational paths were faltering, four of the young people here went to university. However, family allegiances and responsibilities provided a strong pull back into the community. All four remained in the north of England, with the three young women attending universities in or bordering the city and only two of the four making the break and leaving home to study.

Age and the life course took on a different meaning in this locale: early (teen) parenthood was a strong marker of adulthood, ill health (arthritis, heart attacks) a marker of 'old' age (in early 40s). Young women in their early 20s without children or a partner were considered unusual. For young women wanting to 'get on', youthful pleasures were often a luxury they could ill afford, holding many threats to their future, that of pregnancy in particular. Part-time work often had an impact on school performance, particularly for young men (who tended to have access to better paid jobs in the informal economy).

In keeping with standard research knowledge, the nature of the research site (together with its physical distance from the researcher's base for much of the study) meant we lost touch with more young people here than elsewhere; only seven of our original sample of 20 are still involved and these are mostly young women. Close-knit communities within the estate meant we were able to learn about some of these young lives through those who continued to participate in the study. These links may yet result in renewed contact.

The physical distance between these two sites reflects the stark contrast that existed between them in terms of environment, resources and atmosphere. Yet such contrasts could also be found within one city as Sheena McGrellis explains in the context of Northern Ireland.

Northern Ireland – a city in transition

A representative sample of young people growing up in Northern Ireland would have brought us to the small towns and rural areas, to the working-class inner cities and middle-class suburbs. It would have included young people living in border areas and young people from the travelling community and minority ethnic groups. For, while Northern Ireland is typically represented in the media and beyond as a homogeneous area, there are many voices and different experiences of life. Looking in from the outside, Northern Ireland is often associated with conflict and violence, sectarianism and religious bigotry. The permutations of life are overlooked in the sweep of this broad brush. In the Inventing Adulthoods study we did not set out to capture a representative sample of Northern Irish youth, but rather to give voice to the experiences of a diverse group living in one particular area. Against the backdrop of significant social and political change, their stories highlighted and echoed the complexities of growing up in a divided society and the challenges and opportunities presented by the unfolding (and faltering) peace. As the political leaders and community representatives worked towards political resolution and social stability, young people sat exams, sought out part-time work, grieved the death of relatives and peers, made and lost friends, negotiated access to expanding leisure spaces and journeyed into adulthood, and into a world significantly different from that experienced by their parents a generation before.

For despite the stop-start pattern of the peace process, and the reiteration of old political lines and positions, Northern Ireland has changed extensively over the 10-year period since the beginning of the project. As a researcher moving 'home' during this time these changes were experienced both at first and third hand. Being part of a longitudinal study offers the luxury and privilege of 'walking alongside' and piecing together biographies over time. In the building of these jigsaws lies the story of the researcher, if only as a small jigsaw piece.

Placing people in Northern Ireland in terms of their religious or ethnic background is second nature to most living there and ascertaining such information can shape the nature of a social encounter and the level of engagement. From initial meetings with young people in schools it was clear that researchers were not immune from such an attribution process. In early focus group discussions, identity positions were both ascribed and assumed by the young people, and indeed by the researchers. Identities and positioning loomed large in the Northern Irish research site.

The significance of ethnic, religious and gender identities featured extensively in the narratives of the young people over the years. It was part of their education, work and leisure experience and hung as a backdrop to the stage they chose to or were commissioned to act on. In the early rounds of the project, when the political landscape was changing most dramatically and a mixture of hope and fear abounded, young people voiced the sentiments of their communities. Growing up in a Protestant enclave or coming from a Republican community influenced how life was experienced and regarded. Hard-line views and prejudice were often voiced and excused. Losing a relative through violence, witnessing street conflict or experiencing harassment were all raised in discussion as reasons for continued fear, mistrust and segregation. Segregation in school, housing, and leisure was for most of the young people in the early stages of the project the norm, except perhaps for those who were part of the small minority (4%) who attended an integrated school and even their level of integration was largely confined to the school experience. For them, and others, experience of space was such that Catholics largely lived and socialised in one area and Protestants in another.

While it would be misleading to present a picture of happy integration, time has changed the social landscape for many young people, and we have watched and listened as attitudes and behaviours have sometimes transformed. With the expansion of the leisure industry, a growing drug culture, and perhaps the gradual secularisation of a very traditional society, opportunities (and willingness) to mix have increased, and with it the level of social integration that young people of this generation enjoy.

Although small advances in social integration are made on the home front, many continue to leave the province. Some of the young people admitted that sectarian and narrow-minded attitudes prompted their decision to leave. Others left purely for higher education or better work opportunities. While unemployment figures for the region are currently on a par with the UK average (5%), wages continue to be the lowest within the UK. Job losses and limited employment opportunities in the area where the research was located (even for part-time temporary work), prompted many young people in the study to seek out employment elsewhere. Extended family networks beyond Northern Ireland and a culture of emigration made leaving a viable option.

At the time of writing, new efforts are being made to kick start the peace process and restore devolved government institutions. Such efforts are unlikely to generate excitement among the young people in the study who became increasingly apathetic and disinterested in the political situation. Hopes and fears expressed in the early phase of the study were often concerned with the political situation and the threat of violence. The fact that such themes receded over time is perhaps one indicator that times have indeed changed.

In 1999 the Northern Irish interview sample included 23 young women and 19 young men, and in 2006, 15 young women and 12 young men. It has been easier to keep the middle-class participants in the study, and the relatively geographical mobility of young people from Northern Ireland has also proved a challenge.

Finally, Sue Sharpe, will introduce you to the remaining two research sites: the leafy suburb and the inner city site.

The 'leafy suburb', an affluent area near a commuter belt town

The young people growing up here benefit from a place that has the feeling of greenery and space, yet is quite close to a small but thriving city, or within commuting distance of a larger city. It is rural but far from remote and has been very attractive to families with a good income level. The area is sprinkled with well-kept villages where roads of large detached houses are often edged by an additional maze of small streets containing more modern and almost suburban housing. Clearly many families here are materially well resourced, and this is perhaps reflected in the high proportion of intact families, with only a few reconstituted families or single parents. They live in houses, rather than the flats or bedsits found in more urban areas, and many are house owners, rather than tenants.

Public transport is by bus or local train but it soon becomes necessary to have a car. Growing up in a village, even one within striking distance of town, means that young people are dependent on parents for lifts, which they find very frustrating. This makes learning to drive desirable if not essential, and several of the sixth formers (aged 16–18) involved in the study had acquired cars (usually through their parents), many of which were parked along the road outside school. One young woman turned heads on two occasions by arriving to meet me driving a noisy jeep, and a few years later, a racy red Chevy. Transport also affected social life, as it was hard to negotiate going to the nearby city, or even friends' houses without parents' help. At younger and more dependent ages, social life revolved around friends' homes and local parties. Over time it transferred to pubs, restaurants and clubs in the nearest town. Young people did not feel the need to 'hang around' public spaces, although several complained how little there was for young people to do there.

There was a significant smattering of students with working-class backgrounds, many of whom lived in council houses in or around the villages. What appeared absent, however, were black or minority ethnic members of the community. With this mainly middle-class population came a relatively high level of educational aspiration and all were encouraged to stay on into the sixth form. Most of these young people went on to university or art colleges, some took vocational courses, and several dropped out. It is perhaps significant that those who left school earlier or dropped out of a college course came predominantly from working-class backgrounds.

While the young people were still attending school, our interviews usually took place there. The school was very accommodating and some young people chose to be reinterviewed there even once they had left, often observing how 'weird' they felt to be back in a different capacity. Others were happy to invite me to their houses after they had left school, which cast some extra light into their home and family lives. Many of the larger villages have rail links, and when I visited to interview, I travelled by train to the nearest station and took a taxi. It was always the same family taxi firm, from whom, to my bemusement, I was also able to buy duck and hen eggs to take home. For the first round here, we interviewed 20 young people: nine young men and 11 young women, the majority of whom were from middle-class families; by the final round there were 14 participants left, as we had lost three young men and three young women.

The atmosphere of the area was one of affluence and non-violence and the crime rate was low. Young people here expressed little sense of local community, despite living in relatively compact village environments, which probably related to the commuting nature of work. Many talked of returning eventually when ready to 'settle down', while also becoming aware that they might not be able to afford the constantly rising house prices.

The inner city site, situated in the south of England

Environmentally, there are several contrasts between the inner city site and the affluent commuter belt area. For example, the school where we made our early contacts was embedded in a mainly residential area, near a station and a very busy main road. Unlike the other site, there was no feeling of being surrounded by space, although the walk from the station took me past a small fenced area containing both worked and neglected allotments. The tiny school car park was barely big enough for the teachers, and it was unlikely that even the few students lucky enough to possess a car would be able to park there. In the event this was not a problem, as most pupils lived either within walking distance – some I visited were just across the road – or a short bus ride away. Transport was not a real problem for young people here, as there were buses and trains available to get all over the city if you had enough money for the fare. The low level of car ownership in this area contrasted sharply with that seen in the more rural commuter belt location.

The area that young people here inhabited had an industrial feel to it, although there is little industry left. Surrounding the school was largely local authority housing, and most of the young people's families lived in such rented accommodation in the area. In contrast to the school in the commuter location, the faces were not only white, but also reflected family origins in the Caribbean, Africa, Cyprus, China, Vietnam, India and Pakistan. Their backgrounds were mainly working class, and many of their parents were employed in the service industries. They themselves took part-time work as soon as possible, and much of this was in local shops or markets. For their social life, relatively few went to clubs or similar venues, and while there was no shortage of cinemas and other entertainment on offer, money was always a concern and the prohibitive cost of public transport further limited these kinds of activities. Although being part of a large conurbation implied a certain level of urban crime, the young people did not express significant concern about violence.

Being within a large cosmopolitan city, this location appeared to offer our sample of young people a wide variety of social, educational and occupational opportunities. The school they attended was progressive, and pupils were given considerable encouragement to go on to further and higher education. Pupils over 16 were eligible for Educational Maintenance Allowances; a relatively small weekly payment designed to enable and encourage attendance. There was a small sixth form area but many went on to do A levels (university qualification/final school examination in UK) and vocational courses at the local college, or combined some courses at school with those at the college. About half of the small group of young people attending here made it to university, although one dropped out to have a baby. The remainder who did vocational and similar courses did not find these very useful in finding work, and at the last count were either in the process of seeking jobs or had taken work quite unrelated to any qualification they had gained. Unlike the more affluent location, parents here were less well resourced and although usually emotionally supportive, could not generally play a significant material or networking role in supporting their children's aspirations. However, some of the young people had found the teachers in the school to be helpful in this respect. The fragmenting nature of familial relationships in society was reflected in our group of young people from this city environment: only one came from a household with both birth parents; one from foster parents; and the rest from reconstituted families or single-parent households. At the start of the project there were 14 young people in this site: five young men and nine young women, and over the course of the next four interview rounds we lost two young men and four young women.

Conceptual themes

In writing this book we have attempted to let young people speak for themselves as far as possible. This has been very difficult given the volume of interview material that we are working with. For some young people we have up to five individual interviews that may be as long as 3 hours each, plus a range of other research evidence including extensive field notes by researchers, focus groups, questionnaires, diaries and class work. This means that as authors we have condensed material, summarising subtle changes that may have taken place over years, or making comparisons based on our knowledge of many cases. This process of condensing may involve speaking for young people in the form of case studies but the words used in extracts are their own. The move from young people's voices to the voices of the researchers involves selection, interpretation and the use of concepts and theoretical frameworks. Researchers are not without values, feelings and investments and we have tried to include the researcher's voice (in the form of extracts from field notes), enabling readers to glimpse how those involved in a study such as this come to form interpretations. Researchers also change over time in the same way as young people. We have come to understand that these changing feelings and thoughts are a crucial form of understanding that we have attempted to use in our research process.

The conceptual framework with which we have been working in the course of writing this book is two fold.

Ideas that we brought to the research process

Late modern theory

We were interested in this research in engaging with a group of 'late modern' theorists that includes Ulrich Beck, Anthony Giddens and Zygmunt Bauman, particularly with their suggestion that traditional social divisions such as gender and social class may be eroding. Our engagement was a critical one, directed by questions about whether such changes had in fact taken place and whether and how inequalities may be created in new forms. Over the course of the study we were able to draw on a growing body of empirical and theoretical scholarship that interrogated the claims of late modern theory. Throughout the book we will often return to the ideas of Giddens, Bauman and Beck, working with and against them in order to make sense of changes over time and differences between young people's lives. We are assisted in this process by critical scholarship in the area of gender studies (Walkerdine et al., 2001; Adkins, 2002; McLeod and Yates, 2006), social class (Skeggs, 1997, 2004; Reay and Lucey, 2000; Gillies, 2005; Reay et al., 2005), 'race' and ethnicity (Alexander, 2000; Nayak, 2003) as well as a growing body of debate within the field of youth studies as to the value of late modern theory (Furlong and Cartmel, 1997; Cohen and Ainley, 2000)

Although late modern theory tends to operate on a large scale historical canvas, we have also drawn some more human sized concepts from its tool kit, including the notion of the 'reflexive project of self' that we have used to frame our study both theoretically and methodologically (Giddens, 1991). Through this framework we explore how individual young people make and remake their biographies over time, and the factors that shape this process. Again we have engaged in a critical dialogue with these ideas, exploring the role of timing, resources, and social location in the process through which young people imagine who they could be and attempt to gain recognition for these selves.

Social capital

During the 10 years that the study has been running we have seen theoretical ideas come into and go out of fashion. Politicians in western industrialised countries have become enamoured of the concept of social capital in recent years, and it has underpinned much UK government policy-making. Enhancing social capital is seen as a magic bullet to solve difficult policy issues including changes in family forms, declining, alienated and socially excluded communities, and a lack of political and civic involvement (Edwards et al., 2003). The third phase of the Inventing Adulthoods study was funded within a broader programme of work that explored the value of the concept for understanding family life and we draw on the concept in our examination of education, work, family and community experiences of the young people in the study. Definitions and uses of social capital in the social sciences fall into two social theorising traditions. It can be seen as a concept that deals with problems of collective action and integration, or as one that deals with social injustice and inequality (Kovalainen, 2004; Adkins, 2005a). Commentators identified with the integration strand (Coleman, Putnam and Fukuyama) stress collective goods of reciprocity, trust and co-operation, 'features of social organisation, such as networks, norms and trust, that facilitate action and co-operation for mutual benefit' (Putnam, 1993: 35). Putnam has elaborated the concept to include inward looking 'bonding' social capital, which links people into families and communities, and outward looking 'bridging' social capital, which makes links across different groups. From this perspective, bonding social capital is negative and associated with social exclusion, and bridging social capital is positive and links with social inclusion.

The work of Bourdieu, which deals with inequalities in society, is often used as a corrective to this strand of work by those arguing for equality and social justice (e.g. Reay et al., 2001; Skeggs, 1997). Bourdieu generated a typology of different forms of capital (economic, social, cultural and symbolic) to discuss the reproduction of class inequalities in society. He was concerned to show how social and cultural capital are linked with economic capital, the fundamental resource in capitalist societies. For Bourdieu, social capital does not arise automatically in networks of association, but must be worked for on an ongoing basis. It is 'the product of investment strategies, individual or collective, consciously or unconsciously aimed at establishing or reproducing social relationships that are directly useable in the short or long term' (Bourdieu, 1986: 251). It is also 'the sum of the resources, actual or virtual, that accrue to an individual or a group by virtue of possessing a durable network of more or less institutionalized relationships of mutual acquaintance and recognition' (Bourdieu and Wacquant, 1992: 119). Each of these approaches has its critics, particularly those who see bonding and bridging social capital as more complex than perceived by those in the social cohesion school (Raffo and Reeves, 2000; Leonard, 2004; Reynolds, 2004), and those who see social capital as a minor element in Bourdieu's approach (Savage et al., 2007).

Most recently there has been a move to bring together social capital and late modern perspectives in an attempt to empirically capture and describe everday practices of 'sociality', shaped as they are by situated class cultures (Bauman, 2000; Franklin and Thomson, 2005). So for example, Valerie Hey (2005) has written about the 'offensive' sociality of the new middle class (involving self-conscious networking) and the 'defensive' sociality of the disadvantaged in which practices of sociality first secure survival while sometimes also reinforcing exclusion. While this distinction echoes that between bridging and bonding social capital, the shift in language from being towards doing also reflects a political shift from understanding inequality as located within individuals and communities towards an understanding of how inequalities are made and remade. The qualitative longitudinal method is ideally placed to show these processes in action. In the Inventing Adulthoods study we have taken a critical stance towards the concept of social capital, drawing more widely on the ideas of Bourdieu in order to explore the full range of resources available to young people: material, social, cultural and symbolic. Our method has enabled us privileged insight into how such resources are accessed in practice, shedding light on how their recognition and exploitation are entwined with personal, family and community factors, and subject to individual, social and policy contingencies.

Ideas that we developed through the research process

We have also developed ideas through the research process, working inductively, and creating concepts in order to capture aspects of and patterns in the data. Traditionally youth studies and youth policy have broken young people's lives down into component parts: health, crime, education, work, and so on. Our approach has been holistic. We are interested in every aspect of these young people's lives and how these fit together and interact. At each interview we ask young people about what they perceive as being important in their lives and what has happened since we last met. At the heart of our study has been the attempt to gain insight into the relationship between the unique life (biography), the context within which it is located (structure), and the processes that it is part of (e.g. history, social mobility, intergenerational transfers). About 5 years into the project we developed a conceptual model of individual action. This was serendipitous, the outcome of our struggles to create a practical and conceptual model for analysing multiple biographical interviews.

In attempting to make sense of how and why young people moved between identities over time, why they did or did not make choices, we came to a simple yet subtle formula. It begins with the importance of competence: the feeling of pleasure that derives from doing something well. These feelings are dependent on recognition from others. The argument is that if a person is recognised as competent, then they are likely to invest in a particular area of their life. If we take a biographical approach that understands young people's lives holistically, then investment in one area (say work) is likely to be matched by disinvestment (or less investment) in other areas (say family commitment). The different biographical fields that are in play depend on the young person's social location, and the likelihood of recognition. Resourcefulness depends on the resources available to that young person, both in the present and the past. It is a model that can be understood at a relatively simple descriptive level, but which also has the potential for more social and psychological depth as we explore the dynamic and contradictory processes involved in investment, disinvestment and recognition. Certainly individuals are not simply free to choose who and what they want to be. We introduce this model in Chapter 2 and return to it throughout the book as a way of making sense of and comparing young people's biographies.

Another set of conceptual tools grew out of our attempts to understand young people's lives in relation to the contexts and communities within which they lived. Through ideas such as local 'economies of mobility', 'cultures of violence' and 'meanings of success' we sought to capture the extent to which locality provides more than a backdrop for young people's lives, but also the collective context that shapes values and meanings – what Bourdieu described as a 'logic of practice' (Bourdieu, 1977). Individual young people are not determined by their localities, yet their options and identities are constrained or enabled by them. These concepts capture something of the spatial environments within which young people live their everyday lives and which affect who or what it is possible for them to be in the here and now. These concepts also capture the boundaries between local constructions of conventional behaviour and that which is seen as breaking with con-vention and likely to result in censure of some kind. Crossing these boundaries might include things as varied as being 'the only one' to go to university, engaging in mixed reli-gion friendships in Northern Ireland, or using the internet to discover a gay community outside your small rural village.

A third set of conceptual tools grew out of our attempts to understand young people's lives over time and in relation to historical and temporal processes. Although each round of interviews provided us with a snapshot of a community and a cohort of young people, when we focused on individuals and followed them over time, we found that different things came into view. This shift in perspective moved us towards understanding ways that traditional inequalities are being remade not simply as structure but as mobility (Urry, 2000). So for example, when we tried to think through how it was that a particular indi-vidual became the only one of her peer group to go to university, we tended to look more closely at her family background, to intergenerational continuities and resources and to wider processes of social mobility. We also came to understand localities as situated within temporal and historical processes over the course of the study. This was more obvious in some places than others. For example we saw particularly dramatic changes to the econ-omy and leisure facilities in the Northern Irish site over the 10 years of fieldwork. Elsewhere, changes to the local economy were also important, and waves of new govern-ment policies focused on community regeneration, education, work and anti-social behav-iour all had an impact on the lives of those in our study.

The structure of the book

The book begins by spelling out what a biographical approach to adulthood means, arguing that in changing social and economic times, such an approach is vital to capturing both the holistic and dynamic character of young people's lives. Here we explore the importance of temporality in the ways we think about young people. This may include understanding them as part of a historical 'generation' or in more timeless terms as at a stage in the 'life course'. We explain how the repeat interview method invites young people to create a series of retrospective accounts of the past, and to project themselves into an imagined future. One way of making sense of the resulting material is through the conceptual framework of the 'reflexive project of self' (Giddens, 1991). Through a series of longitudinal case studies we introduce a set of conceptual tools including the idea of 'critical moments' and 'resequencing' of transitions. By following young people's projects of self over time, we introduce our own model of action in which a sense of competence, and recognition of that competence leads to investments in particular biographical fields and practices.

In the second part of the book we approach young people's lives through specific areas of public concern suggesting how attention to locality and biography can enrich and complicate established perspectives. Chapter 3 begins the part by looking at education, and reviewing developments in education policy that seek to expand numbers in higher education. Drawing on the experiences of young people in the Inventing Adulthoods study we show how young people manage the new demands of extended dependency and student life. We also explore how young people and their families negotiate competing notions of success in deciding whether to invest in education and social mobility.

In Chapter 4 we then turn our attention to the world of work, describing how the effective disappearance of the youth labour market has affected the transitions of young people – particularly the working class. Nevertheless 'work' continues to be a central part of most young people's lives and we explore how they balance the demands of part-time work, study and domestic responsibility. By taking a biographical perspective we show how blurred the boundaries are between different forms of labour, and the pleasures as well as perils that being a 'worker' may offer young people.

In Chapter 5 we draw on the lives of the young people in the study to explore the effect of locality on young people's experience of and response to violence and crime. We explain how 'cultures of violence' characterise certain areas and how young people employ coping and survival strategies. In the second part of the chapter we focus specifically on the experience of young people in Northern Ireland where sectarianism provides a symbolic system through which territory is demarcated. Focusing on the very different ways in which young men and young women experience these spaces we explore how violence is for some young men a medium through which they seek to construct masculinity and defend territory.

In Chapter 6 we turn our attention to young people's experiences of illegal drug use and engage critically with the discourse of 'excessive appetites' that mark policy agendas in this area. Stepping back from the popular constructions of media representation we listen to the accounts of young people in order to explore the place of drugs in their biographies. We suggest that although gender and social class are important they are not sufficient for understanding the different place and meaning of chemical culture in young lives. Employing our own situated model of action we show how competence, recognition and investment, and their operationalisation within different biographical fields, provide a dynamic account of how and why some young people invest heavily in the leisure and pleasure landscape. We suggest that the fact that some young people then 'get stuck' while others 'take a flutter' can be explained in terms of the social, cultural, economic and emotional resources they are able to access.

In Chapter 7 we think about how young people's 'well-being' can be understood through a biographical approach. Choice, extended dependency and the demand that all young people are involved in purposeful activity, may affect young people's well-being in various ways. We show how experiences of illness and bereavement can operate as 'critical moments', changing the course of young lives. We also draw on our study to demonstrate dramatic inequalities in well-being, with the accounts of young people from disadvantaged areas characterised by stories of ill health and bereavement. We examine the significance of stress, depression and eating disorders, exploring how the resources that young people are able to draw on may shape their emotional and psychic resilience.

In the third part of the book we move from an agenda defined by policy and the popular representation of youth to consider categories that have salience for young people themselves. Through their own voices and stories we interrogate the nature of an increasingly individualised culture, identifying new axes of inequality in young people's lives. In Chapter 8 we begin the section with a discussion of 'mobility', suggesting that notions of being mobile/flexible or being stationary/stuck are central to the ways that young people understand themselves. Mobility operates at many levels including the material (getting around independently), but also at the level of culture and fantasy – as young people identify with places and products associated with more cosmopolitan and less local identities. Factors such as sexuality, gender, ethnicity and disability also have an impact on how mobile we are and whether we are recognised by others as mobile or not. By focusing on how individual young people make their own transitions from youth to adulthood we explore change over time and the importance of the cultural as an arena for the remaking of inequalities.

In Chapter 9 we consider how feelings of 'belonging' may be understood as a crucial dimension of inclusion and exclusion. Belonging involves a relationship to place, neighbourhood, homeland or nation. But it may also involve a sense of belonging to a faith or community. Despite the impact of processes of secularisation it appears that religion is becoming an increasingly important signifier of identity. Interest in 'new' as well as established religions and alternative expressions of spirituality may constitute a new form of politics or meet the same needs as an involvement in politics may have served for an earlier generation of young people. Drawing on case study material we show how politics, religion and ethnicity are interwoven in young people's biographies, and can be simultaneously constraining and give a sense of security and direction.

In Chapter 10 we explore 'home' as a core element in the young people's experience, biography and identity. The transition to adulthood can be understood in terms of movement from a family of origin to a family of destination. At a very basic level 'home' lies at the core of young people's lives and is the main way in which they are able to access resources. Those with disrupted families and unstable homes can be disadvantaged emotionally, materially and structurally. In this chapter we explore what 'home' means to different young people, and how its meaning evolves over time. We comment on how young people handle changing family obligations and how family responsibilities such as parenthood can transform their lives.

In Chapter 11 we consider the importance of couple relationships in young lives. We suggest that relationships no longer follow a linear trajectory with ordered events, that is, form a relationship, get married, reproduce. Although young people consider relationships to be very important, for many 'settling down' is projected increasingly far into the future. The extent to which they rely on a couple relationship in the 'here and now' depends in part on the other kinds of resources that they have access to, particularly family resources. Through case studies we illustrate the established finding that what is considered to be 'choice' in relationships is often consistent with specific class and cultural expectations.

Chapter 12 explores 'sociality' and the value that many young people place on friendship, social networks, knowing and being known. Beginning with a discussion of young people's use of new technologies (including the internet and mobile phones) we consider how locality, resources and young people's own resourcefulness play out over time to create new forms of adulthood.

We have written this book collectively, with different members of the core team leading on particular chapters to which they lend their own distinctive voices. In writing the book we have been conscious that we do not begin to do justice to the richness of the material that we have accumulated for each individual. By focusing on a particular area of their life (often a problematic one), or a particular moment, we have inevitably represented people in ways that they may not see themselves, or want to have themselves seen. The data is far from being exhausted and we are exploring a range of possibilities for sharing the young people's stories in ways that have integrity. Here we have changed all names and any details that may reveal real identities. Life, like longitudinal studies, continues to flow. In stopping to write this book we are fixing the Inventing Adulthoods young people at a certain point in time. But their lives continue and we hope that we may yet return to find out how their stories unfold.

Chapter 2

Inventing adulthoods: Resources and resourcefulness

From 'youth' to young lives

Young people are often understood in very general terms, with little regard to the diverse pathways and detours that their lives take. On the one hand they are lumped together as a generation – defined historically by the time of their birth and the events, values and opportunities that shape their world. In popular commentaries we hear of 'Generation X', and the 'Millennial Generation', the latter raised on information technology and consumption, 'slackers' who face extended dependency on their parents and live in an era of downward social mobility.

On the other hand 'youth' is also seen as a phase in the life course that we all experience, involving a notion of developmental stages leading from dependent childhood to independent adulthood. From this perspective, 'adolescence' can be seen as a period of experimentation, when identities are tried for size, and boundaries tested, and through which external forms of authority are internalised to become a self-regulating adult (Erikson, 1968; Kroger, 1996). In this model, rebellion and a degree of conflict are normalised as part of a typical process. Elements of both these approaches characterise views of young people that focus on how this particular generation are stuck in an extended adolescence, avoiding responsibility and adulthood (Calcutt, 1998; Du Bois-Reymond, 1998; Gordon and Lahelma, 2004)

These approaches powerfully influence how we understand young people and the category we call youth. Both also encourage us to think in very generalised ways about young people's experiences. The generational approach is attractive, allowing those who are older to see themselves as a generation with shared experiences, perhaps of lost childhoods of simplicity, freedom and safety, and to distinguish themselves from current teenagers. This view discourages the perception of diversity in either age cohort, by concentrating on the similarities and often generalising the experience of a minority to the majority. The life course perspective also defends us from recognition of the specificity of experience. The universal model of development is a powerful narrative, and provides a lens through which we interpret what we see and hear as well as how we understand our own biographies. In retrospect and with the benefit of hindsight, we may reconstruct experiences as 'phases'. This standpoint paradoxically enables us to both identify with and separate ourselves from young people's experience in the present.

Temporality is integrally involved in how we understand youth and young people but an approach that emphasises generation runs the risk of defining young people mainly by time, reading into them their era. A 'baby boomer' or a 'gen xer' can become a caricature of a historical period. In contrast, the life course perspective defines young people 'out of time', in an a-historical model of 'normal' development, although critics of this approach have thoroughly demonstrated the extent to which such 'norms' are in fact a product of a very particular time and place (Griffin, 1993). The developmental narrative is also told from the position of the adult, relegating those it describes to the narrative past, not yet reaching the place of personhood. Sociologists of youth and childhood have consistently criticised this perspective for preventing us from looking at, listening to and recognising the present tense, the lived experience of being young (James et al., 1998).

So is there another way? The methods and theories that we use to research young people inevitably construct the way that we see them. The Inventing Adulthoods study used an approach relatively unusual in youth studies, a qualitative longitudinal design. We interviewed young people repeatedly over a period of years, each time asking them to describe their lives, what had happened to them since our last meeting and inviting them to describe their hopes and fears for the future. Our aim was to follow a group of 100 young people over a period of 10 years. This enabled us to see processes of change and continuity, and at each interview to capture the version of self that individuals were themselves forging. Biographies are told backwards (retrospectively) and each time we met with the young people they retold us their story from a new position, yet the study also followed young people forwards (prospectively) by asking them about their hopes, fears and expectations for the future. In order to capture the immediacy of young people's accounts we turned to the concept of the reflexive project of self.

Remaking the past: The reflexive project of self

The notion of the reflexive project of self was introduced into contemporary social theory by Anthony Giddens (1991) as part of a wider argument about the erosion of tradition and security in late modern western cultures. Giddens argued that it is no longer possible (if it ever was) to simply seek to be like our parents or reproduce the models of adult life around us. There are no jobs for life and we no longer follow gendered fates as typical men and women. In a flexible, post-industrial economy, we each face the task of inventing ourselves, of deciding who we are and what we want to be.

Giddens's ideas have been roundly criticised, charged with being too simplistic or optimistic; with generalising what might be the experience of a minority to a majority (Skeggs, 2004); for ignoring the resilience of tradition, inequality and continuity in contemporary life (Jamieson, 1998); and for conflating stories of agency with a theoretical notion of a disembedded individualism (Mason, 2004). These are all sound criticisms that temper the claims that we exercise real choice over our destinies, even if we may want to and feel as if we do. But does the notion of the reflexive project of self assume that we have choice? Perhaps we can also understand it as referring to the process through which the appearance of choice and control is created.

One of the intriguing aspects of the concept is that it generalises to us all the condition of uncertainty, experimentation and immediacy that is so often attributed to children and adolescents in a developmental life course approach (Holland et al., 2000; Plumridge and

Thomson, 2003). For Giddens, the condition of late modernity is one where there is no simple destination for growing up. We are all in the vivid present, attempting to get somewhere, but to an elusive place. Adulthood does not exist, it has to be invented. The notion of the reflexive project of self has its roots in phenomonology – a field of sociology that focuses on the present and on situated action. The question that is posed by this approach is how do we manage to propel ourselves into the future. Schutz (1982) describes this process as centring on a dynamic relationship between 'because' and 'in order to' motives, the former looking backwards, the latter looking to the future. Giddens elaborates this position, arguing that one of the most important tools we have for the creation of identities is the telling of narratives of the self. Explanations of the past and intentions for the future are articulated via these narratives. The reflexive project of self is then the process 'whereby self-identity is constituted by the reflexive ordering of self narratives' (1991: 244). These narratives are 'occasioned' (being closely tied to the circumstances in which they are told) and draw on existing narrative repertoires that reflect the cultural and social resources that young people have access to.

The notion of the reflexive project of self provides a central focus for the Inventing Adulthoods study. The young people in the study (and the adults researching them) each have their own reflexive project of self. The interviews and other research encounters undertaken with young people are records of these ongoing projects, shaped by the way that they order and reorder narratives of the self. Yet what are the mechanisms through which these narratives are reordered?

Critical moments

A wide range of commentators have drawn attention to the consequential character of particular events in individual biographies. Denzin (1989) talks about 'epiphanies' within narratives. These represent interactional moments which leave marks on people's lives, altering their fundamental meaning structures. Others talk of 'turning points' (Mandlebaum, 1973) and 'breaks' (Humphrey, 1993). Anthony Giddens employs the concept of the 'fateful moment': 'times when events come together in such a way that an individual stands at a crossroads in their existence or where a person learns of information with fateful consequences'. For Giddens the key element of a 'fateful moment' is that the individual considers the consequences of particular choices and actions and so engages in an assessment of risk. Fateful moments can be potentially empowering experiences, with consequences for self-identity and future conduct, so that 'consequential decisions once taken, will reshape the reflexive project of identity through which lifestyle consequences will ensue' (1991: 143). In the Inventing Adulthoods study we use the term 'critical moments' to describe events in young people's lives that they or we the researchers considered to be highly consequential. While Giddens's fateful moments, are moments where 'the individual considers the consequences of particular choices and actions and so engages in an assessment of risk', critical moments are different in that they are not necessarily recognised as significant at the time but only with hindsight. The value of the longitudinal approach is that the significance of critical moments can be revisited and revised over time. A focus on critical moments draws attention to the significance of biography and the configuration of timing, resources and resourcefulness. The longitudinal approach enables us to understand how things that take place in a young person's personal life (for example a bereavement) can have consequences that go beyond that sphere (for example affecting their school to work transition).

The kinds of situations/events/experiences that our young people identified as critical moments were extremely varied. They included family related situations, moving (house, school, town, country); illness and bereavement; and events associated with the education system both formal (exams, changing schools) and informal (bullying, relationship with teachers). They also included situations that can be broadly defined as 'trouble'. These generally involved being found out in some way and included among other things, drug taking, and illegal or criminal activity. Leisure and consumption were also an important source of critical moments with young people pointing to the importance of getting a mobile phone, learning to drive, going to the pub or clubbing for the first time and accessing new groups of people. Rites of passage that were identified included 'coming out' as lesbian or gay, passing a driving test and discovering or rediscovering religion. Relationships were an enduring source of critical moments, with changes in friendship circles, girlfriend and boyfriend relationships, and sexual experience providing important biographical reference points.

It emerged that the lives of some young people were particularly vulnerable to events beyond their control (illness, violence, family disruption, etc.) while others may be more likely to report critical moments relating primarily to internal changes. These might involve rethinking the self after a period of depression, the impact of a break-up of a friendship or intimate relationship, or regret after a one-night stand. It is also clear that some critical moments are more consequential than others and for some people rather than others, depending on resources and timing. In practice it is the configuration and timing of these events that becomes significant, and the extent to which young people are able to respond with resources and resourcefulness. There is also a process of accumulation at play over time so that it is possible to be drawn into spirals of decreasing and increasing agency. In the chapters of the book we will touch on many of the critical moments identified above. Here we provide two short examples to demonstrate both the value and the limitations of this approach.

Lorna: turning a crisis into an opportunity?

We first met Lorna at 16, when she gave us an account of being excluded by a group of friends at her predominantly white middle-class school in the leafy commuter belt area. The event centred on a party at which Lorna was assaulted. She told her father and the police became involved after which the situation escalated, and her erstwhile friends denied that Lorna had been attacked. As Lorna explained 'at this point everyone turned against me 'cause I had done a bad thing, I had gone to the police'. Her excommunication from the 'in crowd' was so extreme that it forced her to adopt a new identity. Rather than seeking to be popular she decided to buckle down and study, do well in her exams and to move on. Lorna was proud and defiant, explaining: 'I beat everyone else in this school ... everyone saw me getting on with my life and that made me feel important, that made me feel like I don't need any of you lot.' Lorna's subsequent decision to go to college rather than the sixth form was undoubtedly shaped by her experience of exclusion. Unlike the majority of her peers who had progressed from school sixth form to university, by her third interview she was working as an office temp, having completed a vocational qualification at college. She was highly conscious of how her trajectory differed from many of her peers and expressed considerable anxiety about the relative merits of the higher education versus the work-based route to professional work status. Yet to what extent did Lorna's fate turn on the rift with her school friends and to what extent was it a response to other powerful underlying biographical forces? Over time we came to know more about Lorna and her relationship with her family. She had a complicated relationship with her father, a successful self-made man with little formal education. She admired his achievements but also struggled for independence from him. Apart from a stint as a model in her early adulthood, Lorna's mother had never worked. There was no experience of higher education or university in her family. Could we also think about why the fall out with friends became such a critical moment in Lorna's biography? Could it be that Lorna's solidarity with her parents was tied up with ambivalent feelings of belonging and a valuing of employment over education?

Robin: sailing close to the wind

We met Robin aged 13, a young man growing up in an isolated rural area who cultivated a bad boy urban identity. Robin had a supportive yet divided family and moved between living with his mother and stepfather and his father and stepmother. At 16 Robin convincingly described a critical moment. He had been caught smoking marijuana at school. The subsequent events included a desperate attempt by his parents to prevent him being excluded from school and his own re-evaluation of his identity and likely destiny. Robin explained: 'I look back now and think how pathetic I was. I knew I was going down a bad track, but I didn't care.' But by his next interview Robin had reverted to his dope smoking bad boy identity. He subsequently rejected a traditional 9–5 work future and built a following as an club promoter and alternative entrepreneur. He also developed a growing problem with drugs. His critical, or fateful moment may have risked his expulsion from school, but it did not represent an enduring identity. Moreover, our initial reading of him as a middle-class boy from a broken home was revised when we became aware that elements of a rural working-class identity that were always present later moved to the centre of his identity, providing useful resources and networks in his chosen path. In retrospect Robin's critical moment appears not as a turning point, but as part of what was to become a pattern of confession, self-inspection and experimentation.

Critical moments are important, and they play a central part in young people's narratives of self and in the ordering and reordering of these narratives in their reflexive projects. But critical moments are not the whole story. We are not simply authors of our own destinies, but are located in time, space and social structure. The longitudinal character of the Inventing Adulthoods data has helped us to place young people's reflexive projects of self into context, and to shift attention from the character of particular critical moments to the resilience and resourcefulness of young people in the face of them. Over time we have attended both to the portrayal of critical moments, but also how these are reworked and reflected on, with the expression of regret and wonder over issues of timing and opportunities taken, missed and lost. We have also become increasingly aware of the significance of slower intergenerational dynamics that are played out over time. In the next section we turn our attention from the present towards understanding how young people imagine the future, and how this is constrained by structural and intergenerational forces.

Imagining gendered adulthoods

There is a powerful sociological and political narrative that suggests that western society is undergoing a process of rapid change. At the heart of contemporary narratives of change are two linked phenomena – a process of de-industrialisation and of the movement of women into the workforce. Together, it is argued, these phenomena have transformed public and private life, and what it means to be young. Commentators tend to divide into optimists and pessimists. The former tell a story of gain: democratisation, choice and an increasingly fluid and open society. Pessimists tell a story of loss: of innocence, certainty, security and cohesion. The reality of social change and continuity is messier and more complex. Whether we believe that things have changed or not depends in part on the time period we select and the markers of change that we recognise (Zerubavel, 2003). The stories that we tell about change are shaped by our current concerns (Vickerstaff, 2003; Goodwin and O'Connor, 2005). As historians and sociologists are aware, it can be misleading to read accounts of the past through contemporary lenses.

The term 'late modern theory' is used to refer to a number of commentators who are engaged in exploring the ways in which society is changing. The term encompasses Anthony Giddens who suggests that we are witnessing a process of detraditionalisation, where individuals are increasingly free to construct reflexive identities that in the past were defined by tradition and social institution. It also includes the theory of individualisation proposed by Ulrich Beck (1992) arguing that in broad terms we are moving from 'normal biographies' where we fulfil pre-existing roles and life plans, to 'choice biographies' where we are responsible for who and what we become. Late modern theory is not always optimistic, including in its number those such as Zygmunt Bauman (1992) who suggests that western societies are moving from a situation where we were all citizens (however faulty) to one in which we are all consumers, with a corresponding loss of meaning and value.

Late modern approaches to the lives of young people have emphasised intergenerational change and the view that the predictable life patterns of the past (which tended to be powerfully shaped by social class and gender) have eroded, leaving young people faced with the challenge of forging futures without a map. Beck's distinction between 'normal' and 'choice' biographies has been employed by many youth researchers to make sense of increasingly fragmented pathways in the transition to adulthood (Du Bois-Reymond, 1998; Dwyer and Wyn, 2003). These distinctive biographical paths are distinguished by gender. Du Bois-Reymond talks of a 'gender specific normal biography' where young people 'aim for a clearly defined profession and employment at an early stage and enter fixed relationships in order to start a family – or at least they intend to' (1998: 66). She contrasts this with a 'non-gender specific choice biography' arguing that although gender is losing its determining influence as part of the process of detraditionalisation, in practice the pull of tradition still operates, and is most acutely felt by young women, who are more willing to accommodate their careers to family demands than are young men.

Other commentators such as Ann Nilsen and Julia Brannen (2002) are more wary of adopting these conceptual tools, arguing that the distinction between normal and choice biography is too simplistic, and drawing attention to the continuing significance of structural inequalities, which provide the parameters within which individual choices are made. They suggest that the resources on which individuals draw may be critical in how choice *appears* to them, noting that 'when structural forces and personal resources, such as gender and social class, support one another, there is a tendency for the structural resources to take on an 'invisible' quality' (2002: 42).

All of these accounts generate a sense that we are moving from a society in which identities and behaviours were clearly mapped and collectively understood (if not always followed) to one in which there are multiple maps, few agreed routes and high levels of anxiety about whether individuals are 'doing the right thing'. Although gender, ethnicity and social class may no longer operate as a shared point of reference for navigation, they continue to be important in shaping young people's lives and chances. Despite the appearance of meritocracy, research suggests that there is less social mobility today than a generation ago (Schoon et al., 2001; Blanden et al., 2005). Old forms of inequality such as class, gender and race are being remade in new ways. For example, Walkerdine and colleagues suggest that the choice biography should also be understood in terms of self-regulation, observing the continuing salience of social class where 'the most seductive aspect of self invention of all lies in the possibility of the working class remaking itself as middle class' (2001: 121). Beverley Skeggs (2004) also draws attention to how it is only the white middle classes who are assumed to 'have' a self that can become a project. What Giddens and others describe as 'reflexivity' – a self-conscious conversation of self with self – has more or less value according to who performs it. As Lisa Adkins (2002) explains, it is generally white middle-class men who are rewarded for displaying forms of reflexivity while these are assumed to be 'natural' when displayed by those who are less privileged.

Mapping the future

In the Inventing Adulthoods study we were intrigued to find out what maps (if any) young people drew on to imagine the kinds of men and women they might become. To explore this we asked young people to complete 'lifelines' that included a number of discrete elements (home/housing, education, work, relationships, travel and values) and interviewees were invited to predict their situations in these areas in 3 years' time; again at the age of 25; and finally at the age of 35 (Thomson and Holland, 2002).

When we looked across the lifelines we found both expected and surprising things. Despite the view that life maps are proliferating we found some consistency in young people's expectations of the future. Most expected increasing independence in relation to housing tenure, relationships and work. There was a higher expectation of independence in relation to housing for the middle-class compared with the working-class young people. Educational aspirations were relatively high in general, but in the whole sample more middle-class than working-class young people and more young women than men expected to go to university, with levels of educational aspiration also differing by locality.

The most striking pattern to emerge in the lifelines was in the area of personal lives and relationships, where almost all of the young people expected to be married or in a steady live-in relationship with children by the age of 35. This seemed to be the lynch pin of imagined futures, whatever the trajectory leading to it, which varied considerably. This normative model can be more easily realised by young men within a traditional framework, but for young women it is more problematic. For them, severe tensions exist between expectations of relationships, and high educational and occupational aspirations. So although the goal of a traditional model of 'settling down' to marriage and family is common, it is a destination reached by a variety of routes, if achieved at all. The model is shifting and under pressure, a message coming most clearly from working-class young women, who feel that they must take on the role of both male and female in the traditional model. They must combine career with family, as both breadwinner and primary carer. The model is under least pressure from the middle-class young men, but what is also surprising in this time of change is the power of the normative model and how few young people are pushing against the constraints, and imagining a different future. Given the dramatic changes and expansion of choice that are supposed to have taken place as part of detraditionalisation and individualisation, we were surprised that young people struggled to find new stories to tell about becoming adults.

Drawn from the discussion of lifelines in interviews, the following case studies illustrate just how varied paths into the future can be for the young people in our sample, and how hard it is to think of alternative futures outside a traditional framework.

Monique: Doing it all?

Monique was 17 at her first interview, and her future lifeline reflected the centrality of the domestic field in her current construction of adulthood. She was living in a flat with her single mother, brothers and sisters in the inner city research location. In 3 years' time she saw herself as still living at home but saving for a place of her own. She explained the financial sense of buying rather than renting, saying that she wanted her 'own shack' by the age of 21 – or 22, adding, 'why shouldn't I?' With the desired house forming the centre to her plans in education and work, she explained 'that is why I need these pieces of paper, so I can get the job that's gonna give me the money I need'.

At 25 Monique said she would 'like to have my own house and a couple of kids – somewhere nice', adding, 'I'm only having two kids.' At 35 she saw the same situation as at 25. Monique articulated all of the basic components of her future plans through the home/housing element of the lifeline, having a vision of her goals that was most clearly expressed in her house for her children.

The education element of her lifeline elicited a more contradictory account. When interviewed she had just started at a college of further education having passed two of the seven final examinations that she had taken at school. In 3 years' time she expected that she would have finished education, and said 'I wanna have a couple of pieces of paper' (qualifications). She then found it difficult to bridge the gap between 3 years and the age of 25. She mused 'if I really decide I wanna be this social worker', then elaborated that 'right now I'm thinking I don't wanna do no more [education], but I know that I'll have to do, so –'.

Her confusion over education and its part in supporting her wider aspirations can also be seen in the work element of her lifeline. In 3 years' time she imagined herself doing voluntary work with children and the elderly that would support her ambitions to be a social worker and was already applying for such positions. When asked whether she would also be undertaking paid work she was forced to confront a contradiction between her present and future identities. She first asserted that she would not, but then reflected, 'I've gotta – how will I have that house if I've got no job'.

When the interviewer suggested that perhaps she would still be working in her present job at McDonalds, Monique was horrified: 'NO WAY – not when I'm 20. I'm not working in no fast food joint when I'm 20 – when I should have a good job.' At this point she returned to the secure point in her lifeline – that she would be a social worker at 25 – and tried to work through the implications and consequences of this. In order to get there she would have to complete her access to social work course, and may in fact have to work to support herself through that period. The fragility of her work lifeline was compounded by her view that at 35 she would probably be considering a career change, given that 10 years in social work would be highly stressful.

In her relationship lifeline Monique predicted that in 3 years' time she might or might not be in a relationship. If she was it would not be serious, but nor would it be casual. She was clear that at 25, 'I'd like to be financially secure, with a stable partner, that can be a good parent'. The relative priority of her commitment to her children over her partner in her anticipated future was confirmed by her plans for 35. She did not plan to rely on the continued presence of the partner, and explained that she might live 'with my kids' dad', and while she would 'like to be with the same person', she would be happy to be in another relationship with a person equally as nice. Her reticence in investing in a couple relationship contrasts with her openness towards motherhood.

The final element of the lifeline, 'values and priorities', reconfirmed the centrality of family to Monique's projected future. In 3 years' time, she said, her priorities would be 'me and money', but would include responsibilities towards her current family. At 25 she would be most concerned with 'My job and my family', observing that if she had children by that time she would be thinking mostly of them, again only interested in a couple relationship if it was 'good'. At 35, family would still be the priority. 'My own kids. My own family, my nuclear family as it's called. My job, if I've still got a job. My relationship with my kids and like their father, or their stepfather, or whatever. Their step mum, whatever. I don't know, I might swing both ways when I got older, who knows.'

The two motifs of economic independence and motherhood form the heart of Monique's anticipated future. It is striking that apart from the moral support of her mother, she expects little help in achieving this future. While many young people in the study made plans that relied heavily on material support from parents or partners, Monique imagines a future that is all her own work. It is hardly surprising that there are some practical contradictions in her plans, particularly in the earlier stages and in relation to education, and it is here that her plans are least formed. She herself recognises that she will only 'hang in there' education-ally with her mother's dogged support, as it is an arena of her life in which she is least confident and competent. The centre of her imagined future is her three-bedroomed house, yet neither the work nor education lifelines make it clear how it will be possible for her to secure and support this household.

It is productive to compare Monique's lifeline with that of Edward. If Monique's lifeline is led through the field of the domestic and the motif of her own home, then Edward's is led through the field of work and the motif of 'career'. Significantly, this facilitates what appears to be a less contradictory, and certainly more traditional trajectory into adulthood.

Edward: Having it all?

When first interviewed, 17-year-old Edward was living in a detached house in the leafy suburb, with his white, middle-class parents and brother. The home did not lead in his imagined future, but fitted in with career plans, and did not represent a major emotional investment until later. In 3 years' time he saw himself living in student halls as it would be 'more convenient'. If he stayed on at university to do postgraduate research then he would still be living in halls at the age of 25. If not, he said he would be 'in something very small and unpretentious, with a kitchen, bathroom, bedroom and little else', concluding that all these plans ultimately 'depend on what I'm doing career wise'. At 35 Edward hoped for 'a fairly nice house, probably retail value of £100,000 – depends on how my career is going', adding that location would depend on the demands of his job.

Edward's education plans were detailed and instrumental. In 3 years' time he would be at the end of his second year at university. At 25 he would either have finished full-time education and be 'doing a couple of courses on the side', or he would be doing 'a postgraduate course or a law conversion course if I decide to go that way'. At 35 he observed that 'Education will probably have finished for me.'

It was Edward's plan for work and his position within the hierarchies of employment that were the most detailed, and appeared to be the site of his greatest imaginative investment. In 3 years' time, he said, he would have a summer job with the company where he spent his gap year, providing him with experience for his desired career. At 25 he would either be doing postgraduate study or be in 'a starting job' – and noted: 'I'll have only been a couple of years out of university and no matter how fast I rise I can't expect to be anywhere above low management at 25.' At 35 he expected to be in middle to upper management, within either academia or research.

The detailed planning that characterises Edward's lifeline in education and work disappeared when he predicted his intimate life and relationships. In 3 years' time he felt he might be attending university parties and might have a girlfriend, yet dismissed the train of thought with the comment: 'I don't know, I haven't thought about it in particular. I've always assumed it'll happen to me.' He was however able to describe an imagined future at 35, when he would 'probably be married, if I'm ever going to be married. I might even have kids at 35.' He was unable to imagine his intimate life at 25, suggesting that it would be somewhere between the two. Marriage was symbolically important, Edward explained: 'Call me old fashioned if you like but I like the idea of actually getting an official marriage, [...] I'd want to get married rather than to have a long-term relationship, I'd want to have children in marriage.'

The character of Edward's imagined future becomes clear in the values element of his lifeline. In 3 years' time his priority would be getting a good degree and 'studying very, very hard', but not offending his girlfriend too much. At the age of 25 his priority would be to advance his career, again 'without offending anyone close to me'. At 35 his priority would be to 'settle down', to 'put down roots', in his words 'to reproduce and let your genes carry on'.

The social locations of Monique and Edward's lives are worlds apart, but there are some striking continuities in their lifelines. Both dreamt of their own home and family and imagined this as the result of their own labours, not 'settling down' through the unfolding of a couple relationship. In this sense they both have relatively 'individualised' imagined futures. Yet the timing of this central motif of 'settling down' distinguishes their lifelines, and makes Edward's version more achievable, banished as it is into the distant future. For Monique, the identity of mother and the appeal of competence and authority within the domestic domain had immediate appeal and so complicated her plans for economic self-sufficiency. By disregarding relationships in the present and foreseeable future, Edward was able to assume a gendered division of labour in which his role is simply to have the career and to make the money. Relying as she did exclusively on her own resources, Monique was faced with an almost impossible task of planning relationships and emotional commitments, alongside a career that could support these goals. The temptation to embark on family life before she had the means to support it is clear, but such plans have their own logic.

In a sense the present provides the resources from which these imaginings of the future are made possible. Young people not only imagine very different futures, but how they do so is shaped by their experiences and social locations. Giddens (1992) has pointed out that the ability to 'colonise the future' through such imaginings is highly consequential for the character of social change. Certainly, young people drew on very different resources in this project.

Despite their different imagined futures Monique and Edward are also constrained by a resilient model of adulthood anchored in notions of 'settling down'. While there is evidence of reworking of traditional gender identities, it is difficult for young people to imagine a future outside a normative model of the 'proper thing to do' (Nilsen and Brannen, 2002). Commentators have pointed to growing disjunctions between a gendered reality and a discourse of individual choice. Sharpe reflects on the changes she has observed in young women's expectations over twenty years, concluding that they still 'bump' up against reality and 'men who have not accommodated the changes and developments in their lives' (2001: 180). Women also have an investment in heteronormativity (institutionalised, naturalised and normative heterosexuality) illustrated by Skeggs' (1997) powerful account of the relationship between heterosexual feminine 'competence' and respectability – a theme that is evident in Monique's investment in home life as a site of competence and pleasure.

In seeking to make sense of our data we have been looking for a theoretical account that provides space for an understanding of the 'logic' of particular formations of class, sexuality and gender, while also enabling us to place these identities within a dynamic context of social change. Monique is struggling with the contradictions of the choice biography in a direct way, trying to 'do it all', have a career, be economically independent, and to have a family. She does not make a heightened investment in the couple relationship in response to the uncertainties of individualisation (as suggested by Beck and Beck-Gernsheim, 1995), but in the identity of 'mother'. We can understand her as seeking to navigate beyond the heteronormative model of adulthood – by privileging motherhood, downplaying the couple relationship and questioning her future sexuality. But this still leaves her with the practical difficulty of making it on her own. We see clear tensions in her lifeline between her imagined future and her present circumstances, and the uncertainty of how to bridge the gap. She does not introduce the idea of resequencing events, becoming a mother and later returning to education and career. Although this is an increasingly common pattern for young women, it is yet to achieve any popular legitimacy. So while Monique has a relatively detraditionalised gender identity and subjectivity, the social and cultural possibilities are not in place for her to realise them in a simple way (Bjerrum Nielsen and Rudberg, 1994).

Our longitudinal study has enabled us to explore how young people's expectations of the future mesh with their practices, highlighting the significance and consequentiality of the investments that they make in the here and now, for their future lives. In this way young people's aspirations can be read as reflecting their values and investments rather than seen simply as maps for a presumed future. A focus on resources, investments and the kinds of stories that young people can tell (and those that are difficult to articulate) can help us understand the particular dilemmas that they face. In the next section we bring these elements together to propose a dynamic model of action.

A biographical approach to youth transitions

As we sought to understand how young people invent adulthood over time we realised that they felt adult in different ways and different contexts, and thinking of themselves as adult was related to their feelings of *competence,* and the *recognition* that they received for that competence (see also Honneth, 1995). We described the major arenas of their lives where this was played out as *fields*, which we see as locations within which adult identities can be developed.[1] For the young people in our study the most important *fields* were: education; work; leisure and consumption; and the domestic – which includes family, relationships and care. The specific content of these fields changed over time. For example, the domestic includes family of origin and relationships within that; as they grow older, this field will also include sexual and partnership relationships, and any family they may build themselves. We distinguish these fields for analytic purposes, but in practice they are permeable and overlap. For example leisure may be a feature of relationships at school, college, work and home. What is important is that *fields* represent arenas of a young person's life through which adult identities can be accessed and constructed.

In Figure 2.1 we see the relationship between the fields and dimensions of autonomy and adulthood – self, relationships and practices, and citizenship.

While the basic relationship between dimensions and fields holds for all the young people in the study, as indeed for all of us, each particular case has a different weighting and

Figure 2.1   Dimensions and fields

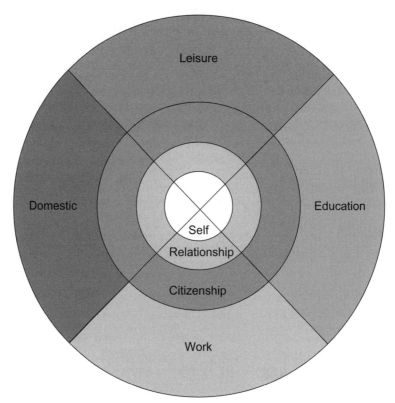

balance. The size of each field relates to its significance in the construction of identity, rather than the amount of time spent, although there may be a relationship between the two.

In taking a biographical approach we found that it was important to explore the opportunities for competence and recognition in these different fields in young people's lives, and to acknowledge that independence in one field may be associated with dependence in another. Competence as an autonomous consumer, or experience of sexual relationships could be associated with living at home in economic dependence. The balance between competence and recognition in these fields changes over time not only through changing circumstances and opportunities, but through investments in these fields made by young people in response to their experiences.

A biographical approach over time

Young people are pulled by competing versions of adulthood: one stressing independence, autonomy and pleasure and the other relationship, interdependence and care. The choices that confront them are structured by gender, locality, ethnicity and social class. The choices that they make are highly consequential for subsequent processes of inclusion and exclusion.

In order to bring this biographical approach to life and this chapter to a close we will return to the case of Monique discussed above, and by doing so we can relate her expected future to her continuing experience.

At the age of 17, living at home, Monique's views on adulthood were dominated by her diminutive size and the fact that she looked younger than her age. Her size constrained her positions within fields, limiting the range of leisure activities in which she could participate. While her size made her feel childish in relation to her friends, she felt adult in the domestic sphere through her significant responsibility for the childcare of the children in her extended family. Monique also worked on Saturdays at McDonalds in the centre of the city, which provided her with some financial autonomy realised in the domestic field. She contributed directly to her keep by buying the electricity card for the household, financing her mobile phone and buying her own clothes. She was proud of paying her way and relatively self-sufficient but as we saw earlier, was determined not to be stuck in this sort of job by the time she reached her 20s. Monique's ambition was to be a social worker. Having gained just two examination qualifications she recognised that she must concentrate on her education and at the time we interviewed her was at college undertaking a vocational qualification while also attending her school sixth form. She expressed frustration with her inability to secure sufficient support from her teachers and was aware that her application and interest in her course were slipping. Monique had not had a serious romantic or sexual relationship, again putting this down to her childlike appearance.

There were clear contradictions between the dimensions of Monique's construction of adulthood in the different fields of leisure, work, education and the domestic. While she felt adult in the domestic sphere and through work, she was effectively excluded from participation in the leisure pursuits of her peers by her size. She found it difficult to secure the identity of a successful student or to negotiate more equal relationships with her teachers. While Monique understood that she needed to stay in education to achieve her longer term plans of being a social worker, in practice she found empowerment in the shorter term in the domestic field.

We interviewed Monique several times after this first meeting and although it would not have been possible to predict what would happen in her life, our conceptual framework helped us to understand the logic of her trajectories. For a while Monique hovered on the edge of dropping out of education, her energies being increasingly drawn into pleasure, leisure and boys as she grew enough to get into clubs and bars. Yet she refocused on her ambition to become a social worker and managed to get into university through an access scheme. University proved to be disappointing for a range of reasons and Monique did not get on well with, or fit in with, fellow students. Her energy continued to be located in her neighbourhood, her old school friends and her boyfriend. By the end of her second year she was pregnant and planning to transfer for the final year of her degree to another university after her baby was born. Although she had been offered an unsuitable council flat, she was living with her mother, staying sometimes at her boyfriend's home.

If we consider Monique's own predictions for her life we can see that she is managing to make progress on all fronts – she is gradually accumulating the necessary education and qualifications, she has her baby, and sometimes her man. She does not have the house and may have to wait, yet the sequence was always a problematic feature of her narrative. In educational terms her trajectory may seem chaotic, yet seen from the perspective of Monique's investments, her own sense of competence, it makes a great deal of sense. Hers is a choice biography, yet one shaped by material circumstance and cultural formations.

Monique's identity is firmly located as a strong black working-class woman. What 'counts' as competence and recognition is experienced through this lens (Reynolds, 2005).

Conclusion

In this chapter we have outlined the components of a biographical approach to understanding young people's transitions to adult life, introducing ideas and examples that we will return to throughout the book. We have shown how our thinking changed over time and why 'temporality' is central to the arguments that we make. Young people are faced with the task of 'inventing adulthood' precisely because the material and social conditions have shifted significantly over the course of a generation. Late modern theorists suggest that these changes mark a new relationship between the individual and the social in which we have greater agency, more choice and consequently more anxiety. Others suggest that these are changes in appearance only, that life chances continue to be determined by forces beyond the control of the individual. What is clear, is that in a diverse and socially unequal society such as the UK, there is no single experience of 'youth' and though young people might share dreams of independence and autonomy, there are many different routes to adulthood.

Young people today must make themselves into adults in a relatively piecemeal way. By looking at their 'projects of self' within which there are 'critical moments' – points at which it is possible to change and rework the stories we tell about ourselves – it becomes possible to understand the work that young people do in the here and now in order to claim a sense of adulthood. Looking at their life maps it becomes apparent that although the staging posts towards adulthood are fragmenting, there is little institutional support for the kinds of resequencing of life stages in which many young people engage. In taking a biographical approach to understanding youth transitions it is possible to see the logic of young people's biographies as underpinned by a subjective sense of competence, and recognition of that competence by others including peers, family, institutions and professionals. It is the experience of such recognition (or its absence) that underpins the investments and disinvestments that these young people make.

Note

1. In choosing the term 'fields' we have been influenced by Pierre Bourdieu's concept of the social field. However, in our case the field is first an arena of the biography, which may then map onto a field in the social world (for elaboration see Thomson, 2004; and Thomson et al., 2004).

Part 2
From public agendas to joined up lives

In Part 1 we introduced our study, indicating the advantages of a longitudinal, and joined up, holistic approach to young people's lives. In analysing and writing about the study it has been necessary to engage with youth studies and youth policy as it exists. We have therefore tried to contribute our holistic perspective to specialist and fragmented areas of knowledge and research. This has been challenging for us and for those working in these fragmented areas, since the kind of biographical material we produce tends to fail many of the conventions and standards that shape particular knowledge communities. We have noted, however, that the biographical approach developed through the Inventing Adulthoods study seems to be gaining recognition in research and youth policy, and speaks directly to practice (Chamberlayne et al., 2004; Jones, 2005).

We also introduced the concepts we are using throughout the book, including the idea of young people constructing their adulthoods through the experience of competence and recognition in the areas of education, work, leisure and consumption, and the domestic. Researchers, policy-makers, parents, media and other commentators on young people generally agree that these are major areas of concern that affect the experiences and behaviour of young people. All of these groups have different ideas about what is happening and what should be done about it, but they frequently intersect in recurrent moral panics. It is to these areas of policy concern and moral panic about young people that we now turn.

Media representations of young people tend to the spectacular, feeding moral panics about drug and alcohol use, violence and criminality, these representations themselves feeding into public understanding of young people's lives and often seemingly into policy. Drawing on our biographical approach, the major impetus of this part is to understand how young people are constructed and construct themselves differently through activities and relationships in different social and institutional settings, and in doing so to move beyond the dichotomy between spectacular public and more private 'ordinary' understandings of young people's lives.

Each chapter takes a particular policy area, placing it in a broad structural and policy context. We use the experiences of the young people in the Inventing Adulthoods study to illustrate how the multiple intersecting features of individuals and families, social and structural elements (class, gender, 'race' and ethnicity) and policy play out across their lives. The first two chapters focus on two traditional institutional and policy fields, education and work. They explore the relationships between changing education and work policy and practice, and young people's engagement in and passage through education and work in a context of social change.

Although work and education are not entirely excluded from moral panics about young people, the following two chapters move onto the staples of such responses, crime, violence and substance use, and young people's consumption of leisure and pleasure. We link our critique of moral panic approaches with others, recognising that an increasingly diverse and fragmented media has led to 'a much more sophisticated way of representing social and political issues to the public' (McRobbie, 1994: 218). Our chapters on violence and chemical culture provide a wider window onto the stuff of moral panic, and explore the contribution of a longer view of young lives to dominant understandings of youth. Finally we examine the effects and implications for young people's physical and mental health of their pivotal location in relation to policy, media, and market as laid out in this part.

Chapter 3

Education

Introduction

Nam: What do you think, do you think education is more important or being happy with life?

INT: I think happy is pretty important.

Nam: Yeah you see, did you have a good time at university?

INT: Providing you know, I mean education can contribute to being happy … with what you say about money and stuff like that.

Nam: Providing okay that you've got a decent full time job that you enjoy that has average income of 11,000 a year … which is not a lot but you're happy with it, and or … you can go to uni having a stressful time you know, all this debt and shit, you know – what would you prefer … ? Happy in life you see, a lot of people do that, they work full time … they quit education you see but that's a stupid thing to do, because you know you'll never make a lot of money. There's a part of me that says yeah education is good and another part of me says enjoy life while you can you see.

(Nam, 20, 2003)

Nam, a working class young man in the inner city site expresses the ambivalence that many of the working-class young people in the study felt towards education. His parents, migrants from south-east Asia, wanted him to have the good education that they had been unable to achieve; he wanted to have fun. He recognised the problems that university might pose for someone like him, potentially stressful and leading to debt. But he felt that without an education he would be unable get a well-paid job. In this chapter we look at the expansion of higher education in the late 20th and early 21st centuries in the UK, and the ways that the lives of young people have been affected.

Our initial access to the young people in the study was through schools that were in very different and socio-economically varied localities, providing different conditions for life. As the study has progressed we have followed the young people through their final year examinations and post-16 decisions about further and higher education. During the period of the study there have been many changes in education policy in the UK, for example the development of Education Action Zones, Excellence in Cities, mentoring of working-class young people, and the introduction of Educational Maintenance Allowances (EMAs). These policies targeted poorer or potentially socially excluded groups, and aimed to facilitate the broader expansion of numbers of students in higher education. In our study, the school in the inner city site grasped every opportunity for improving the opportunity of working-class young people to get into further and higher education, including mentoring, scholarships, and being part of the EMA pilot study. The school on the disadvantaged northern estate also made great efforts, and in each case we saw a number of the young people going to university against the odds. Often they would go to a local university, a new or modern university, or by route of a college of further education. Even if an opportunity to go to a more elite old university existed, the social and experiential (and often physical) distance to be bridged between that type of educational establishment, and their home and community, and the fear of loss of support from family, friends and community led the young people to take the more local options.

In this chapter we draw on the experiences of the young people particularly in the sites vulnerable to social exclusion and subject to the tranche of policies discussed here. But first a broader review of education policy in relation to higher education in the UK.

Education policy in the UK: Expansion in the 20th century

In the second half of the 20th century, the education system in the UK underwent considerable change. A post-war political consensus based on a commitment to full employment and the importance of the welfare state, with general support for a reforming education policy, began to fall apart at the end of the 1960s, and the economic recession of 1971–73 provided the final blow. The period had seen an extension of education through the tripartite school system introduced in 1944, which created grammar, technical and secondary modern schools. As time passed and its effects became more apparent, this system was roundly criticised for reproducing the hierarchical class structure of the UK, but it *had* provided opportunities for working-class young people to gain both a secondary and occasionally a tertiary education. However, when Halsey et al. (1980), compared trends in access to university before and after the Second World War, it appeared that the situation was perhaps slightly worse in class terms immediately after than before the war. Crucially, means-tested grants, and the provision of full fees were introduced in 1960, and 3 years later the Robbins Report argued for the immediate expansion of higher education to enable all those with the ability and qualifications to have access (Robbins, 1963). These moves led to a rise in university entrants of 150 percent by 1989 and was followed by ongoing expansion of higher education. In 1938 the proportion of the 18-year-old population entering university was 2 percent, in 1948 it was 3.7 percent, and by 1996 the figure was 33 percent. On taking office in 1997, the New Labour government pledged to increase the proportion to 50 percent by 2010.

Such a massive expansion of higher education required a range of policy measures, particularly in the light of an overall drop in spending on education after the Conservative party took office in 1979 (although a downward trend in expenditure began in 1976–77). A two-pronged approach was employed, with a particular squeeze on capital expenditure and the physical fabric of schools, and a total change in the funding of higher education, as part of the process of 'marketisation' instigated by a Conservative government. This process became general in western industrialised societies, as a result of the ascendance of the New Right in politics. In the Education Reform Act of 1988 (which also introduced the National Curriculum), polytechnics and some colleges of higher education were removed from local education authority (LEA) control, and constituted as competing corporations resourced through another funding body. So it was the case that between 1989 and 1992, polytechnics alone accounted for 50 percent of the growth in student numbers. In the Further and Higher Education Act 1992, funding was linked to student numbers, and the binary divide between polytechnics (vocational) and universities (academic research and scholarship) was removed so that polytechnics could call themselves universities and award degrees. In what can be seen as a third prong, various benefits and grants were removed from students throughout the 1980s, and in 1990, maintenance grants were frozen and student loans introduced.

Following this trend the New Labour government passed the Teaching and Higher Education Act 1998, which included new and expanded arrangements for loans, abolished maintenance grants and introduced tuition fees for undergraduates. Subsequently, the government ran into considerable opposition by proposing to deal with the under-funding of universities by enabling them to charge top-up fees of up to £3000 a year, but this measure was put into place in 2005. These policies raise the spectre of student debt, and government policies for financing universities in general seem to be at odds with their plans as stated in the White Paper *The future of higher education* (DfES, 2003) and elsewhere, to widen access to families who might see university as beyond their reach, or who had no previous experience of university education like many in our group of young people (Chitty, 2004; Mizen, 2004).

Claire Callender has done considerable research into student finances (Callender and Kemp, 2000; Callender and Wilkinson, 2003; Callender and Jackson, 2004) and concludes that current government policies in this regard have a detrimental effect on poorer students from lower class backgrounds. She argues, first, that debt is unequally distributed: students who are poor before going to university are more likely to be in debt and to leave university with the largest debts, better off students are less likely to have debts and leave with the lowest debts, and so poorer students take more responsibility for the costs of their education than wealthier students. Second, that debt deters university entry and fear of debt is greatest amongst the poorest, with serious implications for government policy. And third, that there are class differences in the changing real value of family and student support, showing that the main beneficiaries of the move from grants to loans are wealthier students. Between 1998 and 2003 financial support from parents fell by 18 percent in real terms overall. It has fallen most (20%) for students from the highest social classes, but they received 15 percent more from the changed student support system; students from the lowest social classes saw their parental support grow by 2 percent, but their income from student support fell by 4 percent in this period. Middle-class families might also be better able to manage the burden of loans. In our study we had an example of a middle-class young man who was able to invest his student loan, whilst supported by his parents, and his own savings.

Finally, Callender argues that students are increasingly reliant on paid work to augment their income, and that those most dependent on work, and working the longest hours, come from the poorest families, with a detrimental effect on their education. This was certainly the case for the working-class young people in the Inventing Adulthoods study who were attempting to pursue further and higher education. Gill Jones also points to differential family support. 'Parental encouragement to stay on in education or to get a job depends both on local traditions and on family belief in the education ethic or the work ethic … Support for students entering HE [higher education] may depend on both the level of cultural capital in the home and the financial circumstances of parents' (2002: 29).

Maisie, who grew up on the disadvantaged northern estate sees the gap between government rhetoric and the actualities of struggling to get a university degree with little or no support:

> But some people – not everyone – but you have to really struggle. And it's a shame because it's like they make it so hard for you to go. Really hard, and I just really think – but I don't think normal people are supposed to go to university, the way they work it out. (Maisie, 20, 2003)

Egerton and Halsey (1993) conclude their study of access to higher education over the 20th century by identifying three major features: it was a period of considerable expansion; there was a significant reduction in gender inequality; but there has been no reduction in relative social class inequality. Less attention has been paid to access to higher education by minority ethnic groups, than has been to class and gender as differentiation factors. Modood and Acland point out that despite their disadvantaged situation 'most minority groups are producing greater proportions of applications and admissions to higher education than the rest of the population' (1998: 37). But while in recent years there has been a rise in members of most ethnic groups gaining entry to university, with gender differentiation within this overall picture, falls occurred for Caribbean and black African applicants (see too Reay et al., 2001, 2005; Platt, 2005).

The expansion of higher education in the 20th century did lead to more working-class and poorer young people gaining qualifications through schooling and even university, but it has been argued that this was an effect of expansion rather than of targeted attempts towards greater equality (Paterson, 2001). In fact there is a general consensus that expanding higher education has benefited less bright wealthier, middle-class young people, rather than the brighter working-class, and that the situation on working-class access to education has worsened in more recent years (Metcalf, 1997; Schoon et al., 2001; Galindo-Rueda et al., 2004; Machin and Blanden, 2004). Machin (2003) indicates changes in the 1990s, reporting that in 1991–92, 13 percent of children from the lowest social class went to university but by the end of the decade, after the introduction of tuition fees and abolition of the student grant, the figure dropped to just 7 percent. Over the same period, participation by children from the professional classes increased from 55 to 72 percent (Blanden and Machin, 2004). There is also evidence to indicate that class and ethnicity affect the sector of higher education that young people enter, mapping onto the hierarchy of higher education institutions. For example, figures for 1998 indicate that minority groups were disproportionately entering the new or modern rather than elite universities: students of Caribbean origin were over-represented by 43 percent, Asians by 162 percent and Africans by 223 percent in this sector.

As we can see then, there is good and bad news about the expansion of higher education in the UK. The situation has been improving for young women, and for middle-class young people (who were always advantaged in this regard). It has varied little despite government policies, access is currently declining for working-class young people, and amongst those from different ethnic groups there is variability.

As suggested earlier, many of the specific efforts of policy targeted towards more socially excluded groups have come into play during the years of the study, but as Nam indicated at the start of the chapter there is some ambivalence amongst those young people as to whether higher education is a sensible route for them. Two examples of academically able working class young women from our most disadvantaged site help to illustrate some of these points.

Two trajectories into further and higher education

The two young women grew up in the large, physically isolated and economically disadvantaged housing estate on the outskirts of a city in northern England. An area with a reputation for violence and gangs, it has many of the characteristics of social exclusion and a history of policy responses to that situation. Levels of unemployment and crime are high; health is poor. Much of the employment in the area is relatively low paid and unskilled, and opportunities are generally considered to be better for women than for men. The research period saw the school that the young people were attending declared one the UK's 500 'failing schools', despite the obvious commitment of the teaching staff.

When we first interviewed the two young women in 1999 they distinguished themselves from the rest of this local sample by a desire for social mobility demonstrated by their professional ambitions. They saw education as a route out of the estate. Over the course of our interviews with them, they engaged in contrasting strategies to pursue these ambitions, and faced different obstacles. Each of the cases presents a situated balance between individual and wider resources, and access to support and social capital. They demonstrate that for young people from economically deprived backgrounds, individual resources of ability and ambition do not necessarily translate into educational and occupational success. We also saw that the 'costs' of social mobility and that community-oriented values, investments and identities – bonding social capital – can militate against social and geographical mobility. Lauren's route was riddled with ambivalence, with the pull of community and her lack of motivation to resist it playing a strong part. Maureen showed an increasingly steely determination and a realisation that you need to get out of a disadvantaged community in order to get on, with all the costs that entailed.

Lauren

Lauren was academically able, always seen as bright in her school, and strongly attached to her family and community. Her highest professional ambition, at 16, was to be a psychologist, and she saw education including university as providing the pathway to this ambition. Her family gave her considerable support: her father provided his 'princess' with material support and social capital through contacts for work (like all the young people on this site, and most in the study, Lauren worked throughout her education); her mother provided emotional and practical support and advice, intervening at key moments to alter Lauren's trajectory. A critical moment occurred before Lauren's first interview in 1998 (aged 14), when her beloved grandmother died. Illness, accidents and bereavement played a part in this story, quite typical for young people in this site. Her grandmother provided a strong value base for Lauren, and was part of a rich vein of adult female culture on which she drew to construct her own identity. Nan remained an important influence throughout, and Lauren said she always asked herself 'would Nan have done it that way' leading people (and Lauren) to characterise her as having 'an old head'. However just prior to an interview in 1999 Lauren went through 'a bad patch'. She had been in a relationship with a 'bad boy' who had gone to prison, and had been drawn into the criminal and drug culture of the estate. She had been at risk of succumbing to the dominant form of femininity in the locality (involving early pregnancy), and was slipping back in terms of school work. Her mother intervened and helped her get back on track at this point. Lauren said that her mother was her 'saviour' who 'sat me down and we had a chat about it all, she put me right really. Helped me see where I'd been going wrong. I knew anyway really, but you know … we sorted it out'. Lauren reasserted herself as a good pupil. She then did very well in her final examinations at school and went on to college to do four A level courses (required qualifications for university entry).

But after a few months at college Lauren lost confidence and became very stressed. Her mother intervened once more, suggesting that perhaps she was not a paperwork but a more practical person and should give up college, steering her towards training and work in 'hair and beauty'. Lauren was interviewed for the study mere days after the decision to drop out had been made (in 2001), and was clearly in a state of great uncertainty. Her interviewer commented that 'A sense of instability and chaos, linked to rapidity of change underpinned all Lauren's interviews' (Researcher Notes). Lauren had considerable personal resources to draw on, being able, having a strong work ethic and a desire to succeed through her own efforts. Despite having a different boyfriend at each interview, and being linked into the community in this way, she was determinedly avoiding the more usual female route through early pregnancy that her peers had followed, and planned to have children 'in 10 years' time'. She had resources to draw on in her family and community, but these bonds pulled her back to more limited horizons. At this point it was looking increasingly less likely that Lauren would realise her academic potential and pursue the university route.

Between 2001 and 2004 there was considerable contact with Lauren, and one arranged interview in 2002 was called off since she was very ill. A final interview was arranged in 2004 when Lauren was 19, and things had changed again, she had reinvested in education and was in the second year of a Nursing Diploma at university.

> Lauren: Yeah well I'm at uni now.
> INT: You're at uni?
> Lauren: Even though I didn't finish me A Levels, but training to be a nurse instead. So I've always wanted to do it really deep down I think.

She related this choice back to caring for her grandmother. But cliff-hangers persisted in this new educational route; Lauren was not totally happy with the teaching on the course:

> It's alright. I enjoy it, but the teachers aren't the full shilling.
> … Some of them, no some aren't. Apparently they're all qualified nurses, but I wouldn't trust any of them to look after me. (Lauren, 19, 2004)

And at this interview she was awaiting exam results that would dictate her future:

> So um if we fail it this time, we get a re-sit, if we fail the re-sit you're off the course. …
> So I don't know what's gonna happen. But I know – I mean me and [friend], we just
> went home and cried, because we knew that we hadn't passed it anyway. So it's just
> a case of waiting to see. (Lauren, 19, 2004)

As with many young people from her background, Lauren struggled to get onto, and
maintain an educational route, and her passage demonstrates the interplay of agency,
structure, resources and resourcefulness, contingency and social policy (the provision of new
routes into nursing) at play in the individual biography. The strategy that Lauren has pursued
also suggests that she is working within the confines of the possible with her locality. It is
interesting to note that a friend of hers from the retail outlet in which she worked is also
pursuing the nursing diploma with her, and another school friend is doing nursing training
elsewhere in the city.

Maureen

Maureen and Lauren were close friends, but in contrast with Lauren, who valued her strong
links to community, Maureen quite clearly considered that she had to get out in order to get on.
Her 'take on the future has not changed in some ways throughout the study: she has always
seen education as her key route to an adult life beyond her local world and university has been
part of it. She has never been clear on the detail of her career, but a profession has always
been assumed' (Researcher Notes). She also had the ability to pursue this route, although her
determination and self-confidence increased over time with increasing evidence of her
academic ability. One of her strategies was to defer the physicality and pleasures associated
with the teenage life to achieve her educational and occupational ends, although her mother
intervened to ensure that Maureen did not get involved in dangerous local leisure worlds, in
order that she might avoid the risks of low aspirations, sex, crime and other pitfalls. At 16
(2001) Maureen talked about 'having to wait to do anything with me life beyond education' and
of having little space in her life for fun, boys, pubs and clubs, whilst these were things that she
would have liked to pursue. One of the costs of Maureen's strategy was the need to defer
active heterosexuality and womanhood until they held less of a threat to her desired future.

   Maureen's parents had split up when she was 6, and she regarded her two homes style
of living, having a bedroom and family life with both her mother and her partner, and her
father and his partner, as a positive resource. The homes were in less disadvantaged areas
on the estate, and the physical separation helped Maureen to maintain her emotional
separation from the community. Although both mother and father had grown up locally they
were socially mobile within the locality. Her mother has been a consistent, indeed an
insistent support for Maureen, and both father and mother have motivated her to want to
leave the estate behind and pursue her education. Maureen seemed to draw implicitly on the
cultural capital of her social worker father, who 'had his chance to go to university' but did
not. Her own strategy was to sever social connections with the community, including a
break-up engineered by her mother with our other case study, Lauren, quite early in the
study (when both were 16). They have each pursued their different routes, one drawn back

into the community, the other totally rejecting all ties, and coincidentally arrived at the same university.

We also missed an interview with Maureen in 2002 and caught up with her in 2004 when she was in the second year of a law degree. She was uncertain what she would do with her degree, but removal from the estate was still a prime motivator. Since the last interview in 2001 she had suffered a falling out with her mother and had left home with her sister. Although her mother retracted the next day, the young women had gone to stay with their father and stepmother until the university term began. Maureen experienced growing feelings of independence whilst at university, the first year in halls, and the second in a shared flat with girlfriends, including her sister. The interviewer observed that 'She is now a confident young woman ensconced in her student lifestyle' and evidently enjoying some of the pleasures that she had eschewed earlier in her education. She has broken bonds with her mother, but her father provides her with financial support, although as she points out, she is one of the few on her course who have worked throughout. 'She seem to be making her own way now, supported by the "friends for life" that she has made at university' (Researcher Notes, 2004).

In the trajectories of these two young women we can see reflected many of the issues discussed in this chapter and book about policy – expanding higher education and the possibilities this can provide for alleviating social exclusion, about social mobility and its tension with the type of social capital that bonds you to community, about bridging social capital out of the community, and the costs of different trajectories for individual lives. Both of the young women had ability and considerable support from their families, and yet still their route could be fraught. Lauren seemed at the last interview to have worked out a way of balancing the pull of community, with a less high achieving path through education, although still insecure in relation to ultimately gaining a qualification and her desired profession. Maureen has stayed with her determined journey of both social and geographical mobility.

These case studies were from the most disadvantaged site in our study. We turn now to look more generally at the experiences of the young people.

Young people in Inventing Adulthoods: Education and ambivalence

In our model of adulthood, education, work, the domestic arena, and leisure and consumption, intersected in different ways. Young people who invested in education looked forward to the recognition that educational achievement can bring, and ultimately to a career and financial security. 'Traditional' transitions were still enjoyed by some of our young people, particularly those in the middle class, on the privileged path to professional careers. And, as we have seen above, some young people followed less traditional and less supported working class routes into further and higher education (see also Maisie in Chapter 4). Those who failed to secure a sense of competence and recognition in education might follow several routes: they could seek accelerated adulthood by leaving school and entering work as soon as possible, they could focus on the domestic domain, start a steady relationship and 'settle down', or, they might attempt to stay forever young, to have fun and pursue leisure. But one route that has become increasingly common, and featured in different ways in our group, including Lauren, was to struggle to maintain a connection with education, building a portfolio of vocational courses, which might in fact lead nowhere, whilst also working in dead end jobs – a yo-yo transition (Du Bois-Reymond and Lopez Blasco, 2003: 23). In our sample, two of the young women in the inner city site undertook vocational qualifications in office/business skills that they saw as giving them no real benefit in the working world, while two in the leafy suburb followed a trend to take vocational qualifications in leisure and tourism, but ended up in work totally unrelated to this area.

Balancing education and study with other aspects of life was another important theme, and young people drew on various resources to manage this. Some successfully juggled many activities, and they were likely to be able to draw on practical and financial support from parents – lifts to and from work for example could ease this balancing act. Parents also used sophisticated strategies in this process, for example encouraging their offspring to give up paid work as exams approached and rewarding them with increased allowances. Young people often talked about not risking educational attainment in order to pursue serious relationships; getting the balance right between study and social life or 'life'. Work and education appeared sometimes to be competing rather than complementary goals, and the allure of an independent income was strong.

A pattern of postponing the demands of intimate relationships and the pursuit of a particular type of femininity also emerged in young women's accounts, especially in relation to desires for social mobility through education. They needed to avoid the negative social capital that could bind them to community; to leave their locality in order to achieve this aim; to get out in order to get on as we saw in the case studies described earlier.

The pattern of combining education and work that the young people pursued in school continued into further and higher education. Sometimes the motivation was similar: to have their own money and not to be a burden on their parents – linking to the resources of the domestic sphere and family. In other instances the work they did enhanced their educational route. Edward and Francis for example took vacation placements that complemented their work ambitions, and could lead to an actual career. Monica, a working-class young woman in a largely middle-class school, carefully planned her gap year in order to earn enough money to be able to buy a car, in which she could drive from home to her chosen local university.

Our research sites were chosen to reflect socio-economic diversity, and of the 70 young people interviewed for a fourth time at age 18–24 in 2002, 20 (29%) were at university (a few more were at college, one was having a gap year, and one middle-class young man had dropped out). Of those at university, nine were working class, eight of whom were young women. Most of these were the first in their family to go to university, so it could be said that this group do reflect the expansion of higher education and the improvement in access for young women. Many of the young people in the study as a whole placed a high value on education, and expressed this in a range of ways, for example seeing education as a good in itself, not a means to an end. Others did see it as a means to the end, the aim being a good job and reasonable income; some valued school, some preferred further education and higher education. Shannon, for example, a working-class young woman from Northern Ireland, valued education, believing that it is very important in Northern Ireland, and that some people there become 'study freaks … they just love to do degrees. I think a lot of people can get addicted to studying and do not know what to do with themselves once they get a degree.'

In contrast, although Carol, a middle-class young women in Northern Ireland, had a great social time she 'didn't really enjoy the academic side of school'. Her approach was highly instrumental; she was 'at university to get a good job' and was not particularly enjoying her course:

> I'm not there to enjoy it, if you know what I mean, which I don't know if that's a good or bad thing … if I was financially secure and not have to go and work academically, I would jump at the chance … I'm interested in what I'm doing at the moment, but I wouldn't say I'm ecstatic, I absolutely wouldn't die for it … The first year is more kinda theory-based and you don't have a lot of scope in the actual practical side of it. But um so I'm hoping (laughs) that it'll be a bit more interesting in the next few years. (Carol, 22, 2003)

Nat, a middle-class young man in the leafy suburb, was similarly instrumental, with his choice of course providing a back-up in case he could not decide what he wanted to do:

> But computing is basically – and I knew what it would be when I chose the course – it would be a back-up if I never realised what I wanted to do, or found something. So I suppose that's what it will be in the end – a back-up – not my first choice but something. (Nat, 21, 2003)

There were very few who thought that education had little impact or meaning in their life. In the earliest part of the study, a group of young men in a pupil referral unit and so excluded from school for behavioural reasons, all subscribed to education as one of the most important things in life despite the fact that it was clearly not working for them. A number in the study as a whole felt that university was not necessarily a good route for them, or that they and others could do just as well in work and earnings without it. As we have seen, some were ambivalent about the value of education, and others felt they personally had made the wrong choices, either of university, or of specific subjects.

Although Karin, a working-class young woman in Northern Ireland, valued education and had made the right choice of university, she felt that she had made the wrong choice of subject because she would not be making a contribution, would not be changing anything. The experience of going to a third world country made her realise that there is more to the world than Art and Design:

> I just thought kind of going to India kind of opened my eyes and stuff as well about how, I don't know, naïve or something we are here about what's going on everywhere else. I always wanted to do something about that there but I'm not going to be doing anything at least for the next 3 years I'm going to be a student I'm not going to be helping anybody except myself. (Karin, 19, 2003)

Edward in the leafy suburb, developed the argument about university not being for everybody in the context of a critique of government policy:

Because of this misguided emphasis on qualifications as pieces of paper, there's a feeling that you have to go to university if you want to get ahead in life, and people who aren't temperamentally suited to university life are deciding to go through 3 years of something they don't enjoy and ending up with a debt – or ending up in less satisfying jobs than they could be doing otherwise. And it's this decision, it's the way people are almost forced to choose between the lesser of two evils at a very early stage in their lives that leads to the homogenisation I believe ... People are being forced to do things in order to meet government targets rather than because it's likely to do them or society any good at all, and that's a mistake. (Edward, 20, 2002)

Conclusion

This chapter and the next, on 'Work', are linked, given the age of the young people in our study, and the numbers of them remaining in education. As a group they illustrate some of the themes we have discussed here. The expansion of higher education has mainly benefited the middle classes (who themselves have also expanded) but the working-class young people in our group who have made it into higher education are mainly young women. Although many have resources of material, social and cultural capital, particularly in the middle class, others have fought bravely against the odds in their attempts to follow an educational route. They have had difficulties balancing the demands of education and the rest of their lives, but are differentially aided through family support and other resources. And, for many, education and work often seem to be competing goals.

Government policy has seemed to be based on contradictions. On the one hand they want to get more young people into higher education, particularly those whose families do not see higher education as being for them. On the other, they place obstacles in their way through student loans (rather than grants) and top-up fees, which the evidence on student finance suggests have a particularly detrimental and deterrent effect on poorer students from lower class backgrounds. A further contradiction emerges in the aim to develop social capital in communities at risk of social exclusion, and the promotion of an individualised pursuit of social mobility through the vehicle of education. We have seen in our case studies that in many instances the bonding type of social capital that binds a young person to their community or family, can limit their possibilities for pursuing the individualised route to social mobility, and that they need to get out of such communities to get on. Or to put it the other way round, the promotion of individual opportunity, of geographical mobility and flexibility, continually undermines traditional community ties. We have also seen the determination that young people demonstrate in pursuing education, with limited resources to draw on.

In the next chapter we will look more closely at the nature of the world of work that the transition from education leads the young people into, and the way that work is entwined in their lives throughout.

Chapter 4

Work

Introduction

Traditionally, 'youth transitions' referred to the transition from school to work for the bulk of the population, or from education to work for the minority. In the UK, for example, between the end of the Second World War and the mid 1970s the employment market was relatively stable. A large proportion of young people (over 70%) went directly from school into the labour market at the minimum school leaving age, and other markers of the transition to adulthood – leaving home, marriage and family – followed soon after. Only a minority were destined for an extended period of education, training and work (Ashton and Field, 1976; Bynner, 2001; Mizen, 2004). These experiences (and work destinations) paralleled the social class distribution in the UK.

In fact the social class and educational background of parents is the major consistent element affecting the education and work chances of young people that emerges from the literature on youth transitions (Bynner et al., 2002; Fenton et al., 2002; Jones, 2002; Ball, 2003; McNeice et al., 2004). It continues to the present, with certain variations in relation to some minority ethnic groups (Platt, 2005). This resilient relationship provides some evidence for the contention that individualisation does not mean the disappearance of inequality, rather its remaking in new forms (Skeggs, 2004). Perhaps all young people face more uncertainty in the current climate, but the one certainty is the resilience of the importance of background, and the concomitant resources available as a result of that positioning. Recent commentators have noted that narratives about processes of individualisation and choice have obscured this relationship and that young people have a tendency to blame themselves rather than social or economic factors for any failure to achieve educational or occupational objectives (Furlong and Cartmel, 1997; Roberts, 1995).

Over the last three decades, in the context of a major restructuring of the UK economy, recession and technological change, the youth labour market collapsed (Morris, 1994; Johnston et al., 2000; MacDonald and Marsh, 2001). Successive UK governments moved in different ways, with different motives and differing levels of success, into policies to provide training and education for young people, with, as we have seen in Chapter 3, a leading current policy being the expansion of higher education to encompass 50 percent of the relevant youth population. The changing public and policy agenda operates with a lag in relation to young people's actual needs, regarding young people in this context as 'problems' and usually producing policy solutions to these perceived problems in a piecemeal fashion, often with unintended consequences. All of these changes in the economy and government policy agendas have had great impact on young people's lives and differential effects in relation to social class, gender and ethnicity.

In 2001 in a White Paper entitled *A new impetus for European youth*, the European Commission (EC) spelled out the more practical considerations for policy that the situation of young people gives rise to (EC, 2001). First, youth is lasting longer and young people reach the various stages on the route to adulthood at later ages; second, there are non linear paths through life where various life-roles are becoming confused, and young people move between them, or hold several at the same time – for example having a job, being a student, living with parents, being a parent; third, traditional collective models are losing ground as personal pathways become increasingly individualised. Du Bois-Reymond and Lopez Blasco (2003) argue that there is a mismatch between policies developed to help disadvantaged and excluded young people across European countries, and the (post)modernised transition they are actually experiencing. These authors also take a biographical approach to the study of young people, arguing that they need to reconcile different aspects of what might be considered broken or disrupted trajectories but which are in fact linked in their own biographies:

> In young people's perception, the transition to work is linked with all the other decisions they take, or want to take: for example, where to live and with whom, what kind of work corresponds to their capacities and interests, and how they might continue with education while working. (2003: 24–5)

For young people themselves, work in its many forms is an integral part of their lives and their understanding of adulthood, and that lost youth labour market can still exert a powerful hold on their own (and their parents') imaginations. In this chapter we draw on young people's accounts from the Inventing Adulthoods study to illustrate the part that 'work' plays in young people's biographies and identities.

From youth unemployment to work as a biographical domain

Youth studies were traditionally very interested in employment and unemployment; with how young people acted as a reserve army of labour; their impact on wage levels; and how youth employment fluctuates according to wider economic fortunes (Bradley and Hickman, 2004). The feminist critique of youth studies encouraged more attention to be paid to consumption, the domestic and the personal (Griffin, 1985; McRobbie, 1980). This shift in attention also coincided with the period of economic restructuring referred to above, in which the full time permanent 'employment' that had marked the destination for the transitions to adulthood for young men, slid increasingly out of reach. A new holistic approach to the varied pathways into adulthood, calling on all aspects of young people's experience, has emerged (Coles, 1995, 2000; MacDonald et al., 2005), and is exemplified by our own study.

Raymond Williams writing in 1976 explored how our understandings of 'work' had shifted; from the notion of general productive activity which might include work around the garden or house, to a more specialised focus on paid employment. Changes in the economy and in social theory suggest that we may be returning to the broader focus implied by a productive definition. The changes in the economy include de-industrialisation, an increase in the service sector, and flexibilisation. In a globalised world based on free market economics, flexibility is demanded at the level of companies, employers and employees. Employees need to be sufficiently flexible, technically equipped and well trained to be able to adapt throughout their professional life to different tasks, contexts and requirements (Castells, 2000). It is argued then that this 'new economy' is becoming increasingly more virtual, reflexive, flexible and networked. Within the new economy there has also been an erosion of the distinction between the public and the private spheres. A major contributory feature here is increasing female participation in the labour market, which has led to attributes and activities previously considered part of the private sphere to be included in the public world of work, and the reverse. For example emotional labour, often carried out by women, takes place in the workplace, while caring for others, previously hidden in the home, is recognised as work.

The flexible field of work has bred a 'new sociology of work' to explain and describe its changing characteristics. From this perspective, there are blurred and shifting boundaries between different forms of work: public and private, paid and unpaid, formal and informal. Work is seen as embedded in other social relations; orientations to work are shaped by gender, class and culture; and attention is drawn to the increasing importance of understanding work on the margins of public spaces (Pettinger, et al., 2005). Glucksman (2003) adds to this conceptualisation by stressing the significance of connections between different work activities. This highlights interconnections between work activities across the economic processes of production, distribution, exchange and consumption; connectedness between work activities in different spheres; changing boundaries between what is work and what is not; and, the regulation and organisation of time in social processes such as work. It is this uncertain space that young people enter as they make the transition to work. Education and work are entwined in their lives, and as we saw in Chapter 3 almost all are convinced of the importance of education for their future work and life chances. A biographical approach that does not fragment young people's lives can provide a basis for a better understanding of their experiences, and potentially the provision of better solutions for the problems that beset them in changing economic and social conditions and in the 'new economy'. The 'new sociology of work' can also provide an integrative approach beginning with the changing meaning of work. These issues are discussed further in this chapter.

Connections of another kind are also important for the individual seeking educational and employment success in this context. Social capital, networks of association, and socially negotiated ties and relationships involving trust and reciprocity provide important resources in this search. Social capital concerns the values that people hold and the resources that they can access, which both result in, and are the result of, collective and socially negotiated ties and relationships (Edwards et al., 2003; see too Chapter 1 'Introduction'). As we saw in Chapter 3, access to social capital can interface with processes of social inclusion and exclusion through bonding social capital, the strong ties that can limit an individual to a closed, local system of contacts; or bridging social capital, weak ties that can enable an individual to access resources and opportunities beyond their immediate environment and relationships. Strong ties and bonding social capital may make it possible for individuals to survive poverty, yet it may also hinder their ability to escape such poverty (MacDonald and Marsh, 2005).

Work in our contrasting locations

The UK is diverse in terms of labour markets, and our research sites were different in this regard. Before discussing the place of work in young people's biographies we will give some indication of levels and types of employment in the labour markets in each of these localities at the time of writing.

The population in *Northern Ireland* is one of the youngest in Europe and in our research site almost half of the population are under 25 years old. The unemployment figures have dropped over the past 10 years and in January 2006 the Northern Ireland unemployment rate was 5 percent. But the rate for 18–24 year olds was higher at 11 percent creating some difficulty for young people in finding jobs. Seventy five percent of the 14,000 young people who leave to take up university places in the UK do not return. The 'brain drain' continues to be a cause for concern, and academics within the local university system blame the ceiling on local university places, arguing that 40 percent of those who leave do so due to a lack of local places.

In the *rural area*, employment in agricultural and manufacturing had declined in the two decades before the research began, although a relatively low-wage economy was still highly dependent on agriculture and related industries. Development of the service sector, had not involved a major increase in financial and business services and provided low wages. Low unemployment figures overall conceal significant pockets of high unemployment, disaffection and social exclusion. There was a strong work ethic amongst most of the young people here and most found no difficulty in finding part-time jobs whilst at school and college.

Historically, manufacturing businesses provided the majority of local jobs in the area of the *disadvantaged estate*, but its decline and a number of regeneration initiatives had seen a growth in service sector work concentrated in hotels, restaurants and transport. This area was in the top 10 percent most deprived local authorities of the Indices of Deprivation in the 2001 Census. The overall unemployment rate from the same source was 5 percent compared with 3 percent for England and Wales. Thirty five percent of the unemployed in the area were long term.

The *inner city* site was in the top 20 most deprived local authorities in the Indices of Deprivation and this and the disadvantaged estate offered the greatest contrast with the *leafy suburb*, which was in the bottom 5 percent of the Deprivation Index. The unemployment rate in the inner city site (Census 2001) was 6 percent, and 30 percent of these were long-term unemployed; in the leafy suburb it was 2 percent. There were higher levels of education in the leafy suburb, and a higher proportion of people in occupations at the top of the occupational scale than for the UK as a whole. Eighteen percent in the leafy suburb had no qualifications, compared with 29 percent for the UK as a whole; and 53 percent were in the top three levels of work, compared with 40 percent for the UK.

Working a way into adulthood

We turn now to the experiences of the young people in the Inventing Adulthoods study, first examining their experiences of paid work, then work experience, and the meaning of work to them through the study over time, and consider their access to social capital. From our emphasis on location, it has also become clear that varying local labour markets affect the access to work opportunities of the young people.

Experience of paid work

Our initial group of young people had considerable experience of paid work, despite their tender age, although the amount of work they did varied by age and by location, reflecting the local labour market. We were surprised to find that over a quarter of the 11–16 year olds (28%) held a part-time job. This varied across the sites and those in the affluent commuter belt (43%) and the isolated rural area (43%) were more likely to be working part time. Young men were more likely than young women to have part-time jobs (30:25%) and to work longer hours. Age was also important. Across the age range the rate of those working went from 13 percent to 45 percent. The weekly hours worked ranged from 1 to 44 and again the number of hours increased with age; in the oldest group (15–16 year olds) 35 percent worked more than 11 hours a week. Delivery (21% – papers, buns, drinks) and retail jobs (19% – fast food outlets, supermarkets, pubs, restaurants) accounted for the majority of part-time jobs mentioned. There were local variations with most (21%) of those in the rural area involved in the farming industry, 20 percent of those in the inner city school working on market stalls, and 28 percent of those with part-time jobs on the deprived estate looking after children. The type of work tended to support gender division, 87 percent of those doing babysitting and 73 percent of those doing cleaning being young women. Like others, then, we have found that high levels of part-time work is a specific feature of the lives of young people at school in the UK (Hobbs et al., 1996; Mizen et al., 1999, 2001; Bolton et al., 2001; Bynner, 2001).

Work Experience: An opportunity or a reinforcement of marginality?

Whilst at school, some of the young people were provided with work experience and/or job placements, where they spent 2 weeks or more working in a real work environment under supervision. These experiences produced varying effects and consequences. For most, work experience tended to reinforce inequalities, and our data raises questions about its limitations as a universal policy measure. It rarely had a transformative effect – those with the right kind of social capital, (the best personal, family and school/teacher networks) were able to derive most from placements in terms of gaining labour market knowledge, developing new networks, and building their curricula vitae. In contrast, those who were least well resourced and least well networked tended to end up in placements that reflected the part-time jobs that were available to them locally. Some of the young people thought they were treated as slave labour and given boring, mundane tasks, or alternatively dropped into difficult situations and left to sink or swim, here, for example, working on a switchboard in a bank:

I only done it for about three days – and then I couldn't do it any more, because it was they had – they were like asking for things that I didn't even know about, so it was like – kept getting stuff. – It was really difficult. I mean the first day, they showed me all the basics, but then they left me on my own to do it by myself, and I didn't know what I was doing so. (Janis, 16, 1998)

For some, it had been their first glimpse of working life, and offered insight into what it might be to be adult, which some welcomed and others did not:

You had to be more independent and just, if you don't do the work then it's – a problem. In school the teachers, if you don't do the work the teachers will tell you to do the work and they'll just kind of tell you off and stuff, but the work, if you don't do it, it's only affecting you really. It's different that way. (Brenda, 16, 1998)

Work experience could lead to a part-time job, a re-think about future work plans, or confirm an earlier career choice. It could also provide information about labour market opportunities, enable young people to find their niche, or possibly provide a depressing insight into the monotony of certain jobs. There was variability in the resources that schools put into work experience placements but they did find most of them, with more or less care in matching the person to the job, or knowledge of what the work entailed. Other placements were found in the same way that later work would be found, through family and contacts. In this way it reflected the levels of access to types of work that they might expect in the future, given their economic and social resources.

The experience of Jean, a middle-class young woman in the rural area, illustrates some of these points. She found her placement helping to teach in a primary school through social contacts, and used it as a means of reflecting on her own position, at the juncture between youth and adulthood. It provided her with an opportunity to step back from her role as a pupil and see things from a teaching perspective. She and her mother had actively sought out, and used, friends and contacts to secure a position that would overcome the lack of ethnic diversity in her part of the country and give her opportunities to work with children from different ethnic backgrounds:

Yes, definitely, it was definitely worthwhile. (Jean, 15, 1998)

The meaning of work over time

Both traditional and more flexible approaches to work and the labour market were expressed by the young people in the interview in 2000. Some talked in terms of being flexible, of having a good varied curriculum vitae (resumé), taking risks and building up qualifications, and of the necessity of being able to change jobs and transfer skills. Others (young men) seemed to inhabit another era when they talked about the continuing allure of having a trade, and the security this could offer you in the labour market over a working lifetime.

We found that the young people attached a range of different meanings to paid work. For example, it could be a way of learning about how to fit into the adult world, a means of developing personal confidence and authority, of reducing dependence on parents, gaining an insight into social hierarchies, keeping out of trouble, a key milestone on the path to adulthood, or a means of making new friendships.

Work could also be seen as a form of leisure. Part-time work in particular could provide a space for making new friends, spending time with existing friends, having a laugh, or spending time in an area of special interest (e.g. a skateboarder who worked in a board shop). For some young people, their time in part-time employment can be seen as a transference of leisure time from one sphere into another. The process of becoming more confident, earning an independent income, learning how to speak to people, mixing with different types of people were all associated with work by young people, and were attributes they used in expanding their social lives. All of these elements could be seen as contributing to feelings of competence and maturity and so the forging of adult identities.

At the interview in 2003, the situation had changed in that most of the young people had left school for further or higher education, or the labour market and so were engaging in some kind of paid work. The meanings that they attributed to work, resonated with their earlier views. They valued the financial rewards, although a number asserted that the money was not that important, but enjoyment of the work certainly was; they valued what their workmates could offer them in terms of friendship and fun. Flexibility, easy access and familiarity were valued by some, and others saw their work as a vocation, expecting satisfaction from work that contributes to the welfare of people in need. A lower-middle-class young woman in Northern Ireland spoke of having a vocation for nursing:

> I suppose the hours and the amount you have to do and you're really involved in people's lives and I suppose you have to put people before yourself. (Lena, 20, 2003)

Cynthia, working class in Northern Ireland had enhanced her self-esteem:

> And I like it like that because you feel kind of trustworthy and everything it makes you feel as if you're worth something and you are valued in your work. (Cynthia, 18, 2003)

For Francis, a middle-class young man in the leafy suburb, work and self were integrally linked:

> I don't want to work for a company that I'm not – I don't think I'll be happy with. So I'm willing to postpone things and make sure I get the right one. (Francis, 24, 2003)

A sentiment echoed by Jade (18, 2003), a working-class young woman in the inner city site: 'Choose a job you love and you'll never work a day in your life.'

Access to resources and support: Social capital

In the interview in 2002–03 when their ages ranged from 18–24 the young people were asked questions about their social networks and the benefits that might accrue from those contacts, including who they could turn to if they needed various types of support around issues relating to education and work.

The major source of support for the young people at that point was their family, parents in particular, who provided emotional, financial and social support and resources. They also provided a network of contacts through which their children could secure information and help with educational choices, and work.

For Edward, a middle-class young man in the leafy suburb, family is a safe back up:

> I'm glad I've got them there as a back-up. I'm pretty confident that if I ever got in a real mess, if I ever got in a very bad situation financially or emotionally or whatever I'd be able to turn to them for support. I would almost certainly be told, 'I told you so'. (Edward, 20, 2002)

Clearly young people without this parental backdrop of support for whatever reason could face considerable difficulty. Others in their social networks who also provided support and resources at this time included friends, wider kin, people in their workplaces, communities, college and university teachers, and members of the social services, including social workers. They also drew support and developed networks through relationships, youth culture, the gay scene, sport and the internet.

A couple of the young people in our study pursued their leisure time activities into work, and developed useful networks in the process, sometimes incorporating members of their family. Patrick, a 20-year-old lower-middle-class young man in Northern Ireland, for example, was very well networked in the music business, with supportive uncles in different towns who were in the same business. He obtained all manner of practical and other support from his wide networks. Samuel (aged 20, middle class in the leafy suburb) regarded networking as his main skill, and gave up university after a year because, 'It's about who you know not what you've done'. By that time he had developed the skills and contacts he needed for his planned future in the entertainment world, as he explained here:

> *Samuel*: A very good network, especially for what I'm going into, I know every-one there is to know.
>
> *INT*: Hmm yeah, so you could say – would you say you were really well networked?
>
> *Samuel*: Yeah very. It's what I've always wanted to do, it's the only skill I really have is networking.
>
> (Samuel, 20, 2002)

The examples of the well networked in our sample tended to be middle-class young people, although in a range of circumstances. They also tended to be flexible and their networks spanned different age groups and communities – local, family, educational, work, leisure – and a range of activities, from bell-ringing to volunteering. These types of networks can be theorised in terms of 'weak ties' and 'bridging social capital' as they enable an individual to access resources and opportunities beyond those of their immediate environment and relationships. Many of the working-class young people in the sample were also well networked, aspired to social mobility, and were resourced by their families. But many others had 'strong ties' and 'bonding social capital', networks that tended to link them into family, community and locality, rather than providing broader opportunities for contacts, education and work (Fukuyama, 1995; Putnam, 1998). The poorly networked tended to have fewer resources in general than the well networked, and often little support on their route through education to work, as we see in some of our examples in both this chapter and the previous chapter on education.

Certain young people, generally from middle-class and well-supported families, may be in a position to translate their social and cultural assets into viable educational and work strategies. They may be able to find ways of maximising the value of part-time work by building networks and cultivating the right kind of work experience that translates into symbolic material for curriculum vitae, and opportunities for gap years and future work. Others have to be reflexive in order to survive. They are likely to have the wrong kind of part-time jobs (that interfere with their ability to study), and the wrong kind of work experience that reconfirms the limits of their social worlds and those of their parents. They are likely to be tempted by the type of recognition offered by full-time work and the access it provides to forms of consumption otherwise deferred into the indefinite future. What is supposed to be the 'normal' trajectory of school followed by higher education is enormously demanding, ruthlessly exposing resources and resourcefulness (Skeggs, 2004).

Three biographical routes into work

Three young people in different locations help to illustrate some of the themes of this chapter: the different local labour markets, the importance of social networks, the differential requirements and demands of the new economy in relation to class and location, and the subjective meaning of work entwined with life.

Most of the middle-class young people in our study were not in full-time work, but still in university by the fourth, or even the fifth interview. These young people tended to be supported generously by their parents, although many still did part-time or vacation work whilst at university. To a certain extent this could be seen as a traditional middle-class trajectory leading to a secure professional career for some, and perhaps for others a situation where they will have resources and are able to make choices according to their needs and preferences (Du Bois-Reymond and Lopez Blasco, 2003). In our study as in others it was the working-class young people who needed to work harder and longer whilst taking their degrees. They would also in general be the ones who would leave school or further education earlier and go into the labour market. We did, however, find middle-class young people who eschewed education at a fairly early age and also ventured into the labour market.

Although we have noted that social class is still an important determinant of life chances we have also seen that class is related to cultural as well as economic factors, and an individual's class can change over the life course. In intergenerational terms too class can be more fluid, as we saw in the example of Robin in Chapter 2. He seemed to be a middle-class young man from a broken home but what emerged on closer inspection as part of his family background was a rural working-class past, which had re-emerged as important for Robin. Lorna too, although middle class, had a self-made businessman father, and an ex-model mother who did not work outside the home, neither of whom provided the cultural capital that a more usual middle-class investment in education provided. Her story indicates a different middle class trajectory, where education does not play a large part.

Lorna

As we saw briefly in Chapter 2, Lorna did not think that university was necessarily a good idea. Like so many others in our study, Lorna had always worked from the age of 14, although she also received support from her parents. The financial support came particularly from her businessman father (retired) who had provided her with cars, in which she has always been interested. Aging from 17–23 across five interviews, in the first interview she was not very ambitious for herself, although thought that she might be more 'career oriented' when she was 25. She left school abruptly, due to a negative experience with peers, a critical moment (Thomson et al., 2002 and Chapter 2), and went to college in a nearby city to do several courses. At the same time she also worked in a pub. By the third interview she had abandoned education and was doing temporary work in various offices. Here she indicates the links between work and social relationships and the relevance of social capital:

> … my really close friend at college, we'd stayed really close and she said oh I'm looking for work so I got her a job there and er … and she started working, and then her dad who works for British Airways and got an amazing opportunity of free tickets to Australia and all the rest of it and so she was like oh I'm going to go and I said you can't just disappear and she said I can, so she told our boss and he said if you come back there won't be a job for you and she said fine and went and shortly after she left I did as well, just because it wasn't the same without having my friend there, she was my best friend, everyone else was nice and everything but it wasn't the same, so I left. (Lorna, 21, 2003).

At her fourth interview she was doing call centre type work and two nights a week in a fast food outlet. At the fifth interview she was working in the service department of a car company, work that she enjoyed, but was looking for similar work with higher pay. Her boyfriend also worked in the same company, and there was a family connection through her father with work involving cars. From the experience of work she described at each interview, it did not seem difficult for Lorna to find work, reflecting the relatively buoyant local labour market.

Lorna is quite independent and takes responsibility for herself, but the type of work she does is more typical of a working-class trajectory, particularly since she lacks qualifications. Her biography may be typical of an emerging trend of downward social mobility among the middle classes, and the impact of those processes that increase the uncertainty and insecurity of young people's transitions. It may also reflect the ways in which gender complicates processes of social mobility. Within Lorna's imagined long-term future, marriage and children were a priority, but not until she is totally organised:

> I want everything sorted out first, I want to be married, I want to be housed, I want everything sorted before I do anything like that. And make sure I can support a child. Very traditional … I wouldn't dare go into it without having a plan, I have to have a plan for everything, you know I'm a very organised person. (Lorna, 21, 2003)

Maisie

In a contrasting example, Maisie illustrates the difficulties that some young working-class people experience as they pursue a university education against the odds, and strive for social mobility. She also exemplifies in her work experiences the characteristics of work outlined by the new sociology of work described above. These are the embeddedness of work in other social relations and the blurred and shifting boundaries between different forms of work: public and private, paid and unpaid, formal and informal. As we saw in her comment in Chapter 3, Maisie sees going to university for someone from her background as a total struggle.

Throughout the time she has been involved in the study Maisie has lived on the same disadvantaged estate with her large family in cramped conditions. Her parents were separated and she cared for her sick mother. Surrounded by poverty, ill health, crime and low aspirations within her local community, Maisie expressed a desire to go to university to do a degree in the creative arts at her first individual interview (aged 17). An unlikely ambition in this context, her desire seemed unrealistic given the resources available to her. Against the odds and with a trajectory that is by no means smooth, she has achieved her aim.

Work has woven its way throughout Maisie's life; unpaid labour in the home; emotional labour in support of her family; and paid labour to support her desire to pursue education, get a degree, and to be a 'consumer'. But the work has also provided support for her, contributing not only financially to her ambitions, but lying at the heart of her identity. Even at school her part-time jobs were focused on her ultimate aims and vision of her future by helping her to buy the materials necessary for her courses. Throughout the study Maisie has held one job, acquired through her father, working as a waitress for a sports club. She loves this job, which has provided her with considerable experience, many contacts, support, and friendship, proving a considerable source of social capital. The competences, confidence and self-esteem she has built in this job have played an important role in defining her identity, and motoring her social mobility. The world of work more generally has provided an important space outside the confines of home and indeed the estate. Much of her paid labour has been in service industries where she also diligently provides emotional labour, and is a good worker (Hochschild, 1983). She has held down multiple jobs whilst gradually building her education. Maisie has always generated her social networks with people outside the estate, as a building block to the life she hopes to live. Each job provided her with contacts and friends, and she described the friends she made at university as 'friends for life'.

Maisie is dismissive of her neighbours, and contrasts her expected life with theirs:

> But then I just laugh because that is what I just don't want in my life. I will – when I'm the one that's got a nice job with like loads of money and a nice car and don't live round here – I'll be the happy one won't I, not them little scallies on the dole? (laughs) … And like I'm not saying that it's that bad around here but, I don't know if you understand what I mean, it's just like I just don't want that, I just really don't want that. And it's just not anything that I'd ever want. (Maisie, 20, 2003)

She is equally clear about what she does want:

> And I really would like to go to university, have a bit of fun when I leave, go away working, but at the end of the day when I grow up I want to have like a nice job, you know, and have a nice house and like a nice family with children and a husband and a nice car and like, you know, just to have a nice life. (Maisie, 20, 2003)

At our last contact she had gained her degree and was going away to work and have some fun.

The boundaries between the public and the private, the paid and unpaid, the formal and informal are blurred and shifting. If we take the case of Maisie as an illustration, it is her job at the sports club that provides her with security and continuity. She works all the hours she can to escape a future of drudgery and domestic labour. College work, housework, relationship work, waitressing are all juggled and implicated in each other. 'Work' is clearly embedded in other social relations, not least the project of social mobility. We can trace the complex interconnections (or circuits of meaning and exchange) between processes of production, and consumption in the different work activities Maisie undertakes. Her domestic and caring labour keeps chaos at bay and her paid employment enables her to fund her education, which in turn provides the promise of a future in which there may be some fun, leisure and consumption.

Ato

A third and final example of biographical routes into work is provided by Ato who we first met when he was 17 years old, studying for a vocational qualification in computing at college and taking some other courses at the school sixth form. At that time Ato was living in the inner city site with elderly Jamaican foster parents, having arrived in the UK as an unaccompanied minor from Africa aged 11. His parents remained in Africa, but his older sister and other siblings were in the same city as he, and he saw them frequently. His ambitions at this point were to take his courses in computer engineering and go on to do a computer qualification. By his third interview (aged 18) Ato was doing the computer qualification and working part time as an usher at a city centre cinema, 3 days a week. He planned to continue obtaining qualifications in computing, culminating in a degree. He also hoped to get his own flat through the council – explaining that he had a good chance because of his fostering situation.

At his fourth interview, aged 20, Ato had left his foster home and was living in a bedsit, arranged by social services, in the centre of the city. He kept in touch with people who had been helpful with work earlier, some of his teachers and workmates from the cinema. He had decided to stop education and computing for while and do something different. A friend told him about a job at a gentleman's club where he secured a post with reasonable pay. At his fifth interview aged 22 Ato was still living in same bedsit, and working at the club. He felt that his job had improved his communication skills, but admited to some feelings of regret about his education. He suggested that he still had a couple of years to decide whether he wanted to return to college and catch up with his computing qualifications, before his training became out of date. He was not at all sure about university. His short-term plan was to stay at the club for 2 or 3 years and then see.

Ato's story shows the different pressures that affect young people's school to work transition, and how easy it can be to drift away from an educational pathway. Having access in the city where he lived to a relatively buoyant labour market gave Ato opportunities for work, and his particular situation gave him access to independent housing at a relatively early age. Yet he struggled to combine this kind of economic independence with education.

Ato's networks are relatively fragile and self-made and cannot simply be categorised as strong/weak or bonding/bridging. At last contact, establishing and maintaining his own home was a driving force in his biography.

Conclusion

In this chapter we have examined how young people's transitions to work have been understood in youth studies and how young people have experienced those changes. The context is an understanding of the changing nature of work and the 'new economy'. As in other chapters, we build here on our emerging theory that it is through the experience of competence in particular areas of their lives, and the recognition of this competence by others, that young people come to make investments of time and energy that have significance for their trajectories (see too Thomson et al., 2004). The investments in different areas play an important part in the construction of identity and adulthood. In taking a holistic approach we conceive of 'labour' in the broadest sense, weaving between activities in different biographical fields. The accounts of the young people from our study illustrate the impact of structural, individual and contextual factors on their trajectories.

We have also sought to show how privilege and inequality are transmitted to young people over generations and through a local labour market. Young people's experiences of work experience, part-time work and combining study, paid employment and domestic labour, suggest the importance of social capital (in the form of social networks and contacts). The extent to which young people are able to make paid employment 'work' for them depends in great part on their existing resources. Yet although we found school to work transitions to be marked by social class, the processes of social reproduction are far from simple. The relative costs and benefits of pursuing education, training or employment are not clear to many young people, and decisions are contingent on a shifting set of personal, economic, social and policy factors. The stories of Lorna, Maisie and Ato all provide illustration of Beck's observation that: 'The reflexive conduct of life, the planning of one's own biography and social relations, gives rise to a new inequality, the *inequality* of dealing with *insecurity and reflexivity*' (Beck, 1992: 98; original emphasis).

Recent theorising on social class suggests that there has been a shift in how class operates, and that 'in various settings of social life, processes of inequality are produced and reproduced routinely and [...] this involves both economic and cultural practices' (Devine and Savage, 2000: 196). In the next chapter we look more closely at some of these cultural practices including the ways that social networks and local reputations combine at the level of neighbourhood to create 'cultures of violence' that provide the real and imaginary backdrops for projects of personal social mobility.

Chapter 5

Cultures of violence

Introduction

In the last two chapters we have considered how social processes and the availability of resources affect young people's educational and work transitions, and how conflicting demands can frustrate social mobility. In this chapter we explore how young people are both affected by and respond to the experience of violence and crime in their lives. We consider the impact of such experience on their transitions and choices, and on the decisions they make, and the effect of growing up in places and spaces where violence and crime are part of the common culture.

Youth violence and crime occupies a large space in the public imagination and policy agenda. The perception in the UK is that levels are rising and that the morals of young people are in some way eroding. In looking for reasons why this may be so, attention often falls on consumption patterns. Young people are thought to engage in a leisure landscape that involves an excess of alcohol, drugs, sex, junk food, (the wrong kind) of television, film, music and computer games. Representations of youth lifestyles as problematic abound in the media, and violence is frequently presented as a result of bad consumption patterns. Young people are portrayed with a broad brush as deviant, dangerous and out of control. A content analysis of local and national press by MORI over a one-week period during the summer of 2004 found that three in four articles about young people were negative in tone, and that the majority were about young men and violence (Goddard, 2004). Given that a sense of ourselves and others is 'constantly refracted through media images', (Brown, 2002) such a negative portrayal not only affects public perception of young people but has an impact on how young people themselves regard their position within society and local communities. Indeed, many young people in the Inventing Adulthoods study felt little sense of acknowledgement in their local neighbourhood, and many felt the glare of negative publicity.

Moral panics

The way in which the media has both responded to and fuelled public anxiety around youth consumption has regularly produced what has been labelled a 'moral panic.' This term was first used in the sociology of deviance in the 1960s and became part of public discourse in the early seventies when Stan Cohen published his book *Folk devils and moral panics: the creation of the mods and rockers* (1972). Cohen described disturbances between groups of young people over a bank holiday weekend in some English seaside towns. What Cohen witnessed was conflict between rival gangs, reported in the media as 'moral panic' – a new generation of teenagers who were out of control, and who posed a threat to the very fabric of society. Such representation of young people, Cohen argued, was the product not only of the events themselves but how these were mediated by those in positions of authority and public office as well as the general public. Mods and rockers in this instance became the 'folk devils' – the scapegoats in a narrative that was being constructed at a time of significant social change. The concept of 'moral panic' has been elaborated by a number of commentators including Hall and colleagues who consider the role of the state and governmentality in fuelling 'moral panics' (Hall et al., 1978). More recently McRobbie (1994) has pointed to a proliferation of moral panics in an increasingly fragmented and fast-moving mediascape. She reconceptualised the moral panic against the changing position of the media in a postmodern society, and considered how 'daily moral panics' are used to construct public policy agendas. The proliferation of moral panics may well reflect the growing sense of uncertainty and insecurity prevalent in a risk society (Heir, 2003). One response to risk is to focus on the future through the figure of the young person. Young people's worlds are constantly under scrutiny and their activities give rise to a regular helping of 'daily moral panics' and while these are typically more diffuse and the 'turnover' fast, the overall presentation of young people remains negative and largely problematic.

The politics and policies of youth crime: From the 'perishing' to 'hoodies'

Concern about young people and 'anti social behaviour' is not a new phenomenon as Heather Shore (2000) outlines in an historical analysis. Responses to such concerns in the UK led to the setting up of the juvenile justice system in the late 19th century, a period traditionally associated with the 'invention' of 'juvenile crime'. In the Victorian age, childhood came to be regarded and treated as a very distinctive stage of life (James and Prout, 1990; Brown, 2002). Amid the significant social change of this time, the role of children in society was critically reviewed. The Factory Act in 1833, for example, legislated against the employment of children under 9 years and brought children into schools as educational reform gathered pace. Part of this move to educate was a response by philanthropists and individuals to take children off the street and to remove the risk of crime to them and others. By the middle of the 19th century the concept of juvenile crime was formalised with the introduction of the 1847 Juvenile Offenders Act, and in the next decade a series of Reformatory and Industrial Schools Acts saw juvenile institutions replacing prisons as locations for young people convicted of crime or 'deviant' behaviour. In some instances children and young people considered at risk of committing a crime in the future were also accommodated in reform schools. The philanthropist Mary Carpenter named these children the 'perishing'. During this period the public focus around youth and crime became increasingly linked to discourses of 'deprivation, depravation, social disorder, and the need for education' (Brown, 2002: 10). As early as 1816, a *Report of the Committee for Investigating the Alarming Increases of Juvenile Crime in the Metropolis* outlined the main causes of juvenile crime as:

The improper conduct of parents
The want of education
The want of suitable employment
The violation of the Sabbath and the habits of gambling in the public streets
The severity of the criminal code
The defective state of the police
The existing system of prison discipline
(Shore, 2000)

This list could well have been drawn together in the 21st century. Indeed, the picture of children or young people in the 19th century as a separate and distinctive group in need both of regulation and education has had an enduring legacy still with us today. Drawing a distinction between groups can promote discourses of difference and deviance, and as Brown argues a process of 'othering' is central to the understanding of youth and crime. Since the mid 1900s young people have been classified according to their specific 'tribes' and these classifications have not only set them apart but have often been associated with deviancy and crime. In his 20th-century 'rogues gallery of young offenders', Sanders (2005) lists 'teddy boys, mods and rockers, punks, skinheads, hippies, ravers, yardies and gangstas' (p. xv), a list to which we could now also add 'hoodies' – the term given to young people who wear hooded tops, making them appear 'faceless' and intimidating. Hoodies have been linked in the public eye with crime, and hooded tops were banned by a number of UK shopping centres in early 2005, a move endorsed by the Prime Minister, Tony Blair. Speaking with reporters, Blair echoed some of the issues raised in the 1816 report mentioned above:

During the election campaign I heard too often people talk about a loss of respect in the classroom, on the street corner, in the way our hard-working public servants are treated as they perform their tasks … people are rightly fed up with street corner and shopping centre thugs, yobbish behaviour sometimes from children as young as 10 or 11 whose parents should be looking after them. (quoted in Tempest, 2005)

Public policies and public opinion

The image of young people as yobs, thugs and vandals, as a group to be feared and who lie beyond the boundaries of citizenship and respectability, continues to be widely and regularly reflected in the media. In turn, the emphasis of UK government policies in relation to youth justice and welfare have, through the years, both reflected and influenced public opinion and the way that young people have been regarded in society.

Over the decades, the focus of UK government policies has shifted back and forth between positions of care and welfare to punishment, reform and control. For example, the Children and Young Person's Act 1933 and Criminal Justice Act 1948 both placed significant emphasis on youth welfare whilst the introduction of detention centres, also in

1948, focused largely on punishment. The expansion of social work services in the 1960s again placed greater emphasis on the welfare of the child and young person. Likewise, the Children and Young Person's Act of 1969 focused on the 'treatment' of children who offended and those who needed 'care and protection' (Brown, 2002: 60). But many aspects of this Act were not implemented and the emphasis on welfare took a backseat during the 1970s; young people brought before the courts during this period were more likely to be sent to detention centres at a younger age and for less serious offences (Millham et al., 1978). As a result more children and young people were listed as delinquent giving rise to a public perception that young people were becoming more deviant and crime more common despite research showing that children's moral values are very similar to those of adults (Holland et al., 2000; McGrellis et al., 2000). In addition, it can be argued that the criminal justice and youth policies pursued by the Conservative party during the 1980s reinforced this perception by promoting the view that young people involved in crime were essentially criminals and should be removed from society and punished. In line with this, more powers were given to police to stop and search and deal with disorderly behaviour – a move regarded as evidence of a further breakdown in society.

Despite a change in government, the trend continued with both the surveillance of young people and the social measures they were subject to, increasing under the Labour party's Crime and Disorder Act (1998), which legislated on Anti-Social Behaviour Orders, Anti-Social Child Curfew Orders and Child Safety Orders. Building on this, Labour launched their 'Respect' agenda in January 2006, which outlined an extensive range of proposals to address 'anti-social behaviour'. These included plans to extend parenting orders (which are given to parents/carers of children who offend, requiring them to attend guidance or counselling sessions or meet other specific conditions) and the introduction of on the spot fines, as well as proposals for a national youth volunteering scheme and the expansion of mentoring programmes.

Interestingly, statistics do not necessarily back up public perceptions of rising youth crime. Two sets of figures are used to monitor UK crime levels – the British Crime Survey (BCS) and Police Recorded Crime reports. While these figures are contested, and are inconsistent, they do suggest an overall drop in crime since 1995 (Dodd et al., 2004). The statistics also show that the majority of crime is committed by people over the age of 18 (Youth Lifestyles Survey, Flood-Page et al., 2000). With regard to gender, the Youth Lifestyles Survey suggests that young men are three times more likely to offend than young women, a pattern echoed in other studies, including the longitudinal Edinburgh Study of Youth Transitions and Crime (Smith, 2004). The Scottish study of over 4000 young people has also drawn links between victims and perpetrators of crime, finding those who have been victims of violence or crime are more likely to offend. A Home Office report on crime found that young people in general (in their teens and 20s) are more at risk of violent crime, assault, and robbery than older people, and young men are more at risk than young women (Nicholas et al., 2005).

The picture of violence across the sites

The Inventing Adulthoods study highlights the different types of violence and crime young people experience across the range of locations, as well as differences in attitudes and responses according to age, class and gender. The findings indicate that violence occupies an important place in young people's moral landscape. Early data from the study is reported in detail in Sharpe (2004) and discusses the presence of violence in young people's lives, and how it was experienced 'in the home, from peers, the police, gangs and crime in the community, and through political violence in Northern Ireland' (Sharpe, 2004: 93).

Two of the research sites in the Inventing Adulthoods study were characterised by 'cultures of violence' – namely the Northern Irish site and the disadvantaged estate. In these localities the level of violence young people encountered (including domestic and street violence) was significantly higher than in the other areas. Attitudes and experiences of violence also differed, with young people in these sites more inclined to express approval for 'revenge', and 'fighting' – regarded as a relatively 'normal' activity. Young people in the rural and commuter areas were least likely to talk of experiences of crime or violence – a pattern that persisted over the course of the study. The nature of violence and crime discussed across sites included domestic violence, sectarian violence, gang violence, race-related and homophobic violence, bullying, and unprovoked street attack.

Where did it happen? The significance of place

... if I was born somewhere else I wouldn't be wile into violence. (Dermot, 15, 1998)

Dermot, who was brought up in Northern Ireland, recognised how place has affected his experience of violence and his attitude towards it. The strength of association between violence and place operates at a number of different levels. At the societal level, for example, it can influence local and government policy, as well as business investment. At a more personal level it can influence our individual responses and perceptions of an area and the people who live there. Reports of violence and crime are invariably laced with information on 'place'. Such information can heighten our reaction or deaden our interest. Are we more shocked, for example, to hear of a stabbing incident reported in a 'quiet rural area' than one reported from an inner city area? Do we react differently to the report of a sexual assault on a young woman in a 'dimly lit alleyway' to one of a young woman in her own home? Do reports of rioting on the streets of Belfast provoke a different response to reports of rioting on the streets of Oldham and Bradford? In short, do our perceptions of, and relationships to, place affect our response to violence, in particular to the victims and perpetrators?

Violence and crime have become linked to urban areas in the public imagination. Space in city living is pressured and neighbourhoods are often characterised according to class, race, ethnicity, and religion while others are 'controlled' by gangs. While these territorial divisions do not appear on any town map, they are drawn in mental maps and are often a visible part of the streetscape. In Northern Ireland, for example, some 'loyalist areas' can be easily identified by the red white and blue kerbs and the proliferation of loyalist and union flags, while the Irish tricolour marks out republican strongholds. While there is evidence that racial integration is increasing within electoral wards in England and Wales (Simpson, 2004), it is also fair to say that within these wards, neighbourhoods or streets are often characterised by people of a particular culture, religion or ethnicity. As areas become distinctive and identifiable they can also become territorialised. Where spaces are contested, young people, particularly young men, are invariably more involved in the defence of these territories, often through the use of violence (Webster, 2003; McGrellis, 2005a). Over time governments have responded to the 'problems' of inner city areas with various initiatives. One such initiative in the first half of the 20th century was to move people from the cities into new 'garden' housing developments. Some of the young people in the Inventing Adulthoods study live in one such development (the disadvantaged estate) and like so many others, they attest to the fact that such moves do not necessarily create havens of tranquillity or alone solve problems.

For those living on this estate the threat of random violence loomed large. Many young people talked of the shootings, muggings, arson, robberies and violent assaults that were part of their growing up experience. Crime statistics for the area are high and are perhaps linked with the high levels of unemployment and poverty present on this estate. The fear of crime in the area was such that some avoided the streets in the evening, streets which were regarded not only as dangerous but as training schools for crime. With cash low and boredom high, crime filled the void and many of the young people were aware of the results. Maisie (who we met in Chapter 4), for example, talked about her brother as a 'bad lot' who was in and out of jail. Her advice to him was to 'get away', to leave the streets and 'get a job'. Sandra, who also lived on the disadvantaged estate, described how her boyfriend was becoming increasingly involved in trouble and 'going bad' as he spent more time hanging out on the streets with gangs.

Although the fear of violence might be greater in urban areas, and crime levels higher, these issues and anxieties also featured in the lives of young people in rural areas. The findings from one Rural Crime Survey (Husain, 1995) found that young people in rural areas had similar concerns about crime to those growing up in London boroughs and that many experienced car crime, muggings and assault. In the Inventing Adulthoods study, those living in more rural areas were just as inclined to express a general fear of crime as those in more urban areas, both in relation to their own neighbourhood and city spaces they were less familiar with. Amanda, from the leafy suburb, talked of her fear of being attacked after dark. She carried a personal alarm but felt she could cope better if she became 'one of those urban types', believing this might harden her to crime and the potential risks. While she had no direct experience of crime or violence, her heightened sense of risk draws on a common public discourse of an increasingly violent society, and subscribes to a fear of 'stranger danger'. Although young men suffer more violent assault it is young women who fear it more (Pain, 1993, 1997).

The one form of violence most commonly experienced by women is domestic violence and this was raised as an issue across all sites but was most commonly talked about in the disadvantaged estate and in the Northern Irish site. Other types of violence within the family were also discussed, with parents' violence towards children accepted to a certain level (Sharpe, 2004). The young people grappled with the moral judgements that these issues raised. Drawing on powerful public discourses they concluded that being witness to such violence in childhood could influence attitudes and behaviour with regard to the use of violence in later life:

> It's like – you know like if you're young and you see your mum and dad fight and argue and they like start hitting each other, when you grow up you'll think that's the right thing to do – start hitting your mum and dad – start hitting your wife. (Mat, 13, 1998)

Those who experienced domestic violence as a power issue between men and women were forced to confront and make sense of the gendered knowledge it produced. For some, the messages that these experiences conveyed on parenting, gender relations, and moral authority complicated their attempts at personal agency in their own lives and practices.

Fay, a young woman in the rural site, had been physically abused by her father as a child and illustrates how young people's experience of violence in childhood can be echoed in their adult experiences. Although she did not talk about this abuse at any length in the interviews, she did talk about the regular beatings she had received at the hands of her boyfriend and how she normalised this experience during the 2 years she remained in the relationship. Classically, she blamed herself for the violence she suffered.

Statistics confirm that young women suffer most from domestic violence and sexual assault. Many studies have explored how certain forms of masculinity are expressed through violent physicality (Willis, 1977; Collier, 1998; Reilly et al., 2004) and the way it is used to achieve and maintain respect, particularly among the working classes (Anderson, 1999). The Edinburgh Study of Youth Transition and Crime found that young men are more likely to be involved in robbery and car theft, and to regard violence as a 'normal expression of masculinity'. The profile of young women involved in violence in the Edinburgh study was more specific: they were more likely to be drug users or truants, to come from lower-working-class backgrounds, or to be gang members.

Gangs were a feature of life for young people in all sites but especially in the disadvantaged estate and the inner city site. They were presented as threatening and protective, restrictive and facilitative. Alf and Owen, like others from the disadvantaged estate, were afraid of and intimidated by gangs in their area, and restricted their movements after dark accordingly. Meanwhile Luu, a young Vietnamese woman in the inner city site, called on family protection to defend her use of space and her family honour, likening the protection to 'a load of bodyguards'. Su, in the same site, talked about relatives in Triad gangs and how violence is used between gangs in the defence of family honour. Defence of family name was one of the most commonly given justifications for violence. What could possibly be regarded as a betrayal of a wider 'family' brought Glen, (who we meet in the next chapter) to the attention of a loyalist gang. Following his parents' separation, Glen left the loyalist area he grew up in to live and socialise in a more Catholic area. As a result, Glen was branded a 'fenian lover' and narrowly escaped violent assault from those who saw themselves as defenders of the wider loyalist family. Gangs, whether they are local street gangs or paramilitary gangs, act to provide moral support for their members and often seek to legitimise their own involvement in violent and criminal activity on this basis (Seaman et al., 2006).

A place of violence: The Northern Ireland site

Northern Ireland has been associated with violence and conflict for many years. The 'Troubles' have claimed the lives of over 3500 people and affected many more through injury, bereavement and trauma. While the paramilitary ceasefires of 1994 heralded a new political era, and a significant reduction in the level of bloodshed, they did not mark an end to all violence or sectarian conflict. While whole communities are affected by such violence it has been young people and particularly young men who were, and continue to be, on the front lines (Crozier, 2001; Reilly et al., 2004).

The youth of Northern Ireland have inherited the legacy of a community torn apart by sectarian and political conflict and have largely made the transition to adulthood in spaces segregated along religious lines. Most have had very little opportunity to engage meaningfully with their peers from different community backgrounds (Smyth, 1998; Murtagh, 2003). Those who took part in the Inventing Adulthoods study lived their childhood and teenage years in the late 1980s and 1990s. Some grew up in contested spaces along community interfaces and were exposed to, and engaged in, a level of sectarian violence that became a part of their social world, and affected their use of, and relationship to, space. Others had little direct personal experience of such violence but their movements and use of space were nonetheless affected by it. And whether on the front line or at a distance, the personal, family and community histories of the Troubles have fed into the hopes, fears and life pathways of all the young people growing up here (McGrellis, 2005b).

While sectarianism dominates much of the discussion in relation to violence and is an established part of youth cultures in Northern Ireland, other forms of violence and crime are also prevalent. Racially motivated crime has increased in recent years as has homophobic crime, and incidence of domestic violence has also risen in the past 10 years (Jarman, 2005). These increases may partly reflect a greater willingness on the part of victims to report such crimes and a greater public awareness generated through increased media attention.

A backcloth of violence

In many ways, the political history of Northern Ireland as well as the current situation, make for a very specific case study on youth violence but the study also has broader implications. It poses questions about the processes involved in the perpetuation of a culture of violence in relation to place; highlights the role of class and gender; and exposes the significant influence that violence, and the fear and threat of violence, has on young people's use of space, place and mobility. The study also offers an insight into how the use and management of space is central to the coping and survival strategies used by young people and how investment in self protection can restrict their mobility, and in turn their opportunities and chances. The link between mobility and social exclusion is explored in Chapter 8, 'Mobility'.

As mentioned above, young men from working-class backgrounds have been especially affected by the Troubles (Smyth, 1998) having filled the ranks of paramilitary organisations, and taken to the streets to 'defend' and mark out territory. A number of young men in the study from both republican and loyalist working-class backgrounds discussed their involvement in community and sectarian violence and how their reputation and family background 'trapped' them in situations that depended on their use of violence as well as exposing them to its consequences. Their personal histories illustrate how childhood experiences of, and exposure to, violence are often reflected in later experiences and transitions, and in their views on the use of violence. Dermot and Stuart, for example, came from different community backgrounds. Dermot grew up as part of a 'big republican family', while Stuart came from a staunchly loyalist background. They both lived in close proximity to each other, but their level of association was limited to the position each held within their respective communities. They were regarded as leaders, enemies, defenders and targets and both accepted that violence was part of their deal (McGrellis, 2005a).

Young people's use of space, their connection to place and to the 'piece of land' they find themselves on, is often bitterly contested in Northern Ireland (McGrellis, 2005a) and our young people told how they avoided, or negotiated access, to certain areas and localities. The location of the commercial and entertainment heart of this city site is in a space regarded as predominantly Catholic or nationalist, which means that many of the young people in the study from a Protestant background did not feel safe to freely shop or socialise there. As well as a fear of sectarian violence, the increase in city centre crime and assaults also deterred many, particularly at night. Recent evidence suggests, however, that this is changing, and that most Protestants are happy to go into the area.

Finding pathways

As outlined above, leisure and consumption are often linked with youth violence, yet the biographical narratives of some young people suggest that it is an area that is tentatively enabling some young people in Northern Ireland, particularly young Protestant women, to move beyond the confines of their own confessional spaces (McGrellis, 2005b). Such movement represents a challenge not only to them, but also to their parents and community of influence. Over the course of the study, young women like Cheryl, who we meet in Chapter 10 and Adele, whose story is told below, made tentative but significant journeys across religious and community divides in pursuit of leisure. For some this journey was made easier by new relationships with work colleagues and budding college friendships. Relationships with young men from the 'other side' represented key moments for these young women in their narratives of place and identity (McGrellis, 20005a). Such challenges and opportunities are less readily available to, or accessed by, young men from similar backgrounds, although there is evidence from the study to suggest that such journeys are more easily pursued by young men from more middle-class backgrounds. Music, DJ-ing, sport, skateboarding, go-karting and art were some of the media used by young people in this category to move across community boundaries.

Violence and sectarianism in three young lives

Adrian, Allan and Adele are young people from working-class backgrounds whose experience of violence and community conflict has had a direct effect on their transitions to adulthood. Growing up they have found varying levels of resources available to them and, at key times in their transitions, such resources have had a significant influence on their outcomes. When we first met these young people they were aged between 14 and 15. At our last meeting Adele and Adrian were both 23, Allan was 21. All three have been victims of violence. As we follow the thread of their biographies we are often taken down unexpected routes. Their narratives shed light on how violence and sectarianism manifests itself through intimidation, expulsion and emotional trauma, affecting connections to community and family. We see how responses to sectarianism and violence can motivate (and sometimes propel) young people between different biographical fields or can limit the expression of their adulthood to one narrow area.

Adele

Adele was brought up in a staunchly loyalist area. Paramilitary activity and internal 'turf' wars between different loyalist groups were commonplace. While she rejected the sectarianism that existed within her estate, she did admit to her own sectarian views. Growing up she feared Catholics and their religion, and as a child was scared to walk past Catholic churches 'in case (she) got blessed and the devil came and got (her)'. Her first encounter with Catholics was through a secondary school cross-community holiday. When she left secondary school and enrolled in a college beauty course Adele's social circle became more mixed. She began to emphasise her 'difference' both in terms of youth culture, and in relation to her family and community values. Although remaining cautious she moved across sectarian boundaries to access live music and clubs and dismissed her parents' disapproval. She increasingly spent more time away from home, and engaged with a new form of sociality that was less bound by the conventions observed by her parents' generation. When she brought her first Catholic boyfriend home she challenged these conventions in a very direct and personal way.

While Adele was investing heavily in the leisure field at this stage, her main goals were to move out of home, to establish herself independently within work, and to escape from the sectarian backdrop of her community. All three desires were interlinked and Adele recognised that all three could be achieved if she channelled her efforts into achieving at work.

A gap of 5 years between interviews, however, brought many changes in Adele's life. A few months after her first interview Adele responded to increased tension at home and a growing need for her own space. In order to qualify for public housing she left her training course, and registered herself as unemployed and homeless. Her need to leave home was such that she could not wait for her original plan to unfold.

Despite her hopes of escaping the violence and sectarianism, Adele found herself falling victim to it. She was housed in another predominantly Protestant estate a number of miles from her family home and because of her ongoing relationship with a Catholic, she was intimidated out of this house by loyalists within six months:

> The night that the windows was put in and I came down the stairs there was three fellas standing with their face covered and says you have to move out now. (Adele, 23, 2005)

Adele was eventually re-housed in a predominantly Catholic estate, where she felt disconnected physically and emotionally from her own family. At our last meeting Adele was vague with regard to her future; her self-confidence, motivation and ambition had all fallen dramatically and she felt trapped in a dependency culture, 'wanting to make an honest living but not knowing how to do it'.

Violence and sectarianism played a large part in Adele's transition to adulthood. She largely rejected, and rebelled against, the culture, values and traditions of the staunchly loyalist environment she was brought up in. She imagined her future in different spaces and set about achieving this through work. However, her decision to give up her course in order to qualify for public housing had a significant impact on her trajectory – knocking her off her work pathway and hurling her into a domestic arena that was fraught with sectarian violence. At last contact, Adele was in a vulnerable situation; she felt trapped and could not see a way out. Having dared to challenge community codes and cross boundaries, she remained excluded, on sectarian grounds, from certain housing areas, felt a stranger in her community of origin, and on the edges of her own family.

Allan

When we first met Allan he was 14 years old and lived in a staunchly loyalist area bordering nationalist and republican communities. Living in such an area had important implications for the way he experienced space; he talked about being 'jammed into your own part of land'. In his early teens the lure of sectarian based street violence was great, representing a localised and accessible version of masculinity and adulthood. His friends supported loyalist paramilitary groups, they defended their space fiercely, and under their influence he supported a Protestant paramilitary organisation. He admitted to being bigoted in his attitudes but although he became increasingly involved in trouble, he discussed in interviews feeling increasingly uncomfortable with some of the activities in which his friends took part.

His parents were clearly concerned about the company he kept and the route he was taking, and actively intervened. They took him on holidays out of the area at times of high tension; they fostered and supported his interest in numerous sporting activities, recognising that these, even more than education, would offer a resource:

> Probably my parents would have influenced me. They taught me all about the paramilitaries and all, like say in case I wanted to join – but I wouldn't. They've took it out of my mind about joining the paramilitaries. They've got me into playing football. Some nights – say there's revision – they still wouldn't care about the revision, they'd let me play football. (Allan, 15, 1998)

While pursuing these activities Allan met other young men from the Catholic community and developed new friendships and attitudes. While he endeavoured to stay clear of paramilitary involvement, in his third interview, aged 18, he continued to present a version of self that was linked to street fighting and despite paramilitary warnings, to drugs. However, under the influence of a new girlfriend Allan decided to cut his ties with this group and 'settle down'. He feared that continued contact could have serious consequences for him and his long-term future.

By the time he was 20, Allan had moved physically and psychologically from the streets he grew up in. He had left training college to take up a factory job, had moved into a flat with a new girlfriend and was about to become a father. Although Allan's identity was in part linked to street fighting and sectarianism, in our last interview he was also keen to realise his masculinity through fatherhood and in the domestic arena. Fatherhood had, he believed, made him more sociable, even-tempered, more confident and optimistic. In his own words he felt 'invincible', 'immortal' and a 'superhero'.

While Allan and his family had little in terms of economic, social or cultural capital to draw on they used the little they had to good advantage. They were astute in their investments in sport, leisure, and relationships. The availability of such support at key times, and the value Allan placed on relationships and fatherhood as a route to adulthood enabled him to move away from the sectarian and paramilitary influences that were so dominant in his community.

Adrian

Adrian was brought up in a working-class Catholic area and attended a Catholic maintained school. Growing up he had as little contact with Protestants as Adele and Allan had with Catholics. Adrian was the oldest of a large family and left school at 16 to enrol on a training course. Having a skill was important to him and from the first interview he placed great value on achieving through work. In the first year of his course aged 17 Adrian found himself involved in a serious violent incident. He was ordered by republican paramilitaries to leave the country for his own safety and did so with the knowledge of the police. For Adrian this type of 'policing' was normal; he accepted it in the same way he accepted the need for punishment beatings and shootings meted out to those involved in 'anti-social' behaviour, although this was the first time he or his family had come into close contact with such 'trouble'.

His forced exclusion from family and community for a year constituted his 'punishment' but also ensured his well-being. Permission to return for court appearances was negotiated with the paramilitaries, and he was subsequently cleared of any charge. Living and working in England gave him confidence and a taste of life beyond the local community. Despite a job offer in his home town, Adrian opted to return to England and take up better paid work opportunities. There he had made friends from all over the world and from different cultures and backgrounds, including 'Muslims and Arabs', and Protestants from Northern Ireland, who were equally exotic to him.

Reflecting on his life, Adrian believed that his forced exclusion from home at 17 and subsequent life experience accelerated his journey to adulthood and propelled him in a direction that had in fact been to his advantage:

> Made me stronger for myself like. I dunno, made me grow up fast too, definitely.
> (Adrian, 23, 2005)

His enforced time in England threw Adrian into a new and unfamiliar world without preparation or planning. He was, however, supported in this accelerated transition to adulthood by family and friends, and with this support was able to turn the situation to his advantage. His expulsion represented an escape from the sectarian youth culture that he was part of and influenced by, and corresponded with a shift in attitude and focus. He became very work orientated, keen to achieve material success, and to learn about different cultures and traditions through friendship and travel.

Conclusion

Young people's experience of public spaces and neighbourhoods is very different from that of adults. Being more active and more visible on the streets they are potentially more at risk of violence and crime. But as we have seen the places and neighbourhoods they grow up in also play a part in the level of crime and violence they are exposed to and are potentially involved in. While structural factors and wider social processes play a part in the presence and level of violence within communities, individual and group investment in place also matter. Violence seems more likely in localities where individuals have a strong investment in place. It is less likely in areas that are more individualised and where space is not so contested, such as our rural area and the affluent commuter site. In two other research sites, Northern Ireland and the disadvantaged estate, the use of space and place was central to young people's biographies, and there was a pervasive 'culture of violence'. It affected their mobility, the decisions they made, and also the extent to which they accepted or justified this violence as part of their lives. Gangs, (neighbourhood, drug or paramilitary), were most prolific in these sites and played their part in legitimising such violence. Although there was some gang activity in the inner city site, young people appeared to be less bounded by the borders of the neighbourhood, suggesting how factors such as diversity and immigration might affect these issues.

As in other studies it was the young men whose lives seem most compromised by violence and crime, although as Jarman (2005) highlights, the role of young women as agents and victims in violence is perhaps less often acknowledged and considered. In an attempt to address this he has explored the possible roles that young women take in street violence in Northern Ireland including observer, victim, restrainer and participant. Within the Inventing Adulthoods study, it is perhaps Adele's story that best illuminates the potential effects of violence and sectarianism on young women's lives. Her position as a victim has been both influenced and exacerbated by the social and structural processes she is subject to and ultimately, at least with the bounds of the study, she found herself unable to escape and override the culture of violence in her community. Although herself a victim of sectarian and criminal violence, Adele believed that sectarian violence had become less prevalent. She attributed this to an expanding drug culture, believing that young people are now more interested in 'getting winged than fighting'. The investments young people make in the drug culture, and the effects of such investments are considered in the next chapter.

Chapter 6
Chemical cultures

Introduction

> Modern ballroom dancing may easily degenerate into a sensuous form of entertainment, and if self-control is weakened with alcohol it is more than likely that it will do so, which might easily lead at least to unruly behaviour and not infrequently to sexual immorality. (*English Life and Leisure* (1951), quoted in Everitt, 1986)

Historically, no aspect of young people's lives has consistently ranked as highly in the popular imagination and public agendas of the UK during the 20th and early 21st centuries, as their collective involvement in consumer-based leisure (Cohen, 1972; Hebdige, 1979; Pearson, 1983; McRobbie, 1991; Murji, 1998; Presdee, 2000). In the context of these 'moral panics', young people's pleasures have been cast as transgressive and criminalised – none more so than the heady mix of music, dancing and various forms of intoxication (often illicit or illegal). The notion of young pleasures as problems was well established long before the post-war consumer boom heralded the birth of the 'teenager' but it was the ever-increasing expansion in the leisure–pleasure landscape that has set this perception in stone. From the threat to national security posed by the emergence of the nightclub, jazz music, dancing and cocaine (used initially by the lower social classes) in London's West End during the First World War (Kohn, 1997), to the spectre of marauding, nocturnal 'binge-drinkers' disrupting British town centres and with it British society in 2006, the history of young people's nocturnal public pleasures has been one of social threat and cause for social control and regulation (Measham, 2004a). Even a collective activity considerably removed from the spectacular canon of youth cultural history – ballroom dancing – was cause for concern in the early 1950s.

This tradition has been integral to public anxieties around social change. Concerns about the new forms of, particularly working-class, femininity made possible in war time and the threat of extending the vote to women under 27 were at the heart of the portrayal of the drug-related deaths of two young women too frail to cope with the freedoms of the 'modern girl' in the years following the First World War (Kohn, 1997: 137). The Inventing Adulthoods research period, also one of considerable social change, saw a familiar replay of old social anxieties and the gendered media stories of youth cultures. The 'single, white female' once again starred in an ongoing tale of drug-related deaths as an innocent victim preyed upon by evil male perpetrators – the source of the drugs, the music and the venues at the root of these young women's decline (Kohn, 1997; Henderson, 1997; Blackman, 2005).

The normalisation of chemical excess: Popular young pleasures and public agendas

Shortly after their re-election in 2005, the UK Labour government launched a multi-pronged 'war on disrespect' which was somewhat reminiscent of the Conservative government's call to get 'Back to Basics' in the early 1990s. Young people, crime and transgressive pleasures – condensed into the spectre of 'yob' – loomed large on both agendas. However, the nature of the cultures reflected in these public concerns and the policy agendas addressing them changed considerably over this period of time.

Whilst consumer-based leisure involving dancing, music and chemical intoxicants had been a central feature of the weekend for a considerable minority of young people for at least half a century (Measham, 2004a: 338), the 1990s saw the commercialisation and growth of cultures with the use of Ecstasy, electronic 'house' music and all night dancing at their heart – further variations of which still persist in 2006.

Research had a role to play in sustaining this image of young people, as an increasing number of surveys and some qualitative studies painted a picture of a burgeoning 'pick and mix' youth drug culture in which the patterns, prevalence and symbolic currency of drugs appeared to have changed from being exceptional to a feature of contemporary everyday life – the 'normalisation' thesis (Newcombe, 1991; Measham, 1996; Henderson, 1997; Parker et al., 1998; South, 1999).

The Labour government's '10-year strategy for tackling drug misuse' (HM Government, 1998) marked a return to the prioritisation of drug use prevention, treatment and enforcement, from a public health concern with HIV and AIDS among drug injectors. Identifying and targeting those most likely to shift into drug dependency and problematic use became a priority of a broader policy framework geared to addressing the social processes through which certain groups become excluded from the mainstream of society (HM Government, 1998; Drugscope, 2000a; Drugscope, 2000b; Melrose, 2000).

Whilst critics of the normalisation thesis argued that actual levels of drug use were exaggerated (Shiner and Newburn, 1997), young people in the UK continued to be characterised in terms of having 'excessive appetites' (Measham et al., 2000). As the new century began, what had earlier been identified as a 'big bang' approach to drinking (Measham, 1996) ousted the horrors and consequences of Ecstasy use from the headlines and 'binge drinking' became the number one popular pleasure posing a threat to the nation. Towards the end of the research period, the suggestion that 'we are drinking younger, longer, faster and more cheaply across the class and gender spectrum' was well and truly established in the public imagination (Levy and Scott-Clark, 2004: 1).

Despite evidence of a 'normalisation of determined drunkenness' (Measham, 2004b: 321), there was no government-led 'war' on alcohol to match that on drugs and 'no attempts to bring down the "Mr Bigs" of the alcohol industry' (Hobbs, 2005: 24). Rather, the main 'dealers' of alcohol worked together with police and local politicians in local policy partnerships.

Landscapes for excess? Transformation and globalisation

The emergence of these discourses and practices of excessive pleasures took place within a transforming landscape. The use of Ecstasy in the late 1980s blossomed, fragmented and transformed beyond all expectation. Its diversification in the early 1990s from predominantly illegal into commercial venues was simply the beginning of a dynamic process that perennially involved a broadening of its impact on mainstream consumer culture (Thornton, 1995; Garratt, 1998; Silcott, 2000; Henderson, 2001; Measham, 2004a; Blackman, 2005). The Inventing Adulthoods study period saw club and bar culture shift to the centre of consumer culture. The spaces of the 'night-time economy' proliferated, coinciding with the entrepreneurial drive within 'dance' culture and with policy geared to developing the 24-hour city and urban regeneration (Measham, 2004a, Hobbs, 2005: 24).

The increasing globalisation of club culture, extended and sustained by investments from for example film makers, novelists and advertisers (e.g. Collin, 1997; Garratt, 1998), was also central to its longevity. Importantly, these successive generations of entrepreneurs connected with the structures of regional and global tourism (Harrison, 1998; Sellars, 1998; Turner, 1999; Pini, 2001) with the result that 'the 21st century has seen the emergence of an international clubbing scene as an organized and rationalized form of public entertainment' (Blackman, 2005: 175).

'Living it large?' Growing up in excessive landscapes

Commentators in the UK have tended to understand the 'turn' to chemical excess within the broader theoretical framework of social change in late modernity (Henderson, 1997; Aldridge et al., 1999; Measham, et al., 2000; Blackman, 2005). Whilst the predominant perspective in this context focuses on the emergence of 'risk cultures' in the face of economic uncertainty, rapid social change and the experience of modernity (Beck, 1992), it has also been argued that these conditions have, in fact, given rise to chemical cultures within which safety – in the form of collective chemical experience – is 'the ultimate high', an 'antidote to the prevailing atmosphere of risk and anxiety' (Calcutt, 1998: 2; Raven, 2001). In a context where 'youth' was increasingly a consumer category, where consumer culture was a central means of identity construction, and the currency of old models of adulthood was eroded, doubt was cast over previous understandings of intoxication as a teenage phase. Whilst there was little research evidence to suggest what proportion of experimental and recreational drug users moved into problem drug use, there had previously been an assumption that a majority of young people who experimented with drugs moved on leaving drugs behind (Ashton, 1998).

The broader picture of how chemical culture figures in young people's lives over time is still sketchy. Very few studies have focused on the complex processes shaping the changing place and social meaning of drugs in young lives and into young adulthood. Rare exceptions – prospective longitudinal studies – have demonstrated the dynamic nature and complexity of the development of drug use and the role of transitions in other areas of life in determining drug pathways, including the transition from secondary school (Measham et al., 1998a; 1998b). These studies have found that, while illicit drug use was a central, substantive element of youth transitions, shared objective conditions in a locality experiencing extreme social exclusion produced markedly different orientations to drugs and drug pathways (MacDonald and Marsh, 2002, 2005). A more gendered picture of experimentation with chemical culture over time has also begun to emerge, suggesting different types of gender gap at different stages of growing up: while more young women experiment with illicit drugs in early teens, young men 'catch up' in their mid-teens and start to 'overtake' in young adulthood (Measham, 2002).

In this chapter, we take a step beyond public agendas relating to young pleasures and explore the complexity and detail of evolving biographies. We take a look at how young people in the study engaged with the landscapes of chemical excess that began evolving when they were babies or small children. In doing so, we draw upon and span a number of discrete and specialist areas of youth studies and policy, in particular those of youth cultural studies and research on substance use (criminological, psychological and sociological). Whilst the chapter mirrors the norms of much drugs research in that it concentrates particularly on those who made a heavy investment in chemical culture, it also breaks with the established paradigm of focusing in on the specifics of drug use then outward to its 'social aspects'. In line with this approach, data on drugs and alcohol were not collected systematically but arose in a number of different contexts in the course of biographical interviews. Our starting point is not drugs as an issue, but the broader fabric of young lives and the complex processes shaping biographies, combining a prospective and retrospective approach over time, and offering a situated account of young lives.

Chemical culture in Inventing Adulthoods: Changing landscapes, attitudes and involvement

One of the studies contributing to the 1990s picture of a popular chemical culture concluded that illicit drugs were used in different ways in different parts of the country and played different roles in different youth cultures (6 et al., 1997). This was borne out by our study, as we heard tales of different leisure and pleasure landscapes and different forms of engagement with these landscapes. In the demographically 'young' city in Northern Ireland, for example, club and bar culture was higher on young people's leisure list and enjoyed at an earlier age than elsewhere. This perhaps reflected a recent and dramatic expansion of its leisure and entertainment industry alongside a parallel (post-ceasefire) expansion in drug markets (once blocked but controlled and policed by paramilitaries). An essential leisure tool for young people, there was a spatial map of the pubs and clubs considered to lie in Catholic or Protestant territory. At the same time, chemical culture provided young people with a vehicle for escaping the sectarian divide. They also talked more and at an earlier age about personal drug use than elsewhere. There were notably different cultures of drug use associated with different youth cultures: a more individualist and masculine 'freak' culture that involved heavy cannabis and alcohol use and revolved largely around the pub and indie music scene; and the more mainstream club scene based around Ecstasy and more open to young women.

Next in line for early engagement in party culture (albeit initially based in rural community centres and pubs) were young people in the rural research site, who shared with their peers in Northern Ireland an earlier engagement in the use of drugs other than cannabis. Although young people in the pub cultural landscape of the Home Counties were more talkative about drugs than their rural peers, their experimentation was largely confined to cannabis until leaving home for university. In contrast, young people growing up in the inner city and the disadvantaged estate were far less vocal about personal illicit drug use of any kind until later in the study, confining discussion largely to the 'druggy' reputation of their respective areas.

In terms of attitudes to illicit chemical culture, the overall pattern revealed in the Inventing Adulthoods study suggests a familiar picture of its changing place and meaning in young lives over time. In their early teens a majority were far more accepting of drinking alcohol and smoking than the supply and consumption of illegal drugs (McGrellis et al., 2000); by the time they started work or further education in 1998, drinking and experimentation with cannabis were largely viewed as a 'normal' part of growing up and a period of youthful fun that would end with adult responsibility; four years later, clubbing and pubbing, drinking and drugs were central to discussions of social life.

At the point in the study when a majority of young people were starting work or further education, just over half had tried cannabis but few had experimented further. Although nearly a quarter of the sample we are still in contact with (n = 70) went on to try Ecstasy and cocaine (n = 16), considerable involvement in chemical culture sustained over a period of years was only evident in a small number. It is to these young lives that this chapter now turns.

Chemical culture in the biographical round

As we saw in Chapter 3, some, largely middle-class, young people in the study assumed and followed academic achievement as a route to a secure future. As a source of additional skills and competence they also invested in work and leisure and tended to avoid relationships (see Chapter 11). Orientations towards chemical culture varied amongst these well-resourced young people but they were generally not impartial to alcohol, some having been allowed to drink in family settings from an early age, and had come into contact with the use of cannabis when younger and use of Ecstasy, cocaine and other club drugs when at university. Their approach to substance use, however, seemed to reflect their instrumental approach to constructing their future: their chemical pleasures were generally limited to alcohol and to particular settings and times that would not jeopardise their main priorities.

For the minority of young people who are featured in this chapter, this leisure landscape became an alternative resource for constructing identity, a sense of competence, status and belonging and, to a greater or lesser extent, a future career. Any initial educational aspirations were linked to popular culture (usually Media Studies) but education was either rejected or abandoned as a route to the future. It was these young people who developed the most excessive appetites for chemical culture. Their careers in substance use, involving the use of Ecstasy and/or cocaine, alcohol and cannabis in particular, varied but were an integral part of this heavy investment in the leisure landscape. A look across these young biographies also suggests that social inequalities and differences were very much at play in chemical culture, the most immediately obvious of which relate to class and gender: those who invested heavily in leisure were largely male and middle class.

Having a flutter on leisure? Chemical culture and middle-class masculinities

For these young men, chemical intoxication was part of aspiring to non-traditional success, defined in terms of material wealth, hedonism, glamour, minor celebrity, entrepreneurialism and, in some cases, a flirtation with 'scam' culture. They were also disinclined towards steady relationships for much of the study, preferring casual sex, singledom and the company of friends (for an analysis of this approach to relationships, see Chapter 11). Growing up, these young men bore little responsibility, relied on their parents for financial and practical support and often confessed to being 'lazy' and/or 'spoiled'.

For example, in the affluent commuter belt, Richard and Sam (aged 16–24 and 16–23 respectively during the study) both looked forward to a future in the cultural industries when we first met them, and both were taking Media Studies. As time passed, they both did less well in education than expected: Richard left school without any qualifications and dropped out of college by 18; Sam made it to university but devoted himself to making contacts, having fun and a first serious relationship, and left university without completing his course (see too Chapter 4). Back in their home town, Sam moved into leisure management, later training in the design field, whilst Richard worked in a bar, went traveling and became involved in the travel industry.

Meanwhile, Naz aspired to an eventual future in business but made little investment in education on the way, leaving college at 19 and working in the family business. Out in the countryside, Robin, whose critical moment (being caught smoking marijuana at school) we described in Chapter 2, fulfilled his aspirations and became relatively successful as a local club night promoter while unemployed, before beginning a management training course.

During the research, all four young men showed a leaning towards the easy life that conflicted with their ambitions – a point noted by researchers in their notes:

Having a good time and getting through life as handy as possible has been Naz's motto throughout the years. He has had a charmed upbringing – he recognises that he has been spoiled by his parents – and that life has been much easier for him than many of his peers.

Richard is still a cool and wayward lad who may succeed in something, but not unless he puts in a bit of effort, something he is possibly a bit reluctant to do.

These young men continued to draw on their parents' resources throughout the research: Sam's father wrote off the debts he had incurred at university and continued to support him even after he set up home independently; Richard's parents continued to bankroll increasingly costly attempts to develop a career; Naz continued to live in the family home in the comfort to which he had always been accustomed; and Robin continued to move between his mother's and father's homes, making no practical or material input into either.

All of these young men began drinking and smoking cannabis in their early teens, moved into Ecstasy and/or cocaine use at 17/18 years, and experienced peaks and troughs in their drug use into their early 20s. For Naz and Robin, however, drugs took on a much more central and consistent role in their lives, defining the critical moments in their biographies over time and becoming integral to their flirtation with 'bad boy' identities. Naz, like Robin, was caught smoking dope at high school but, unlike Robin, was expelled. While Robin spoke of regret and still considered this as a terrible moment in his life 4 years later, Naz appeared unphased. Despite their very different responses, both continued to pursue 'bad lad' identities: Naz living the high life with other affluent young people and supplementing this lifestyle of fast cars and cocaine with 'scams' and drug dealing; and Robin 'hanging out' with local gangsters while building a reputation and making connections on the local club scene.

Although both young men talked in terms of 'reform' when discussing their drug use at various points, bingeing on cocaine in particular was a key feature of their late-teen/early 20s lifestyles, both typically spending £400–500 in a weekend. It was a rocky road for both young men. Naz had a brush with the law for possession in his early 20s. Initially he responded by turning to the gym and reducing his drug intake but this did not last. His cocaine use escalated once again until, 2 years later, he was shocked into giving up dealing after discovering that he was on the hit lists of more than one local gang leader. At this point he embarked on a serious relationship and returned to the gym. Robin's cocaine habit spiralled out of control at 19 after a year or so of unemployment. The loss of his friends and growing drug debts combined with increasing pressure from his mother, prompted him to begin a training course. Long hours, 6 days a week, initially left him little space to indulge in the high life he desired. But although the long hours continued, Robin fell in love with someone who was into cocaine, and by his last interview aged 20 had returned to long cocaine- and alcohol-fuelled weekends. While giving up drugs was a consistent theme in Robin and Naz's stories over time, they were still enamoured with the drug-related lifestyle in their early 20s. By the same age, Sam had relegated his drug use to the past:

[My partner] is very anti-drugs. … And it's funny looking back on my drug days, because it's quite nasty thinking about it, and I think, 'God, why did I do all that?' … But, not my cup of tea any more. (Sam, 20, 2004)

Getting stuck on leisure? Chemical culture in 'poor places'

While Sam, Richard, Robin and Naz clearly over invested in leisure – often at some personal cost – they also managed to incorporate future plans for education, training and career. For others, with fewer resources, the prioritising of leisure often meant a narrowing of the horizon as far as future opportunities were concerned. Alcohol and drug use were a key part of this group's leisure landscape but their investment was not backed-up by financial and practical resources and there was little expectation that education would provide a route to the future. For them, substance use (largely alcohol and cannabis) became an integral part of everyday life and grew in significance as work and education faded into the background.

Glen was an example here. From a working-class, Protestant family in Northern Ireland, he was initially set on doing a media course, but dropped out of college at 17, began another training course and was dismissed for failing a drugs test. A pattern of uncompleted training courses and placements under the UK government's 'New Deal' followed, none of which interested him. Unlike the middle-class young men who could better afford a 'flutter' on leisure, Glen had nothing to fall back on and no-one to bail him out. Most significantly, Glen's housing situation was very precarious and remained so throughout the research period. His parents had split up when he was in his early teens, each moving to a different part of the city and setting up homes with new partners. Neither area felt welcoming or safe to Glen (see McGrellis, 2005a). He developed a sense of 'not caring' about sectarian loyalties and pursued an alternative, more cosmopolitan identity.

Throughout the study (between the ages of 17–23), Glen's dream was to become a successful musician. Against a backdrop of limited material resources, dwindling interest in education and work outside music, and a widening gulf between his dream and the day-to-day reality of life on benefits and dead end training schemes, Glen's investment in this area of competence and alternative family (his band and other musicians) increased. Support from his father was variable over time and while Glen was close to his mother, she was unable to support him materially. In this context, having a steady girlfriend became the other constant in Glen's story, providing him with emotional support and, often, a place to live. This kind of heavy reliance on the couple relationship is discussed more fully in Chapter 11.

Life on the local music scene brought with it a wide network of casual friendships and the social currency of shared drinking and smoking spaces. Glen's alcohol and drug use escalated. At 17, he and his mates spent their pay cheque in the pub and on the week's supply of cannabis. Long drinking binges with friends continued until, at 21, Glen felt he had come close to the edge of alcoholism. He also maintained a daily dependence on cannabis throughout the study. Having tried other drugs such as Ecstasy and LSD, he preferred cannabis because 'it just brings out the more creative side of me … completely insane imagination'. Price was also a serious consideration and he did not get into the cocaine binges of middle-class young men in the study.

Girlfriends were an important controlling mechanism for Glen's substance use. At 19, he 'calmed down a wile, wile lot on the pot', switching from using bongs and pipes (methods for taking much higher doses) to joints because a new girlfriend insisted on this. At 21, he felt had been brought back from the brink of alcoholism by meeting his new girlfriend:

> I don't get up in the morning now and go the bar or go to get drink … during the day or anything, there's no more of that problem any more. … It was starting to get a serious problem, … I scraped all over the first stages, the second stages and just went straight … to nearly to a full blown alcoholic to tell you the truth but I didn't go there like … I met (my girlfriend) and she says 'oh it was you, it was you who done it', it was nothing to do with me at all it was her. (Glen, 21, 2003)

Things seemed to be looking up for Glen when we last saw him (aged 23). He was still in this relationship, his housing situation had improved and his priorities had changed, shifting from a situation where he, in his words, would have sold 'my fucking granny for God sake' for 'drink and pot and stuff' to spending on 'coal first or oil first or food or something like that'. With a relatively secure base, he was making plans for the future. His drug use had changed to some degree as a consequence:

> I've always been living in shit-holes basically like, all me life. And I'm just sick and tired of it like, and sick and tired of fucking living like that, like drinking loads and all that. Like I'm still smoking a lot like, but I'm not gonna stop, and everyone knows that like … so I try to keep it down to about four or five joints in a day. (Glen, aged 23, 2004)

Excessive appetites and young femininities

Taking a look across the Inventing Adulthoods data for continuities/patterns in the ways drugs and alcohol entered young biographies produced a somewhat surprising result: the dominant picture, although a familiar one of drug use as a part of young identities being constructed in and through globalised consumer youth culture, was overwhelmingly one of young masculinities. This suggests more continuity in the ways in which young men invest in the chemical leisure landscape than young women. The final section of this chapter moves on to explore gender differences in the ways that drugs and alcohol 'fit' into young lives through two comparative case studies: Hazel from the rural site (aged 15–20 during the study), the only middle-class young woman who took a similar 'flutter' on leisure in our sample, and Corinne (17–21), a young woman from Northern Ireland with a much higher chance of becoming 'stuck' in leisure through a similar involvement in club drug use.

Both young women were strongly anti-Ecstasy in adolescence (having witnessed its effects on relatives' lives) but started clubbing and taking Ecstasy towards the end of compulsory schooling (aged 16–17 years). At this crucial point, both began a year of 'living for the weekend'. For Hazel, her club-based party lifestyle involved taking 9 Ecstasy tablets per session at its height as well as developing a taste for cocaine and, in her words, 'doing anything for a buzz'. While Corinne confined her drug use to 3–4 Ecstasy tablets per session, both young women began to 'fail' at school and experience increasing conflict at home. Hazel left school after failing most of her exams at 16, continued to work in a series of factory jobs (briefly returning to education and dropping out again) and settled into marriage and the routine of a domestic-based lifestyle at 18. Corinne managed to continue in education and was on course for completing a nursing degree when last in touch. Both young women felt they had put the clubbing and drugs lifestyle behind them by the age of 19 and each became involved in a serious relationship as part of a strategy for achieving this. Hazel, with money tight and a mortgage to pay, was confining her drug use to the odd night at the pub at 20, whilst Corinne, feeling she had little space in her life for leisure while working and training to be a nurse (at 21), drank 'as much as possible' when she was able.

Hazel: 'Why not be content with working in a turkey factory?'

Hazel had a great deal in common with her young male middle-class contemporaries who 'fluttered on leisure': she initially aspired to a non-9–5 lifestyle in the creative arts, came from a middle-class professional family with an emphasis on music and continued to draw on her parents' emotional and material support throughout the study. She avoided steady relationships for much of the time and shared an easy-going attitude to life, denying agency and adopting a fateful approach:

> ... sort of just take life as it is and don't try and make something that isn't going to happen basically ... 'cos I think basically if it's going to happen it will. (Hazel, 17, 2001)

However, her story over time illustrates some important gender differences, particularly relating to the alternative structures for social mobility within youth culture and to family responsibility.

Unlike the young men whose drug stories we touched on earlier, Hazel was expected to take on domestic responsibilities for her two younger siblings as she grew up in a family of two working parents (Henderson, 2005). She also took on a mediating role in her parent's ongoing conflicts from the age of 12. It was a wish to escape the conflict and responsibilities of domestic life, combined with a strong anti-academic attitude and sense of difference from her school peers that propelled her into the spaces of leisure. Her clear aversion to reproducing her parent's lifestyle was also clearly implicated in her resistance to education.

Although Hazel's rejection of traditional middle-class social mobility echoed that of her fellow, male 'flutterers', she did not share the same desire for wealth and success. Having actively embraced non-ambition as a strategy for avoiding disappointment at 17, she simply wished for 'a nice life'. The resources she drew on in this downward mobility strategy were also very different.

Hazel's parents' London origins had contributed to her sense of difference (Henderson, 2005) and, certainly, the club cultural lifestyle provided her with an exciting means of constructing an alternative identity and occupying a different set of 'urbanised' social spaces from both her family and school peers. This route to a life beyond the local served a number of purposes: providing her with intergenerational, and cross-class and gender relationships more in keeping with her cosmopolitan identity; offering a forum for pursuing sensuality, flirtation and sexuality far exceeding the boundaries of the traditional 'settled' sexuality of the rural peers she disdained; providing a source of power and status, as a member of the 'in' crowd at club events; and, importantly (as a podium dancer), a source of income for sustaining her involvement. However, the options and possibilities for constructing an alternative career path through involvement in club culture were much more limited for young women and, despite the advent of the female DJ (Henderson, 1997), did not hold the same breadth of promise for her as, for example, for Robin.

Hazel also opted for another version of downward social mobility as a means of resisting a professional middle-class future. This involved drawing on an aspect of local rural working-class culture: rural factory work. Hazel was initially drawn to the most powerful symbol of 'failure' in the locality – working in a turkey factory – but, after experiencing the brutal culture shift this involved, settled into a wider variety of manual, unskilled work.

From the position of her middle-class and rural background, Hazel did not experience drug use as a risk to her future, simply as a contrast to boredom with her environs and a cultural passport to a world beyond it. Corinne's experience was rather different.

Corinne: 'I don't want to end up on the bru[1]'

Corinne had much more in common with Glen in that she had far fewer material resources to draw on, but the close community she grew up in provided her with extensive social networks and a more domestically based, local party scene. The night-time cityscape became a key tool for Corinne in constructing difference and consciously ignoring the rigidity, restrictions and fear of sectarianism. She was able to move around the city's divided leisure spaces with friends from both sides of 'the divide' and as a young woman was relatively safe in doing so.

There were also a number of things working against the processes that tied her into her local community and its norms (MacDonald et al., 2005). Having seen male relatives living a similar lifestyle to Glen and having experienced its impact on others first-hand, Corinne felt an urgent need to escape this. As a result she invested heavily in education as a route out of poverty and sectarian divisions. Like Hazel, she saw no attractive opportunities in the party scene for a long-term future. Whilst Glen tended to present a positive picture of life, Corinne's story was marked with regret for much of the study; wishing at 17 that she had 'never even touched' Ecstasy, she felt her life was out of control and that the previous year had been 'the worst year of my life' – something she associated with the death of her uncle who was 'like a father to me' and who she felt would be 'ashamed' of her.

A turning point in her drug career came shortly before this when Corinne returned home one night to find her mother drinking and distressed about their declining relationship. Her ensuing resolve to repair this relationship was given a further boost when her teachers requested a meeting with her and her mother to discuss Corinne's changed attitude and achievement at school. At 19, Corinne was describing 3 years of Ecstasy use as a 'wee phase' she had 'got over', having acquired a new, anti-drug social circle and boyfriend and reinvested in education as a route out of her community. At 21, she was still living at home, was close to her mother once more and had little contact with her old friends on her estate. Still with the same boyfriend, she was considering following him to work abroad. Working and studying filled most of her life. Her taste for hedonistic pleasures became heavily boundaried in this context and took the form of drinking 'as much as I can' on rare nights out with her boyfriend.

Conclusion

The bigger picture of chemical culture at the turn of the 21st century emerging from the accounts of those of a more chemically hedonistic bent in the Inventing Adulthoods study contradicts dominant understandings in that it invokes an oddly 'retro' image of the privileged classes dabbling in cocaine use and of predominantly male affairs with chemical culture. This seems a long way from the dominant portrayal of late modern consumer culture of chemical excess as a democratised zone in which gender, class, ethnicity and so on are no longer significant barriers to participation and in which postmodern femininities have played a prominent role. This predominantly middle-class male picture is all the more surprising given that the study sample became more female over time and remained predominantly working class. On reflection, however, it appears to point up a bent for new forms of material and social 'success' entailing downward social mobility amongst middle-class young men. Whilst the working-class young man – historically the 'spectacular star' of previous studies of drug cultures – is almost absent from this picture *in person*, his presence is arguably much more considerable in a symbolic sense. The burgeoning club culture may have produced the phenomenon of 'boys staying home to cook tunes' and with it a plethora of aspiring DJs (Henderson, 1997), but the relative normalisation of certain aspects of the criminal underworld and all things 'scam' within popular culture also contributed to the landscapes for young masculinities, lending currency to 'performing' a variety of 'working-class', 'bad lad' identities (Henderson, 1997; Beynon, 2002).

The bigger picture, however, only reflects the continuities and patterns within young biographies. The Inventing Adulthoods study also enables a shift into the complexity and detail of connected individual lives over time, which illustrates that, although gender and class are clearly relevant factors, they are not sufficient tools for understanding the different place and meaning of chemical culture in young people's developing lives.

Whilst Glen was drawn to a more traditionally sub-cultural identity, his middle-class peers 'bought into' the masculine identities available within more mainstream chemical culture. For Hazel, intent upon downward social mobility, the resources for adopting a working-class identity were not as readily available to her within club culture as they were to her rural peer Robin. Instead she turned to the 'unrespectable' elements of the rural job market. Meanwhile, for Corinne, her changing attitude towards drugs increasingly became an expression of the way she dealt with the tension between her desire to leave behind the risks her socially disadvantaged community posed to her future, and a need to maintain her family ties and position within her community. In rejecting the Ecstasy culture, she confirmed her rejection of a life of limited options and prospects. A less localised version of adulthood, achieved through education, vocation and social mobility, became her primary focus.

Glen's lack of resources meant that his sub-cultural investment led to diminishing options as well as fewer choices over time. In contrast, his middle-class peers were shored up by parental resources and, to differing degrees, this translated into an ability to turn their investment to advantage. This class difference also applied to Hazel and Corinne but worked very differently and with very different outcomes. Although Hazel's middle-class parental resources were crucial in supporting her through her fling with club culture, family origins, responsibility and conflict were, at the same time, the impetus to her initial involvement. Similarly, whilst Corinne shared many of the elements of Glen's disadvantaged Northern Irish background and was the most given to chemical hedonism amongst young women from 'poor places' within the study, her response to her local landscape and the role that her investment in intoxication played in this, was quite different.

Fiona Measham has recently argued that:

> ... for women 'doing gender' through 'doing drugs' allows the possibility of both constructing and challenging traditional and non-traditional notions of femininity. (Measham, 2002: 363–4)

Our case studies certainly suggest this analysis could be extended to 'doing' masculinities and 'doing' class through 'doing drugs'. However, Measham and colleagues have also noted the dynamic nature and complexity of the development of drug use and the role of transitions in other areas of life in determining drug pathways (Measham, et al., 1998a, 1998b). The case studies discussed offer complex, dynamic accounts of heavy investment in the leisure–pleasure landscape, situating engagement in chemical culture in the broader context of an analysis of structural and identity transitions. As such they provide a window on the different place and meaning of chemical culture in contemporary everyday lives, one that provides a refreshing contrast to its place on public agendas. They also suggest that the chemical leisure–pleasure landscape is not only a matter for public concern but also a popular arena in which inequalities are being remade. It is to such questions that the book now turns.

Note

1. Unemployed and in receipt of benefits.

Chapter 7

Well-being

Introduction

We end this section by looking at aspects of young people's well-being, a state that is entwined with most of the other themes explored in this book, both affecting and being affected by the life experiences of the young people involved in the study. Earlier chapters have explored some key public concerns around young people by looking at the broader, complex processes shaping young lives at the turn of the 21st century. This chapter examines the implications of social change for the way young people growing up in a rapidly changing and increasingly uncertain social world, feel in and about themselves – a holistic sense of physical, emotional and mental well-being (or ill-being) – and the impact of this on their paths to adulthood.

As we have seen, the state of the nation is often linked closely in the public imagination with the state of the nation's youth. Health is no exception. Pick up any newspaper and you will find tales of the new generation of telly-addicted couch potatoes, junk food diets and rising obesity. Young people's pleasures have perennially been the staple of public concern and policy remedies, and a public preoccupation with certain 'risk taking' behaviours (associated with but not confined to the young) forms the stuff of contemporary daily life. From this perspective it would be all too easy to conclude that, when not engaged in disrupting British society through teenage pregnancy, sexually transmitted infections or anti-social behaviour, young people are threatening its very future by forsaking physical exercise for life as stop-at-home geeks.

In the past, public agendas have tended to concentrate on the implications of young people's pleasures for those around them, while the emotional and psychological pains of the young people themselves have been relatively neglected. In recent years, however, the media has begun to present young people as more of a health concern, and as being under rising pressure in competitive education and work environments. Reports increasingly describe a decline in their mental and emotional well-being, associated with depression generally, and more specifically with behavioural problems such as suicide, eating disorders and self-harm. Now, they are not only seen as a 'problem' in terms, for example, of violent and disorderly behaviour, but as unhealthy through lack of exercise and obesity, and alcohol and illegal drug consumption. The Department of Health (2004) acknowledged that mental health problems in children and young people 'are associated with educational failure, family disruption, disability, offending and antisocial behaviour, placing demands on social services, schools and the youth justice system'. Some media comment (Bunting, 2004) has also suggested that a failure in parenting involving lack of 'attachment' could account for increased mental health problems, and compared young people to coal-mining 'canaries' in terms of representing an early warning of wider social problems to come.

In the Inventing Adulthoods data, certain aspects of mental ill-health, particularly depression, came into clearer focus when we analysed it at the stage when young people were aged 18–23 years. We felt it would be appropriate to use our biographical approach in developing a more holistic and situated account of these 'internal' aspects of young people's lives as they grow up in late modernity. The notion of 'well-being' has been used in various ways, but it is now generally acknowledged to be more than an absence of illness, and a state that includes a broad range of mental, social and personal aspects. Although we thereby recognise that well-being is an all-embracing concept, this chapter focuses mainly on the mental health issues that emerged from the young people's accounts, which allowed us to monitor their well-being in context, over time, and through their own perspectives.

Young people, uncertainty and mental health

It has been argued that so-called risk taking behaviours such as smoking, drinking, drugs and sex are related to young people's attempts to feel adult in the uncertain landscape of the 'risk' society in which they are constructing their personal and social identities (Furlong and Cartmel, 1997; Miles et al., 1998; Pavis et al., 1998). A perceived rise in psychological disorders among young people has been linked to late modern uncertainty and anxiety arising from: an expansion in possibilities, choices and decision-making (Rutter and Smith, 1995); the extension of education and the financial pressures on students (Rutter and Smith, 1995; Furlong and Cartmel, 1997; Rana et al., 1999); extended unemployment (West and Sweeting, 1996); and poor parenting (Bunting 2004; DoH, DfES, 2004). Furlong and Cartmel (1997) have argued that in late modernity 'young people are forced to reflexively negotiate a complex set of routes into the labour market and in doing so, develop a sense that they alone are responsible for their labour market outcomes'. Good qualifications should lead to good jobs but there is no guarantee; young people with more than average qualifications may not find work, may be forced to enter lower-level jobs, and may experience mental health problems as a result (Furlong and Spearman, 1989; West and Sweeting, 1996). Walkerdine and her colleagues have written of the psychic costs of neo-liberal demands for educational success among middle-class young women (Walkerdine et al., 2001). It has been suggested by psychodynamic theorists that the unconscious, collective anxieties of the wider society may be projected onto young people, who then symbolically act them out, and increasing stress and mental illness in late modern society may be introjected and internalised by young people and lead to 'psychotic anxieties' (Briggs, 2002).

Certainly, the figures on young people's mental health make worrying reading, in particular those relating to students and the young unemployed. In 2004, a survey for the Department of Health and the Scottish Executive suggested that 'one in ten children and young people aged 5–16 had a clinically recognisable mental disorder' (National Statistics Online, 2005). Students are more likely to report increased mental health symptoms than other young people of the same age (Olohan, 2004), with 40 percent concerned about issues related to depression, 23 percent experiencing anxieties, phobias or panic attacks (Grant, 2002), and 17 percent presenting with severe psychological problems (AUCC, 1998). Furthermore, 53 percent of college students experienced depression after beginning college while 9 percent considered committing suicide (Furr et al., 2001).

Rutter and Smith (1995) indicated an increase in depressive conditions which strongly correlate with an increase in suicide and self-harm. In the UK, suicide rates in young men rose dramatically (64%) between 1984 and 1994, with the steepest rises occurring in rural areas (Bird and Faulkner, 2000; Middleton et al., 2003). It is estimated that the rates for young men have gradually decreased since then with the exception of Scotland, where rates are substantially higher than in England (Coleman and Schofield, 2005). National statistics show that more young men (491) compared to young women (134) between the ages of 15 and 24 years committed suicide in 2002. Deliberate self-harm, however, is more common in young women than young men (11.2% females compared to 3.2% males) (Hawton et al., 2002). It has been suggested that the psychological fall-out from extended unemployment rises with young people's age and that unemployed 18 year olds reported much higher rates of suicide than those in work (West and Sweeting, 1996; Gunnell et al., 1999; Hawton et al., 1999). Those in education show a similarly higher rate and, for example, Hawton et al. (1995) showed that over a 14-year period, the overall number of student suicides at Oxford University was higher than that among people of similar age who were not students.

As well as the stresses experienced by young people relating to education and work, there are other stresses such as bereavement that are less subject to the privilege of social classes, although experiences of bereavement may also interact with material conditions and chronic ill health to shape disadvantage. Bereavement experiences in young people's lives may represent a risk in terms of their subsequent educational performance, employment and leaving home, and for personal outcomes such as physical and mental health (Ribbens McCarthy with Jessop, 2005; Ribbens McCarthy, 2006). Research by Harrison and Harrington (2001) showed that 92 percent of young people under 16 reported having experienced bereavement with regard to what they considered to be a 'close' or 'significant' relationship. This is likely to increase by the age of 18 or 25. Many of these bereavements involve the death of a grandparent, but other researchers have documented that up to 8 percent of young people under 16 may have experienced the death of a parent (Wadsworth, 1991; Sweeting et al., 1998), or a close friend (Meltzer et al., 2000). Children and young people often struggle to understand and cope with overwhelming and unexpected feelings following a deeply felt bereavement and may have difficulties in social relationships and lack of opportunities to talk. They tend to take their cues from those closest to them, such as family members, who may seek to 'protect' each other by avoiding painful conversations. This raises issues about general social attitudes towards bereavement and the specific way in which it is experienced by young people as involving a relative lack of power combined with a sense of exclusion from the decisions being made (Ribbens McCarthy with Jessop, 2005).

Eating disorders have also been associated with the impact of 'risk society' on an individual's development of a safe self-identity. In the words of Giddens (1991: 107), 'anorexia represents a striving for security in a world of plural, but ambiguous objects. The tightly controlled body is an emblem of safe existence in an open social environment'. As anorexia peaks in adolescent years (14–19) and bulimia in late teenage years and early adulthood, these conditions have also been linked to young people's attempts to arrest development into adulthood (Rutter and Smith, 1995; Briggs, 2002). Separating from the relative safety of home (see Chapter 10) coupled with embarking on the uncertain journey into independence may pose threats to young people's mental health and well-being. It may also represent a way of trying to feel in control, or of resisting some exertion of power or control coming from outside, such as a demanding parent. Once a disorder associated with middle-class women, the fastest growth in anorexia has more recently been reported among working-class women (Furlong and Cartmel, 1997). And although more adolescent girls than boys experience eating disorders, young men have increasingly been affected (Briggs, 2002).

Psychological 'ill-being' in the Inventing Adulthoods study

Although individual researchers may have been aware of particular cases, it was only when we analysed the round of interviews conducted at age 18–23 that the significance of depression and related mental health issues in the dataset became apparent. Thirteen young people (nine young women and four young men) described experiences of depression and stress linked to education, employment, family situations, and relationships. Almost all the young women were from working-class backgrounds, mainly from Northern Ireland and the disadvantaged English site, while all but one of the young men were from middle-class families living in the affluent commuter site. In addition, five more young women described how they had been affected by the depression of someone they were close to, such as a parent or boyfriend.

Young people living in the disadvantaged estate and some parts of the Northern Irish site were more likely to experience cultures of ill health, poverty, poor housing, unemployment and family breakdown. They found themselves with far fewer material, social and cultural resources on which to draw than others in the study. This harsher landscape with its higher incidence of illness, bereavement and suicide meant there was more potential for 'critical moments' in young people's lives to have a negative impact on their well-being. Figures from the 2004 survey (National Statistics Online, 2005) found the prevalence of mental disorder was higher in lone parent or reconstituted families, and where parents were unemployed or had no educational qualifications, and were living on a low income – all factors which were relevant to the young people in these two sites. Bereavement was a key theme that also emerged in this context and this sometimes changed the young people's approach to life, and their values, confidence, motivation and hence their life trajectories. Meanwhile, while talk about depression was largely done by middle-class young men or working-class young women, only the latter discussed experiences of self-harm and eating disorders. An exception was Hazel, who we met in Chapter 6 and whose experience of ongoing parental conflict underwrote her rejection of education, her subsequent embrace of employment and club culture and, finally, her story of depression (Henderson, 2005).

Young people's well-being, and particularly that of young women, can be negatively affected by having to take the role of carers in their families. Location and gender once more come into play, as exemplified by two young women in our study who come from the more disadvantaged sites, where young people's present and future lives were more likely to be critically affected by having to manage or care for a sick or alcoholic parent or close relative. Maisie's story of inner resourcefulness against all the odds in the northern English estate (in Chapter 4), was one in which her family presented a constant drain on her well-being. With illnesses of her own to contend with, Maisie also took responsibility for her mother's many serious ailments as well as her siblings' drug dependency and violent relationship. Karin grew up in Northern Ireland in an atmosphere of parental conflict, with an alcoholic and depressive father. Alcohol also became an important part of her own social life, and she became subject to bouts of depression, one of which left her a year behind in her college course.

Education: The best days of your life?

There is a tendency for social commentators to imply that depression and other emotional problems are more of a middle-class malaise, often precipitated through pressures for educational success, but both government figures and the Inventing Adulthoods young people suggest diversity across the social classes. Material, social and cultural resources are clearly important in sustaining young people through the educational process, but emotional support (or the lack of it) also has considerable currency. In the case of young men, it is possible that masculine expectations of success and achievement can provide the context for some quite different experiences of stress that may be managed in particular ways. Depression emerged as a significant factor in the lives of several young men in the Inventing Adulthoods study who were going through university, and for whom this path proved tougher than anticipated.

We have chosen to focus on three young men in this educational context: Edward and Nat both grew up in middle-class, materially well-off families in the commuter belt, whilst Danny grew up in a working-class family in Northern Ireland. There were strong similarities in terms of their trajectories. All three went to university, faltered in this path and became depressed, felt they had no-one to turn to, but completed their degree courses. However, their aspirations and sense of themselves, the educational routes they took, the critical moments within these and the resources they were able to draw upon were quite different. While Edward and Danny both had a stable and supportive family and entered university with considerable academic self-confidence and belief, Nat's family breakdown was central to a more rocky investment in education and educational outcomes.

Edward

Edward's high aspirations regarding education and career success were central to his self-identity. Having received outstanding A level results, he aspired to 'getting a first' through 'studying very hard', which he accomplished in the first year. His aims however, were shaken by a bout of depression experienced during his second university year that caused him to miss over half a term of lectures. At this time he even considered dropping out, but continued because he could see no viable alternative:

> But being the sort of person I am I thought, 'What would I actually do if I did drop out of the course?' And if I'd thought of something better to do, I would almost certainly have left … university at that time. (Edward, 20, 2002)

He did not tell his parents or seek help but went home for Christmas and felt much better. Although he subsequently worked hard to make up for it, he was not one of the top students that year. Edward's previous experiences of being a high achiever shaped his expectations (and probably those of others) and it is likely that his depression stemmed from his failure to reach the unrelenting standards he set for himself (Young, 1999). Possibly as a form of self 'protection', he reflected that he had not worked to his capacity and speculated how much better he might have done if he had worked really hard:

> If I'd worked all the time and only ended up with sort of 5th or 6th in the university I'd have had to admit, right, there are these people who are more capable than me. But by not working I could, I could blur the distinction and I could say well yes I could have been 10 or 20 places higher if I'd worked. It was, I suppose it was a sort of insecurity ... and I suppose there was also the fear that, that was the highest I was going to get even if I did work solidly. (Edward, 22, 2004)

The following year Edward was diagnosed with clinical depression and saw his results dropping a grade for that year. This affected his confidence and he postponed his plans for postgraduate study. It is possible that the underlying reasons for his depression were closely related to expectations for academic success (his own and others'), especially the case for people who come from middle-class backgrounds.

Nat

Unlike Edward, Nat did not do well at the examination to qualify for university, and stayed on at school to take a vocational qualification in business studies. Parental conflict in his late teens provided a hostile atmosphere in Nat's home and his relationship with his father was bad. His younger brother had left school and was unemployed, and both brothers smoked a lot of marijuana. Nat's pride and joy was his car, but it absorbed lots of money and he was in debt. Although he passed his vocational qualification and went to university to do business studies, he spent his first year smoking dope, did not bother to take exams, and had to re-do the year:

> I sort of became really sort of withdrawn into myself, and I'd spend a lot of time on my own and um became a little bit unsociable … I dunno, I was really quite depressed. … I was in a downward spiral for a bit and er that's why really I didn't go into university, because I didn't really care or want to – no motivation. (Nat, 21, 2002)

Nat began taking antidepressants but could not be bothered to travel to get a repeat prescription. He was without a job, his father would not give him any money, and he was dependent on cash from his mother. He was left with few material or family resources, and nor did he have a girlfriend or close personal friends for emotional support. By 21, he had messed up two academic years by not going to courses and failing exams, and admitted using dope to block his depressing thoughts and feelings, commenting 'I just became reliant on it to run away and to forget'.

After working hard over that summer, Nat did well in his exam re-sits and could at last move on to the second year. Meanwhile, his family had disintegrated completely; the family home had been sold and its members had moved in different directions. His sense of 'home' was now reduced to wherever he was (see also Chapter 10). Although he now had a well-paid part-time sales job, he still had large debts. Nat moved to a spacious (but more expensive) flat in a nicer part of town and life looked up when his sister came to live with him for a year. However, Nat went on to fail his second year exams and finally left university with a pass degree. The combination of a fragmented family life which could not give him the kind of emotional support he needed, his use of marijuana and his recurring depression have led to a series of failures in someone who is clearly capable of much more. Although things have improved, his financial situation combined with his propensity to take risks in various areas of his life, such as education and career, have made it hard for him to achieve a stable and successful future, and he has found it hard to motivate himself:

> ... you put yourself down, it's difficult to become motivated about things, oh my whole life was tumbling down for a very long time. And I just hit rock bottom, and there wasn't really anything I could do about it ... you're in control but you're not at the same time. You wanna do something about it, but you're not strong enough, or you just can't basically. (Nat, 23, 2004)

Danny

Danny from Northern Ireland was well resourced in terms of family and school support that gave him a great deal of confidence and self-belief. He went from school to an English university where he was extremely enthusiastic about student life. He was the sociable 'Irish' lad and his differences and eccentricities were celebrated. But in his final year there was a definite sense in his narrative that he had lost a lot of social support. His more middle- and upper-class peers had become very competitive and were concentrating on studying. Although Danny had the financial back-up of his parents throughout his degree, he had to work during his second year to supplement his student loan. He continued to work in his final year, taking on more pressure, while his friends just rang their families for more money. He felt left out, academically less able, stressed with the pressure of work, and described how he became 'severely depressed' for about 6 months. Danny distanced himself from his friends, lost confidence, and did not want to 'get out of bed, eat, talk or socialise'. After an incident when he thought his drink had been spiked and he publicly 'lost it', he also ended up overnight in hospital. He did not talk to his parents or doctor about his emotional health.

Danny returned to Ireland after obtaining his degree but found his hook into the local community had been dislodged. He also found it difficult to fit back in with the rules and systems at home and missed his freedom. Unable to track down any of his former schoolmates, he felt he was living like a 'stranger' in his own town, where he seemed to have lost his access to the social life. He also found it hard being unemployed, with no expectation of extended financial support and under pressure to find a job. At last contact he was looking forward to returning to England where he felt more at home and had more social connections.

These three young men illustrate different sorts of psychological vulnerability experienced at an important educational stage in their life paths. Edward had a set of solid friendships at university but suffered from the elevated academic standards he set himself (see Chapter 2); Danny's depression was precipitated in his final year by changes in the bases of his friendships; and Nat lacked close relationships and material, social and emotional resources for much of the study, developing a low level of well-being and motivation, and a dependency on marijuana.

Ill-being, the body and young femininities

A survey published in 2004 (National Statistics Online, 2005) found that at younger ages, boys were more likely than girls to have a mental disorder (age 5–10, 10% boys: 5% girls; at 11–16, 13% boys: 10% girls), while the Mental Health Foundation (2003) suggests that at ages 16–19, the reverse is the case with 6 percent of young men and 16 percent of young women thought to have some form of mental health problem. Young people's well-being appears to be strongly gendered in that young men and women tend to suffer differently from a number of 'disorders'. For example, there is evidence that proportionally more young women suffer from eating disorders such as anorexia and bulimia, and are twice as likely to suffer from a depressive illness as young men, despite the recent concern shown by the media and policy-makers about an apparent rise in depression among young men (HDA, 2001). Whereas, despite media publicity about young women's binge drinking, it is young men who are more likely to be dependent on alcohol or drugs; more commonly show behaviour disorders (10–20% of young men involved in criminal activity are thought to have a 'psychiatric disorder', Mental Health Foundation, 2005); and, as described earlier, are much more vulnerable to suicide than young women between the ages of 15–24.

The discussion of depression by the young women in the Inventing Adulthoods study was notable for the ways that it involved action on their bodies. Of the nine young people concerned about weight issues, all but one were young women. We have chosen three of these to illustrate the issues; all had experienced eating disorders, one of whom also described activities of self harm, and suicidal feelings.

Marion

The first, Marion, developed an eating disorder in parallel with, and possibly as part of, her intense concern with working as hard as she could to succeed academically. She was a plump young woman who was talented in music, and did several part-time jobs to earn money. She came from a large, lower middle-class family whose religion made demands that added to the other pressures that she imposed on herself. She achieved well and at 18 was anxiously working very long hours revising for her examinations that would qualify her for university, although it was sometimes hard to keep on top of her schoolwork as she shared a room at home. She had applied to several universities, and it had been suggested that she apply to Oxford or Cambridge. During this time she lost her plumpness and turned into a slim teenager. But she could not stop this process and by the end of the summer she was in hospital with anorexia, her university education had been put on hold and the future was looking uncertain. The pressures she felt under seemed to have proved too much. Some researchers (Evans et al., 2004) have looked specifically at girls' eating disorders in the context of the formal education system and point to the importance of power, and particularly gendered power relations and the ways that young women struggle for empowerment within them, in any understanding of how such disorders develop. Not eating can then be seen as a way of trying to control the body, in the context of struggling to control other areas of life.

Monica and Shannon illustrate how an emotional crisis, in both cases caused by a split with their long-term relationships, can precipitate an eating disorder.

Monica

Monica, from a respectable working-class family, had been at the same predominantly middle-class school as Marion (but several years earlier) taking examinations to qualify her for university and planning to go there. She had experienced periods of stress and depression in the past, but her current distress took hold when her previously steady boyfriend had stopped seeing her in order to go out with another girl. After some weeks, to her relief he changed his mind and returned, but her confidence had been undermined, she found it hard to trust him, and was constantly seeking reassurance. Meanwhile she had developed a minor eating disorder, and had started making herself sick after eating sweet things. This she said was to punish herself, either for eating them in the first place, or for being jealous about her boyfriend, who knew nothing of this. Monica was not unfamiliar with this condition as her older sister had had a similar eating disorder. She had not confided in anyone except her best friend Jane who did the same thing:

> Well, I don't always eat and when I do I make myself sick again ... I used to do it a couple of times, like if I had too many sweets or something I did it, 'cause I felt guilty,

but lately I've been doing it practically every day, I shouldn't … I think everyone goes through the stage of doing it don't they really, Jane's been through it a couple times, she does it like every month practically so, I mean everyone does it don't they? (Monica, 18, 2000)

Some time later, Monica moved into a flat with her boyfriend and her eating disorder seemed to have disappeared.

From a psychodynamic viewpoint, eating disorders such as anorexia and bulimia can be seen as displaced 'acting out' of societal anxieties about consumption. Briggs (2002) suggests that the uncertainty characterising the external world may take the internalised form of 'psychotic anxieties' that some young people try to control through self-harm and eating disorders, or even suicide. However, Briggs noted that these anxieties only lead to mental health illness when there is a failure of 'containment'. Containment can involve a process during which a person describes their disturbed state of mind to someone who can manage and neutralise their frightening experiences, thus enabling him or her to tolerate them (Spurling, 2004). For young people, containment can be facilitated through an emotionally secure environment usually involving family, relationships and friendships. Monica, for example, would talk about her feelings and bulimia with her best friend Jane, but it was only when she felt more secure and more in control again with her boyfriend, that she stopped making herself sick.

Shannon

Shannon's story illustrates how family experiences may lead to self-harm and how a traumatic ending to a couple relationship can trigger a depressive process. After her parents split up when she was young, Shannon lived with her mother in Northern Ireland. She did well at school and transferred to the grammar school to do examinations to qualify for university, where she found the course work a struggle, and having a working-class background, also felt somewhat socially and culturally inferior. But she passed her exams and got offers from several universities. She had fallen in love with her boyfriend, Al, and went to live with him in an English city. There she took courses at the local polytechnic instead of a more prestigious university. Shannon tried to keep their home together by doing two part-time jobs but Al was a bit of a waster, very possessive, and had a drug habit. They became engaged but soon after that he ended the relationship. She gave up her course and moved back to Ireland to live with her mother, feeling depressed and sometimes suicidal. She commented how her mother hid the paracetamol from her at this time. She lost over a stone in weight and began taking anti-depressants:

I mean I got um a bit sort of really quite thin when I came back after finishing with Al, 'cos I wasn't eating – I never ate for like two weeks, 'cos I was just like crap (laughs) … yeah, yeah and I was put on Prozac and um he basically sort of said that if I don't start eating within the next four weeks that they're gonna – you know, start (laughs) – they joked about putting a tube down my nose. (Shannon, 19, 2003)

After her relationship broke up, she took some time out in Australia where she had a brief but confidence-restoring relationship with an older man. At 19 she was back in Northern Ireland but had decided to make a fresh start by taking a degree in an English university and at last contact was in a much happier state.

Concern with relationships, family, insecurity, isolation, and difference tended to feature in Shannon's interviews, which contributed to incidences of depression, self-harm, and suicidal feelings, triggered when she experienced moments of extreme physical or mental distress. In a later interview Shannon recalled how in her early teens she had reacted to earlier family experiences by wanting to harm herself by cutting her legs, and by developing some obsessive rituals like covering up, and shutting doors, to make her feel safer. Deliberate self-harm is four times more common in women than men, and certainly much more common among younger than older adults. And as we see in Chapter 11 ('Intimacy'), developing a long-term relationship can have a critical effect on a young person's life, but such a relationship splitting up can have equivalent outcomes, inducing, as we have seen, depression in Shannon, and an eating disorder in Monica.

Bereavement as a critical moment

It was not surprising that some of the young people in the study had experienced bereavement in their lives. While bereavement had also arisen for some in earlier interviews, at the fourth-round interview 13 young people (11 young women and two young men) described having lost someone significant in their lives, such as a parent, grandparent, some other relative, or a friend. For some it was through illness, while others described fatal car accidents involving their friends, or friends of friends. There are many ways in which bereavement can act as a 'critical moment', whereby the young person involved is brought up sharply against the reality of loss, and in our group of young people, it sometimes precipitated a temporary or permanent reassessment of their values and priorities.

Neville

Neville, a young middle-class man, provides an illustration of one whose well-being and direction in life was greatly affected by losing his mother. Neville had grown up in Northern Ireland with his parents and older sister until, at 18, when alone in the house with his mother, she suddenly collapsed and died of a heart attack. It was totally unexpected as she had been very healthy, and family life ground to a halt as they tried to take in what had happened. Getting back to normal at college was difficult, but Neville was determined to do well for his mother's sake, and his friends were very supportive.

A year later, life had settled down; he was doing well in college; he had a good relationship with his father; and his sister was engaged. But his grief for his mother was ever present and reinforced by the constant reminders of her in photographs. He found it hard to cope with life and sometimes wished he could escape from everything:

> There's times like I just feel like saying 'Oh to hell with it all' and you know, going away somewhere and just starting again … Okay, a year's gone past now like and it's still as bad ... It still hurts like hell and you know, there's nothing you can do. You can't bring her back. (Neville, 19, 2000)

His loss still loomed large after another year had passed, and he described how he would drive up to the graveyard late at night, park in the car park and talk to his mother's grave. To mark the second anniversary, he had written up the whole event in great detail, which he said was 'just like somebody lifting a weight off your shoulders because I kept it in for 2 years'. He felt that his mother's death had changed him as a person:

> You know, I'm not as out-going as I was before … I think I'm a more emotional person now … I'd be crying a lot more now. Well, I wouldn't be crying at everything … but I wouldn't be as strong as I was before. And I find it hard to get motivated most of the time now. (Neville, 19, 2000)

At 22, Neville had completed his college course but decided not to pursue university even though he had been offered a place (later he did take another further education course). He felt he had lost some of his previous confidence to do well, had let his friends go, and seemed rather isolated. His sister had left home to get married, an event that underlined the absence of his mother. His father had married again and they all moved to a different area. While his father and his sister have moved on and into other significant relationships, Neville has continued to be preoccupied with his mother's death, and this has depressed his thoughts and motivation.

Disability: Working harder at well-being

Neville's situation was complicated by a minor disability that affected his physical coordination, and this seemed to make him more isolated after he left university. Health is a significant resource and its lack in young people with disabilities poses significant challenges to well-being. Graham was a notable example of this. From the disadvantaged northern estate, Graham had a progressive degenerative illness that saw him change from an able-bodied 8 year old to being wheelchair-bound from the age of 12. This made him highly aware that he was physically diminishing whilst friends were growing – the opposite of the usual progress from youth into adulthood.

Graham

Being disabled meant that Graham had a unique set of material resources: an adapted bungalow, disability allowance and a car. His periods of residential independent living also gave him confidence to consider living on his own. But Graham's social resources were largely linked with education and when he was no longer educationally engaged he became much more isolated. Two years spent at college provided access to social life, as well as local authority transport and support workers. But at the age of 19, once education ended, levels of support appeared to diminish as, in a minor way, they had for Neville. His networks beyond the family and immediate neighbourhood had been continually disrupted, and largely ended when he left college. His initial hope had been to get 'a good job with good money' but when even a disability agency failed to offer him anything suitable, he finally lost the motivation to work at all.

One of the networks that remained constant for Graham was his contact with a few other disabled young people. Whilst this provided him with a frame of reference to define himself as 'a wheelchair' too proud to want anyone feeling sorry for him, it also increased the chances of contact with illness and death. Sadly, the only two people he was emotionally close to both died within weeks of each other towards the end of the study. Vulnerable and unhappy with his lot, Graham began to express a great deal more anger towards the lack of equality for those with disabilities – describing his embarrassment at going into the local pub, or queuing for, and getting into, a taxi in the city centre at night. Family had been and remained at the centre of his life practically and materially speaking; he was particularly reliant on his mother for everyday practical support and while increasingly resentful about this, was aware that this dependency could only increase as his body deteriorated. Despite considerable personal fortitude and struggle, Graham was becoming increasingly centred within the domestic domain.

Conclusion

The Mental Health Foundation (1999, 2005) point to the increasing demands on social and other services due to mental health problems in children and young people, and the cost of mental illness in the UK, given as £93 billion per year, will certainly rise if these problems persist into adulthood. As we have seen, a wide range of acute or ongoing situations and experiences may contribute to young people's psychological well-being at any time, and can have critical effects on both their mental health, and their life trajectories. The ways in which young people cope with negative events depends to some extent on the resources that they have available to them. These may vary and can include personal strength of character, family support, material resources, and networks through which to seek help. As Nat and Shannon illustrate, the nature and quality of family or personal relationships can be very significant in how they respond to critical events and in their transitions to adulthood, while Edward illustrates the potential dangers of self-imposed, high educational standards. Characteristics of social class and location can contribute much to this and it is significant that there was a greater incidence of ill health, bereavement, depression and mental illness in the disadvantaged areas (north of England, and in Northern Ireland), where there is also less access to the social capital that could transform young people's trajectories, than in the other sites. The cultures of violence found in these places can also contribute to both cause and outcome, as described in Chapter 5. These violent environments have fostered new forms of material survival, such as the growing claim culture, in which compensation claims are made, for example, after muggings and other street or sectarian attacks.

Simply living in and responding to cultures of poverty and violence serve to maintain levels of social and economic inequalities. Thus further aspects of well-being (or ill-being), which include mental health in particular, can create or accentuate existing inequalities in young people's life potential. In addition to presenting real practical difficulties, they may erode or destroy young people's self-confidence and motivation to succeed in whatever area they may have chosen. As described in the previous chapters, young people are subject to structural and public influences but their well-being is also clearly affected by private and personal issues. These are taken up in the following section that explores aspects of young people's lives such as a sense of belonging, the meaning of home, and the significance of a couple relationship.

Part 3
Biographical projects and the remaking of inequality

Introduction

In this final part of the book we shift our focus from the categories of policy, practice and moral panic explored in Part 2 to those that sprang from our interviews as having salience for young people. Seen through the eyes of the adult world, drugs, violence, health and education were perceived to be the areas of relevance to young people but it was mobility, belonging, home, intimacy and sociality that emerged as most meaningful to young people themselves. These are the things that young people value, that motivate their actions and characterise their accounts of self. We can see these as 'biographical' categories, reflecting the life as lived and experienced, as opposed to the life as regulated via state or policy intervention. In Part 2 we began with the public perspective and worked our way back to the biographical. In Part 3 we begin with the biographical and then explore the ways in which the social can be understood through this lens.

As we argue in Chapter 2, the context within which the Inventing Adulthoods young people are growing up is characterised by rapidly changing structures and expectations. In material terms they are entering a 'new economy' that is becoming increasingly more virtual, reflexive, flexible and networked, and characterised by data, knowledge and service intensity (Castells, 1996; Thrift, 1998; Hardt, 1999; Lury, 2003; Adkins, 2005b). It is also a period marked both by an overall stagnation in social mobility and by movements within fragments of middle and working classes. In intergenerational terms it is an era in which you have to 'move' in order to stay still. Although they operate within highly constrained structures of opportunity, the contrasting biographies within and between localities suggest that personal agency and parental support are central resources in negotiating outcomes and life chances. Our methodology gives us an insight into the work that individuals do on the self over time and how social divisions such as social class are reformed 'around individualised axes' (Savage, 2000: xxii).

The categories that we explore in this part of the book can be understood as the 'hotspots' in young people's biographies – aspects of life that are the front line of the kind of identity work that can make a difference to processes of intergenerational social mobility and continuity. The Part begins with an exploration of 'mobility' a theme that was central to young people's narratives in all research sites, whether understood in material terms of getting around, or the more symbolic or structural terms suggested by the terms 'getting on' and 'getting out'. We suggest that notions of localism and cosmopolitanism are central to young people's biographical projects, and may be a crucial axis of social inequality in the new economy. In Chapter 9 we turn to 'belonging', a term used here to refer to the significance of faith and religious identification for a significant group of young people in the Inventing Adulthoods study, and how the various forms of religious belonging sit alongside the widely documented trend towards secularisation. While this may at first sight appear paradoxical, we suggest that such forms of 'belonging' may be understood as ways that young people invest in the self and new communities of interpretation and support as a way of dealing with uncertainty and social change. The kinds of investments that they make and how these are perceived by others are in turn consequential for their ability to access opportunity. Some religious identities are read as 'stuck' while others may be perceived as evidence of reflexivity.

Traditionally the passage from family of origin to family of destination was understood as a central thread in young people's transitions. In the context of extended dependency, access to family resources are increasingly understood as the most important element in determining young people's life chances. Chapter 10 suggests that 'home' also plays a crucial role in providing young people with a sense of personal security, and the making of a home may be the most satisfying marker of adulthood. The ways that young people negotiate this resource do not map simply onto established categorisations of difference and inequality such as social class, gender and ethnicity. Rather, in exploring home we gain insights into some of the other elements that may be increasingly important in the making of inequality. Intimacy is closely connected to the idea of home and in Chapter 11 we explore the place of the couple relationship in young people's transitions. We also investigate the different patterns of relationship formation that emerge from an analysis of the Inventing Adulthoods young people's lives. These 'tendencies' can be seen as part of emergent biographical paths, closely related to family support and material resource, that cut across traditional class based models of inequality.

In the final chapter on 'sociality', we focus on communication, reputation, knowing and being known as an aspects of young people's lives. We understand sociality as an everyday practice that plays a crucial role in an increasingly fluid social system, observing the way that the control and flow of information is a central part of young people's everyday lives, mediating friendship, relationship with parents, access to social networks and the ability to be geographically and socially mobile (Bauman, 2000). By exploring the changing place of Information and Communication Technologies over time (including the use of mobile phones and the internet) we chart the impact of the digital revolution on the identities and practices of a new generation.

Chapter 8

Mobility

The process of moving from total physical dependence to independence is one of the basic underpinnings of how we understand the transition to adulthood. Learning to crawl then walk, crossing the road, walking to school with friends, learning to drive and travelling alone are widely viewed as stages in a story of social development. The contradictory impulses of mobility and change, on one hand, and stability and continuity, on the other, are also widely viewed as part of the human condition.

Discussions of travel, transport and migration were consistent themes in young people's accounts of growing up in the five contrasting localities captured by the Inventing Adulthoods study. Over time it became clear that mobility is highly salient to young people's lives, whether discussed in pragmatic terms – getting around, public transport, learning to drive – or aspirational terms – travelling, migrating or associating with the music and style of a different place. It also came to the fore as an element in the re-making of inequalities as it became clear that differences in orientation towards physical and geographical mobility were linked to social mobility. Differences in local attitudes and conditions were the most immediately obvious factors. Strong affinities to local community and its norms, for example, could limit what was possible for young people, contrasting sharply with the options and choices open to those with a more global/cosmopolitan outlook. However, these differences were not explained by locality alone. Limited family resources, physical impairment, domestic responsibility and the physical threat associated with certain social spaces were among a wide range of other constraining factors.

This chapter explores some of the different ways that mobility becomes a resource, both in growing up and in intergenerational patterns of continuity and change. It begins with a brief review of thinking around mobility, moving on to look at the importance of locality in shaping particular 'economies of mobility' within which young people operate. The complex and dynamic ways that mobility can feature in young people's lives over time are illustrated through two contrasting case studies. Through Karin and Stan's stories, we suggest the value of thinking about 'cosmopolitanism' and 'localism' as two sides of a coin, competing themes that are not only always 'in conversation' in young people's identities and biographies but also connected to continuous intergenerational processes of continuity and change.

Thinking mobility: Physical, social and cultural movement

The assumption that 'things get better' as a result of economic prosperity and educational policy has a long history. It gained particular currency when the notion of 'getting on in life' was extended to the masses, with working-class members of the baby-boomer generation joining the ranks of the middle classes through access to a grammar school education. In contrast, the contemporary period in the UK is associated with a trend towards downward social mobility and a growing gap between the rich and the poor. As we saw in Chapter 3, policies that seek to expand participation in higher education rely on well-worn narratives of upward social mobility through education. These narratives carry the heavy burden of motivating working-class students and families to make the sacrifices that this route demands. But as biographical examples explored in Chapter 3 and 4 suggest, it may be that a fear of downward social mobility, of doing less well than your parents, is an equally powerful (if rarely spoken) narrative – especially among the middle classes.

Approaches to understanding the link between geographical and social mobility and the reproduction of social inequalities have become more conceptually complex since the classic community (e.g. Young and Willmott, 1957; Bell, 1968) and mobility studies (Goldthorpe et al., 1969; Pahl and Pahl, 1971) first documented forms of working-class localism (patterns of socialising with family and 'old' friends) and middle-class cosmopolitanism (being geographically mobile, maintaining links with family and socialising with 'new' friends and work colleagues). Simple distinctions between working-class immobility and middle-class mobility have been questioned. In the same field, Devine et al. (2003), for example, identify a range of both working- and middle-class locals and cosmopolitans, and suggest that the meaning and value of mobility has been transformed in the course of a generation. Intergenerational studies of the family, rather than the individual, have also revealed complex patterns of chain migration associated with ambivalent feelings about social mobility (Brannen et al., 2003).

Ideas of cosmopolitanism have also been explored in cultural studies, in discussions of the emergence of social divisions based on access to consumption and relationship to place (Bauman, 1996; Hannerz, 1996). For example, Zygmunt Bauman distinguishes between the 'trapped', the 'vagabond' and the 'tourist' and Ulf Hannerz between 'cosmopolitans', 'locals' and 'exiles'. For Bauman, the tourist consumes places yet always has a home to go back to. The vagabond has neither a home nor access to such consumption. For Hannerz (1996), the cosmopolitan is distinguished by competence; possessing 'both a generalised and specialised ability to make ones way in a different culture via listening, looking, intuiting, reflecting'; displaying 'a willingness to engage in difference' yet always knowing 'where the exit is in the alien culture' (p. 103). From this perspective, it may be possible to be a cosmopolitan without ever going away, the key being the cultivation of a particular disposition towards mobility. In contrast, the tourist is portrayed as 'incompetent'; uninterested in participating or gaining the backstage access that drives the cosmopolitan. The exile takes no pleasure in competence, maintaining an emotional commitment to an original home, for existing in another culture is a cost (or necessity) but not a benefit in itself.

Neither Bauman nor Hannerz apply their ideas specifically to young people, but in a study of young people growing up in the Scottish Borders Gill Jones and Lyn Jamieson sought to explore the interplay of migration and cultural disposition (Jones, 1995, 2000a; Jamieson, 2000). The researchers distinguished first between those young people who were 'leavers' and 'stayers', and then asked whether these young people continued to be 'attached' or 'detached'. Thus, an attached leaver may entertain romantic notions of home and a detached stayer may feel trapped and dissatisfied. These distinctions were also understood in an intergenerational context in which wider families were also positioned as locals and incomers. Importantly, they found that these levels of attachment were not linked to class and family background in any simple or direct way.

Understanding mobility demands both that we take the long view, understanding how things play out over time and over generations, and also that we recognise the importance of context. Youth culture is often viewed as the cutting edge of an increasingly liquid modernity within which mobility and communication are crucial resources (Ling, 2000; Henderson et al., 2002; Tully, 2002; Tolonen, 2005). Young people's cultural practices contribute to processes of economic development and social mobility (for an overview see Pilkington and Johnson, 2003). Researchers have shown that urban and cosmopolitan identities are available to young people both within and outside cities and developed economies, and the formation of connections between young people through popular culture has been identified as an intrinsic part of economic and cultural globalisation (Miller, 1992; Leichty, 1995; Sansone, 1997; Ball et al., 2000; Nayak, 2003). In thinking in terms of mobility it is important to keep all of these dynamics in play: the role of youth cultural practice; physical mobility; cultural dispositions towards mobility, and the way these elements form part of local cultures, intergenerational family dynamics and historical trends.

The importance of locality: Economies of mobility

The significance of young people's relationship to local space and place in the processes through which they imagine and remake themselves is a consistent theme of this book. Mobility-related issues – whether pragmatic or aspirational – are no exception to this and arose differently in different research sites, forming a particular 'economy of mobility'.

Northern Ireland

For young people growing up in the embedded working-class communities in our Northern Irish city (where several generations live alongside each other), day-to-day physical mobility was something of an ordeal. As we found in Chapter 5, the division of physical space into Catholic or Protestant areas posed dangers for those caught out of place, particularly young men (McGrellis, 2005a). Whilst coming from a 'known' family offered protection in certain places, it also meant that individuals could be the target for attack and surveillance elsewhere. At the same time, generations of migration meant that young people tended to have knowledge of, and access to, places other than their home town – most commonly Scotland and London for Protestants and London, the Republic of Ireland and the USA for

Catholics. As young people grew older, these connections provided a resource for short-term hospitality, help with finding work and an important imaginative 'escape route'.

Leisure activities could provide young people with access to non-sectarian spaces, but they could just as easily reinforce them. Mixed friendship groups and activities always posed problems of transport and safety. Sport was an important alternative to street life and neighbourhood identities that for young men could take the form of affiliations to para-military groups. However, even when it facilitated travel, participation in sport could be problematic. For example, one young man described how travelling to Glasgow Rangers soccer games in Scotland made him feel even more 'bitter' and constrained than he felt in Northern Ireland itself.

In contrast, middle-class young people tended to mirror their English middle-class counterparts: embracing a more deliberately 'cosmopolitan' orientation. It was common for these young people to adopt education as a means of forging a future outside the province and expressing a desire to 'travel'. They also tended to aspire to own or have access to a car, a short-term solution to the dangers of moving across a divided city. Some explicitly engaged with informal youth culture as a means of transcending local sectarian identities, while others engaged in more formal youth activities, such as orchestras and exchange trips that also facilitated travel abroad.

Leafy suburb

Here, young people viewed travel as a rite of passage rather than a means of escape. Most young people had travelled extensively with their parents, and package holidays with friends marked a symbolic transition at the end of compulsory schooling. The 'gap year' was discussed frequently, envisaged as an interlude between final school examinations and university and a means to accumulate wider life experience. The majority aspired to spend some time living in London after university, returning to their home area to 'settle down'. University was seen as an opportunity to meet new people and make new contacts and young people often chose to attend universities in towns that they did not know, or where they had no pre-existing family connections. Again, having access to a car was a priority for most, living as they did in a semi-rural locality with limited public transport, and part-time jobs were often the means by which young people paid to support their social lives.

Rural area

Geographical mobility was a fundamental requirement of this research site, generally essential for accessing education, work and leisure. Gaining independence from adults in this respect was a highly significant point in transitions to adulthood and was managed in a variety of ways including: finding a friend with transport, working and saving for their own, travelling for hours by bus, or joining those who became adept at travelling the country lanes; walking long distances, hitchhiking, and 'cadging' lifts, often to get to places where they could connect with taxis and trains.

The relationship between social and physical mobility in this rural area was clear at the outset of the study in that young people frequently spoke of moving away from the area and focused on access to quality employment, university and/or a more cosmopolitan lifestyle. However, orientations towards leaving changed considerably over time. An inclination to return in order to bring up children was also widely expressed. Those from working-class backgrounds were more likely to have been born in the area and less likely to express strong desires to leave their locality when they made the important transition from school. With the passing of time, some became more embedded within family and work structures in the more immediate locality, whilst others have had to reconsider this orientation and find work further afield.

Disadvantaged estate

In contrast, many of the young people living here held aspirations to escape the locality for good. Yet doing so was far from easy. Few young people had practical means of escape and discussions of mobility more often had the quality of dreams than plans (Nilsen, 1999). Living on the outskirts of a large city, they often lacked the resources and the confidence necessary to access the city centre. Strategies for escape initially included attending colleges outside the area and moving in with relatives in different neighbourhoods. However, the few who did aspire to go to university generally considered local options. Initially travel was not part of most young people's lives, few had been on school trips or family holidays. Where it did feature it tended to be in the form of dream holidays, or plans to treat parents to gifts of holidays for wedding anniversaries. As they gained access to independent resources through work, holidays and travelling became an important source of pleasure and leisure for several of the young people in this locality.

Inner city

In this more ethnically diverse site, young people had a significantly different relationship with both their locality and their country of origin than did their parents (who were frequently first- or second-generation immigrants from the Far East, Middle East, South Asia, Caribbean and East Africa). For them, making their identity meant engaging in intergenerational narratives of belonging, and notions of 'moving away' or 'escaping' did not have the same relevance. Despite extensive international family networks, only one young woman talked longingly of 'returning' permanently to the country of her parents' birth. Most returned only for visits or pilgrimages. Mobility within the locality varied. Some of the young people moved freely across the city, drawing on its economic, educational, cultural and leisure resources and often accessing ethnically specific leisure pursuits. Others (generally the white working class) were much more rooted within the neighbourhood. Despite a wide variety of choices, few young people who planned to attend university envisaged going beyond the city limits although choice of college often deliberately took them outside their immediate locale.

A brief look across the accounts of young people growing up in our five research sites, then, begins to suggest that localities have their own particular economy of mobility, operating at levels of the material, cultural and fantasy. At the same time, it suggests that young people appear to be tied to the immediacy of physical and social space to differing degrees, and factors such as ethnicity, gender, sexuality and social class also seem significant in this: gay young people living in the rural area were more likely than their heterosexual counterparts to make contact with urban and virtual communities, via the internet, travel and socialising (Henderson et al., 2002; MacNamee et al., 2003); young women growing up in working-class areas of Northern Ireland were more able to move beyond the religiously defined boundaries of the neighbourhood than young men (McGrellis, 2004, 2005a); and middle-class city dwellers appeared to be more mobile than their working-class counterparts, unless the latter were part of a diasporic network.

It also suggests that, whilst the particular 'economy of mobility' a young person grows up in is crucial for shaping their aspirations and actions, as young people grow older they move between different economies of mobility. Increasingly aware of how their locality fits within a wider picture, they draw on whatever resources they are able to access in order to achieve their ambitions. For example, several young people from Northern Ireland went to London in their late teens in search of work. Here they experienced a radically different economy of mobility, sharing houses and working alongside young economic migrants from around the world, and in many cases being treated for the first time in their lives as Irish (many Protestants in Northern Ireland identify themselves as British rather than Irish). On return to Northern Ireland, these new ways of understanding place and identity contributed in turn to the local culture. In this way it would be a mistake to draw any simple distinction between the global and the local. While global forms of culture transcend the specificities of place, they are engaged with differently in response to local demands, and contribute to new forms of the local.

Conversations between cosmopolitanism and localism

Through the following examples we attempt to capture the 'liquidity' of lived experience, and in doing so suggest that cosmopolitans and locals are seen not as two kinds of people but as two sides of the same coin (always in play together). Through privileging the biographical we also privilege the temporal, drawing attention to mobility over time as well as over space (Massey, 1993, 1994). The longitudinal case histories show that it is only through the passage of time that sense can be made of the 'resource' that mobility represents for an individual. If time is understood as continuous then we are also drawn towards an understanding of young people as part of intergenerational chains through which processes of social and geographical mobility are played out in ever changing circumstances (Bertaux and Thompson, 1997). In new economic times, the cultivation of cosmopolitanism may be an important resource for holding onto privilege or in accessing opportunity. As we have seen throughout the book, local networks may act as a two-edged sword, providing community and belonging yet also tying young people into identities and practices that are at odds with educational achievement. Cultivating useful social networks was certainly a priority for young people from the leafy suburb site, and in many of the localities in which we conducted our research, young people assumed that they would have to leave the localities in which they currently lived in order to make their way in life.

Stan – investing in mobility

Stan is a white heterosexual young man, living in an affluent area in a leafy suburb. He was interviewed three times for this study, at ages 18, 19 and 20. The period of the study coincided with a period of intense personal change and identity work for him. When we first met Stan he was entering the first 2 years of post-compulsory secondary schooling, expecting that like most of his peers he would go on to university and a profession. He also articulated his own brand of cosmopolitanism, aspiring to be someone unconstrained by an office job and a mortgage who would drop everything to go snowboarding, scuba diving or to travel the world. Stan envisaged that at 21, if he was not at university, he would 'definitely be in another country'. He located his desire for a cosmopolitan identity in his family background noting in his first interview that travel 'kind of runs in the family'. His father was a business executive who travelled extensively as part of his job. From Stan's perspective, travel 'is in the genes'.

The version of cosmopolitanism that attracted Stan at this point in his life can be understood as a gendered biography in which flexibility, risk taking and 'living in the present' are counterposed with the deferred gratification of traditional middle-class masculinity (Brannen and Nilsen, 2002). While this model resonates with elements of the immediacy that characterises some working-class masculinities, it is also consistent with a particular middle-class male culture of consumption. This is the 'work-hard play-hard' ethos of young men who invest heavily in expensive and high status leisure pursuits and who may well engage in high levels of risk taking (see Chapter 6). Although Stan is not yet in a position to support such a lifestyle his investment in geographical mobility relates to aspirations for social mobility.

The motif of travel and mobility is not just relevant to an imagined future but also to the immediate present. At the centre of Stan's life at the first interview was his fast red car. Stan identified the freedom that driving provided as a critical moment in his transition to adulthood, enabling him to be independent of his family and part of wider social collectivities:

> I went from the person who kind of relies on his parents, didn't really have much of a social life 'cause he could never get out, to someone who could suddenly, whack, you know, I could get everywhere, the sky's the limit and that kind of changes you, 'cause you can get out more and see more people, eh, I think that breeds change so, yeah, that was good. (Stan, 18, 1999)

By his second interview Stan had accepted that he would not be going to university. In fact he had missed his mock examinations because he was on a snowboarding holiday with friends. However, he expressed great relief over this decision, reporting that on the advice of his careers adviser he was considering a future in carpentry, the occupation of his maternal grandfather and something that he had a genuine affection for. In this interview Stan also expressed an awareness of the costs of his father's jet setting lifestyle, observing that his regular absences from the household on business trips had drawn Stan into some of the practices that had once been his father's, such as DIY (do-it-yourself) and providing lifts. Throughout Stan's narratives, we find a more embedded, embodied and domesticated form of masculinity. Here it is possible to see Stan shifting his identification from his 'cosmopolitan' corporate father, to the local artisan masculinity of his grandfather:

> My mum's dad has been a cabinet maker all his life, and I've always been interested in that, playing with wood, and so whenever something like that comes up around the house, a shelf needs fitting, it's always me that does it so, I kinda help that way, things like that. [...] My dad being away a lot, kind of lot of handy jobs that, say something goes wrong and dad's away and mum can't do it, it kind of all falls to me. (Stan, 18, 1999)

At the same time, Stan's commitment to travel is complicated in this second interview by love. He presents himself as so transformed by this commitment that he is no longer able to enjoy his greatest pleasure:

> Yeah, the simple fact is like I went snowboarding for a week and was kind of like, I know it's only a week, but I kind of miss her and stuff, and she kind of, I dunno, being at home and that, would hate me being away for months on end and stuff, so I understand, and I think I'd find it quite difficult and perhaps it might even ruin the whole experience I'd have anyway and so perhaps if I go away and do a 3 year course, and she's finished what she wants to do, then we can go away together ... (Stan, 19, 2000)

Travel is no longer an individual pursuit, but rather it must be negotiated in relation to his domestic plans and commitments.

By the time of his third interview Stan was firmly embedded in heterosexual coupledom, and working as an apprentice joiner. Snowboarding had been cancelled that year, as he could not afford it and most of his friends were 'off travelling'. He had even sold his prized possession, the fast car, in order to save money.

At this point it becomes more difficult to locate Stan in relation to categories of cosmopolitanism/localism, or in the more nuanced model of attached/detached leavers and stayers offered by Jamieson (2000). Stan was a detached leaver who had become a stayer. While his initial cosmopolitan identity was located within a middle-class family tradition, over time his identifications shift towards a more localised sense of self. This had been a particularly reflexive process for him, as he was aware of the contradictions and ambiguities in his narrative. Cosmopolitanism continued to be an important part of his sense of self, yet in many ways was belied by his practice. He was able to hold on to it by presenting his situation as based on choice, and maintaining an open sense of the future in which his partner may join him in the risk biography in which he has so much invested.

Stan is most unlikely to describe himself in terms of downward social mobility, nor as forging continuities with an intergenerational narrative of working-class masculinity. In this way Stan's cosmopolitanism can be understood as a defence of self, a way of making the mundane habitable while also having the potential to be realised in practice (Walkerdine et al., 2002). Stan is neither a cosmopolitan nor a local, but someone for whom an investment in mobility is an important part of identity work.

Karin – moving away, but not really

Karin is a white, Catholic young woman from a working-class family, living in the city in Northern Ireland. She was interviewed four times between the ages of 16 and 19. Again, travel and mobility were central motifs in her accounts of self, and she too can be seen to be absorbed in a conversation between cosmopolitanism and localism – although in very different ways from Stan. When we first met Karin aged 16 she was clear that her future lay outside Northern Ireland. She aspired to follow her two older siblings to university in England, the first generation of her family to enter higher education. Her plan was to study product design in a big Scottish or English city. She spoke scathingly about her home town as no place to bring up children. From the outset Karin was highly mobile within her locality despite the restrictions imposed by sectarian neighbourhoods. She attended a religiously mixed secondary school in the city and actively pursued friendships and activities that enabled her to transcend the sectarian divide. At her first interview this took the form of an identification with skater culture, which she explicitly recognised as a globalised (and thus in local terms non-sectarian) youth culture:

> Once you're a skater, no matter where you go in the world if you meet other skaters you've got a link with them. [...] Skate-boarders are really laid back, they don't care about nothing but their sport and things like that, most of the ones I met anyway, and I really love that kind of chilled out, it's like pure, they're not nerds anyway, they're not lads out there to drink and get into fights, most of them just seem really laid back and cool, things like that. To get in with all those people I think is changing my life. (Karin, 16, 1999)

Karin struggled to find ways to socialise with her mixed religion friendship group outside of school, and with a female best friend in tow she located and gained access to a city centre youth club. Where the working-class neighbourhood youth cultures of the city were characterised by wearing sports clothes and distinguished by the symbolism of Rangers and Celtic soccer clubs, the young people frequenting this youth club had forged an identity as 'freaks' marking them as outside of the dominant cultural divide. While the label 'freaks' was seen by most as a term of abuse, Karin was attracted to the distinction that it provided, observing 'there's freaks in there, but people call me a freak, so why not'.

Cosmopolitanism takes on a very specific character in Northern Ireland, constructed in opposition to the dominant categories of Catholic and Protestant that territorialise local spaces and identities. Being a freak enabled Karin to opt out of these investments, in effect distancing herself from her environment. In contrast to Stan, for whom cosmopolitanism was constructed in opposition to formal academic success, Karin's involvement in youth culture did not come at the expense of schooling. She was always careful to do just enough studying to get by. Although she had no love of school, she recognised from the outset that her passport out of the city and a local future would be education. Her older sister, already at university, was a key resource in enabling her to imagine a more cosmopolitan future:

> I had this big long talk with my sister a couple of weeks ago and she was all – the longer you stay at school it [...] kind of opens your mind and other prospects and if you go to university and things like that you meet different types of people. You travel right. It was all in perfect context when she said it, but you don't hear of someone who's working in this city thinking right I'll go to the Kibbutz for the next couple of months, go to Israel like, but if you're a student in university that's the kind of things you do. (Karin, 16, 1999)

Over the course of the four interviews Karin constructed and defended what in local terms was a highly cosmopolitan identity. She took up opportunities to visit her siblings at university, to visit London with friends, and cultivated a highly sexualised identity at odds with local forms of femininity, explaining that 'I take a pure wee fella attitude to the lot of it'. This determined rejection of the local, and pursuit of cosmopolitanism, was a high-risk path, and on a number of occasions Karin found herself the object of gossip and exclusionary practices by other young people.

Between her third and fourth interview Karin took the opportunity to do voluntary work in India as part of a youth volunteering scheme. This interlude gave her the opportunity to escape what were becoming increasingly difficult relationships with her fellow students and erstwhile friends at the youth club. It also facilitated the forging of an identity that was not exclusively tied to youth cultures and consumption. Karin expressed contradictory feelings about the trip. Initially she argued that it had not changed her but had 'opened my eyes more than they were beforehand, building toilets for a primary school, it really got me seeing the kids and the sheer poverty they were living in'. However, towards the end of the interview she revealed that on returning from the trip she had a serious bout of depression, struggling to find ways back into her previous urban life having lived outside 'closer to the ground'. On reflection she observed 'I've been thinking about this. Going to India, I did learn from it. I know now that I can do things, not how to do things, but that I can.'

On her return from India, a number of big changes took place in Karin's life. She became a much more dedicated student, she began a long-term monogamous relationship (her first) and she withdrew from the active involvement in the youth cultures that had previously dominated her life. The shift in Karin's narrative around education was perhaps not an unexpected one if we consider her continuing refusal to fail educationally. What may be more worthy of comment is her ability to reorient her identity from an oppositional to a more dependent stance. The life plans laid out so clearly in her first interview were still relatively intact. The changes that she made to her plans were subtle yet significant. For example, she no longer countenanced going to university in England as a possibility, citing the experience of friends becoming estranged. As Karin explained, 'hardly anyone comes back' after leaving for university, except for those who fail to stick out the course and 'those people return and don't leave again'. In this discussion of university she expressed much more complicated feelings about leaving her home city than she had previously. Where in the past she had focused herself entirely on 'escape', she now felt torn, both in terms of having a long-term boyfriend, and being the last of her siblings to leave home. Her choice of local universities reflected a desire for 'moving away but not really moving away', observing: 'I never had anything to keep me in here – now I do it's scary.'

Karin was the last of her siblings living at home, her brother and sister both having already made the journey through higher education, to England and into the middle classes. Her positioning enabled her to experience different cultural understandings of success, symbolised by travel and university on the one hand or marriage and work on the other. The costs of both going and staying were high for Karin, each demanding sacrifice. She simultaneously anticipated feelings of guilt about leaving her mother and about her own educational failure, explaining that if she did not see through a university education it would 'break my mother's heart'. There is a sense of obligation that she fulfil the thwarted and wasted ambitions of her parents, who made sacrifices to give her and her siblings 'more':

Although Karin's identity is highly cosmopolitan, she is nevertheless bound by obligations to locality, primarily through the female side of the family. In her final interview Karin acknowledges that although she is not religious and has chosen to be part of 'the art student and freaky community', she will go back to the church and the religious community because her mother had stepped into that when her Gran died. Like Stan, her particular brand of cosmopolitanism has been reworked as her life moves into a new phase and local gendered narratives of family and neighbourhood assert themselves.

Conclusion

Our case studies suggest that in practice young people are pulled by competing forces in relation to notions of home, tradition and fixedness on the one hand and of mobility, escape and transformation on the other. The ways that these tensions are negotiated (though never resolved) at the biographical level is firmly embedded in gendered projects of self through which young people work through the kind of men and women that they can be, drawing on family, community and cultural resources in the process. In this sense, localism/cosmopolitanism can be understood as a single, interdependent term through which feelings about space and associated status can be expressed (Moran et al., 2003; Skeggs, 2004).

Notions of mobility are central to young people's accounts of self as they make the transition to adulthood. This may be in the form of access to an independent social life (through transport), being able to move around your community safely, travel as leisure (in the form of holidays) or movement as a rite of passage in the form of going to a university away from home or migrating for work. The part that mobility plays in narratives of transition is historically and culturally specific, with the character of youth transitions currently shifting in response to extended dependency and the expansion of higher education.

Not only is mobility a central motif in young people's accounts of adulthood, but the different ways that it is manifest reflect inequalities. Mobility means different things in different places and young people within the same locations engage differently with mobility. Terms such as cosmopolitan, local and exile are also useful in that they draw attention to the cultural dimensions of mobility but also show how this is underpinned by material resources. You can be a cosmopolitan without leaving home and a local who travels the world. Yet it is unlikely that you act like a cosmopolitan without economic support.

Chapter 9
Belonging

Introduction

'Belonging' is a word that conjures up rich associations and meanings. For many it is linked with a sense of place, of feeling part of a larger entity, whether family, national or even global forms of community. It implies connectedness and relationships with others, saying something about inclusion, acceptance, and identity. As we saw in the last chapter, 'place' is a key aspect of young people's sense of who they are, and where they might 'go' in life. Ethnicity, gender, sexuality and social class all contribute to 'economies of mobility', which in turn shape the identities that young people subscribe to. In this chapter we take a closer look at religion and politics as aspects of belonging. We explore their place in young people's biographical narratives, and indeed how their relationship to place is implicated in their religious and political identities.

A broad spectrum of belief systems were represented in the Inventing Adulthoods study, with young people coming from Buddhist, Christian, Hindu, Jewish, Muslim and Sikh backgrounds. Some were involved in more alternative practice, and many expressed interest in eastern philosophy, horoscopes, fortune tellers, healers, and psychics. The level of young people's engagement with religion varied. At one extreme there were those like Marion, who attended religious meetings three or four times a week. At the other end of the spectrum were those who attended church for special occasions such as weddings, or to hear carols at Christmas 'as a nice little thing to do'. In between were those whose religion represented a political or social identity, having less to do with spiritual or doctrinal beliefs. Some had no association with organised religion but expressed a belief, or a hope, in a higher order and afterlife, while others described themselves as atheist or agnostic, or 'too much of an individualist for religion'.

The rise of individualism has been linked with the declining influence of religion and religious institutions that for generations wove together the threads of the social, moral and political fabric of society. It is implicated in the secularisation thesis that sociologists of religion such as Bruce (1996) have traced back to the Reformation. The principles of individualism and rationality that emerged at that time, Bruce argues, increasingly threatened the purpose and authority of religion. In traditional societies religious practice and belief were central to the construction and maintenance of community, and the formation of identity, offering an explanation for the meaning of life. In a late modern, pluralist society that is individualised and de-traditionalised, this influence, it is argued, no longer exists.

However, secularisation is not a straightforward process of declining religiosity. Nor is it a theory that can be applied universally, or indeed accepted as an accurate reflection of the state of play in late modern society. The usefulness of the concept itself has been questioned by authors such as Casanova (1994) who identifies three dimensions to secularisation: '… differentiation of the secular spheres from religious institutions and norms, … decline of religious beliefs and practices, and … marginalization of religion to a privatized sphere' (p. 211). The spread of fundamentalism worldwide, and a surge of interest in Pentecostal-charismatic and liberation movements, particularly in Central and South America, for example, pose a challenge for the secularisation thesis. Norris and Inglehart (2004) examined trends in secularisation within a political context in the USA and western Europe, and found that cultural and economic differences are significant, with higher levels of secularisation in societies where people experience greater social and economic security.

There is a general consensus that interest in formal politics is falling, particularly amongst young people. If voting statistics are taken as a straightforward measure of political participation then this assessment is beyond question. However, voting patterns do not necessarily give the full picture with regard to political and civic participation. Gauthier (2003) argues in her review of studies on Canadian youth, that using voting patterns alone to assess political engagement disregards the many other ways in which young people are politically active on local and global issues, from civic volunteering to involvement in protest rallies (see also Roker and Eden, 2003). Findings from the Inventing Adulthoods study suggest, however, that young people are not particularly engaged with politics at this level either. While some talked about taking part in anti-war protests, and others were active around environmental issues, the overall picture suggested a lack of involvement in politics and political activity in the traditional sense. But lack of political orientation did not mean passivity – in line with other research we found that most young people were engaged in constructive social activities, most often what Lister and colleagues call 'general social participation' (Lister et al., 2003; Harris et al., 2003). One of the arenas through which young people accessed the 'feel-good feeling' of civic engagement was through religion. We might well ask if religion could be the new politics?

Believing and belonging

A survey question in the initial stage of this project asked young people to identify what, if any, religion they belonged to, and on a scale of 1–5 to indicate how religious they felt they were. In subsequent interviews the issue of religion and faith came up in discussions around identity, family, community, relationships, politics and terrorism. In the last round of interviews the young people were asked specifically about the role of religion or spirituality in their lives. From the sum of this data it is evident that while formalised religious practice is the exception rather than the norm, young people relate to the presence or absence of religion in their lives in a way that underlines the links between it and identity, community and politics. Despite the low numbers who professed to ritual religious practice, the majority acknowledged a spiritual element in their lives that ranged from having a 'glow inside' when the sun shines, to experiencing serenity in the 'calmness' of a church.

We found marked differences relating to locality. As expected, figures for religious affiliation were much higher among young people in Northern Ireland compared with any of the other sites with almost 90 percent stating religious affiliation. The young people there were also much more likely to describe themselves as being 'religious', with almost three-quarters describing themselves as 'very religious'. Subsequent interviews over the years emphasised the different patterns of religious identification and practice across sites. Those growing up in Northern Ireland continued to express the highest levels of religious affiliation, practice and heritage, although there was also evidence of declining ritual practice. Kitty, for example, expressed strong religious beliefs and defended her regular church attendance when we first met her in a group interview in 1998. Just over 2 years later she had become disillusioned with church teachings and rituals, which she felt were 'out of date' and no longer relevant to her life. At the other end of the continuum were young people growing up in the affluent commuter belt, who were the least likely to be church goers and most likely to be sceptics. However, a number also expressed a belief in a higher order, and one young woman in this site professed to be a witch within the Wicca movement. The young people in the inner city site lived in the most culturally and religiously diverse setting and their narratives reflected an awareness of and interest in the religions and belief systems practised by friends and those around them. Despite such a rich source of references there was less evidence of personal practice; as one young woman commented, 'everyone comes from religious families but no one follows it'.

A picture of intergenerational decline in religious faith and practice was perhaps most evident in the rural setting. Here young people talked about attending church on special occasions such as Christmas and Easter to keep parents, or grandparents, happy. While many professed to a spiritual dimension and a belief in God or 'something', there was less emphasis on denominational belonging – religious practice was something 'inflicted' on them by grandparents. Within these broad patterns were many individual stories, and it is in these biographical accounts that we appreciate more fully the way in which religious and political identities are entwined and how a sense of belonging is mediated through such institutions. For some, religion is ascribed by virtue of birth and heritage, for others it is a matter of active choice. Political identities can follow a similar pattern. In choosing to invest or withdraw from such institutions young people make decisions that affect their sense of belonging and their transitions.

Religion – choosing and losing

Khattab

When we first met Khattab, a 16-year-old young man from a working-class family, he lived with his mother, her second husband, and siblings in the inner city area. He had regular contact with his father, and located himself within a family network that extended to Pakistan where his parents originated, relatives still lived and he returned with his family on a regular basis.

From his first interview the role of religion in Khattab's life was evident, as was the influence of his family on his religious practice and belief. He described his family as being 'very religious' and enjoyed attending the local Mosque with them:

> It's like we go there and we're – like people are chanting and praying and all that. It's all right, I enjoy it. When I go there it's because it's all like relaxing.
> I just like feel yeah, this is where I belong and all that. (Khattab, 16, 2000)

Just as important as his religion at this early stage, was his passion for football and his hopes of becoming a professional player. The discipline required for playing football was sympathetic with the practice of his faith. Both advocated abstinence from alcohol, cigarettes, and drugs, and both allowed Khattab to invest in traditional and compatible forms of masculinity. While the strict religious teaching on celibacy before marriage was perhaps more challenging for Khattab, living as he was in a society where sexual values were very different from those set out in the Koran, he was also able to reconcile this discipline with that required for an aspirant professional footballer:

> So in a way there is a link between my football and my religion because the football keeps me off the alcohol, keeps me off the cigarettes and so, alcohol is a sin to drink in my religion. Also it keeps me off the women because um, what basically what happened to my ex-coach, he had so much women and everything like that, he was professional and then he just flopped from there. (Khattab, 17, 2000)

Although Khattab recognised tensions between the different cultures and traditions that he subscribed to, over time he reduced such tensions by increasingly focusing on his religion as an institutional force from which he drew meaning and recognition. It is perhaps significant that Khattab's investment in religion became more intense as the possibility of a professional football career became less likely. This increased investment in religion also coincided with his university career where he met and became close to other young Muslim men. He was impressed by the discipline these young men exercised in relation to prayer and observance of the faith.

While Khattab was born into Islam and brought up within a religious family, as he journeyed towards adulthood he actively chose to deepen this connection. His experience contrasts with those who although 'born into' religion either chose not to pursue it or actively disengaged from it. Joss, for example, a middle-class young man living in Northern Ireland, was brought up within the Bahi faith but became more and more disillusioned with his religion over the years. He attended meetings and services for his parents' sake but planned to officially disengage from the faith community when he left home. For Joss, religion conflicted with rather than confirmed his sense of identity and such had little place in his transition to adulthood. He disagreed with many Bahi principles and teachings. Making such a definite and active decision with regard to withdrawal was unusual. Although many young people in the study had been brought up within a particular religion, or at least ascribed a religious identity through christening and similar rituals, few officially opted out even if they no longer practised or drew any meaning from it.

In Northern Ireland the majority of young people identified as either Catholic or Protestant. Religion for many there is enmeshed with political and ethnic identities and is an expression of community belonging. Karin who we met in the last chapter identified as Catholic, but was not an active church goer. While she had not been to church for a number of years, like many in that site in Northern Ireland her religion remained a key part of her identity, and was an aspect of her life which would, she anticipated, become more central in the future. This anticipated change was linked to her role, as she saw it, as a woman and was located within a gendered line of faith transmission:

> God I don't feel I'm part of it but see if any body slagged off my church I would break them apart. I am not like practising or anything like that but I know at some stage I will be because my mum was never wile into religion but see since her mum died she's taken over the role as the kind of, especially in Catholic families I don't know about Protestant families but especially Catholic families the granny's always the really, really religious one and then it kind of goes down from the daughters and then the grand kids even less and then as soon as my granny went my mum just stepped into her role. (Karin, 19, 2003)

The role of women in 'passing on the faith' and taking an active part within the church was evident from the narratives of the young people. Across sites, mothers and especially grandmothers, were hailed as the guardians and persuaders of faith, although they seemed to be fighting a losing battle. Here, Anna, who was brought up in a working-class Protestant community in Northern Ireland, explains:

> I would pray but I don't say I'm religious, I wouldn't read the bible, I couldn't tell you the ten commandments but I do believe in God, I just think it's the way people my generation is, it's like my granny said too she doesn't know what's going to happen when her generation goes because there's nobody goes to church and she's true but the only time our church is ever filled is whenever it's Christmas Eve or when there's a christening or something. (Anna, 20, 2004)

Although women did feature in Khattab's account of his religious experience, it could be argued that the more defining influence came from men, especially the young men at his university. Compared to other religious groups in the UK, Islam has the youngest age profile and is the only religious group where men outnumber women (National Statistics Census, 2001). Meanwhile the gender imbalance within the Christian churches in the UK continues to widen with woman making up the majority in church pews (Levitt, 2003).

Given such statistics it is perhaps not surprising that one young man's religious conversion was greeted with shock and surprise by his friends. We met Stan from the affluent commuter belt in the last chapter and saw how his biography shifted over time with respect to his career aspirations and his relationship to place. During the course of the project Stan also 'found' religion and became a practising Baptist. He met his girlfriend through the church and religion became for him a significant point of reference. His 'conversion' could be regarded as a critical moment in a biography that, as outlined in the last chapter, became more 'local' over time. The sense of belonging that Stan experienced through church membership was also tied into his locality, compared with that experienced by Khattab, for example, who was very much aware of his place within a global community.

Having a sense of belonging to a local and/or global community is one of the attractions of evangelical churches that seek to win back those who no longer attend church or to win over the 'seekers' who are looking for meaning and a sense of belonging in their lives. The Alpha programme is one of the most successful evangelising initiatives in the Christian church, and most successful in terms of 'conversions'. Starting out in 1991 from a central London church as a 10-week programme of religious re-conversion or instruction, the Alpha movement spread first nationwide and then worldwide. Judy, a young woman from the affluent commuter belt, followed an Alpha course through the Baptist church her boyfriend belonged to. She came from a non-religious family and they too were shocked when she became a committed Christian. In keeping with the Church's teaching and the values of her boyfriend, Judy complied with a celibate relationship. As friendship or family networks are usually central to the conversion process, it is not unusual that Judy's conversion was linked to her then relationship. A strong family and community atmosphere is invariably promoted within evangelising churches, and new members are commonly wel-comed as 'sisters' or 'brothers'. In the case of the Alpha programme, religious instruction and meetings extend beyond the main church building to 'home churches'– further promoting the family atmosphere and sense of belonging and connectedness. From a biographical perspective Judy's conversion could be seen in the context of the relationship with her boyfriend who introduced her to his church and belief system. It also coincided with her move away from home and from a supportive but protective family background.

While many young people are joining Christian churches through evangelising pro-grammes such as Alpha, in the UK the trend, as noted above, is more typically the reverse. The growing interest, however, in New Age beliefs and Eastern religions and philosophies is widely acknowledged and is evident even within the small sample of young people in the Inventing Adulthoods study. For example, Donal from Northern Ireland talked about his ongoing search for meaning and fulfilment and of his research into Buddhism and Hinduism. He felt the Catholic religion, in which he was brought up, no longer held mean-ing for him. One young woman who was perhaps more involved in New Age movements was working-class Monica who lived in the leafy suburb. She belonged to the Wicca move-ment and practised spells and attended witch festivals. Other young people acknowledged their interest in or experience of Tarot cards, ouiji boards, fortune tellers, psychics, healers and ghosts. Many within mainstream churches see such interest as a reflection of the grow-ing search for meaning, belonging and spirituality in an increasingly individualised and secular society. For the young people, these interests and beliefs often sat alongside more mainstream religious affiliation, or in some cases represented a rejection of parents' belief systems.

Political belonging

While some young people expressed an interest and were participating in alternative reli-gious systems, few, if any in the study, indicated any involvement in formal political organ-isations. Previous research has shown a high level of disengagement among young people in relation to formal politics (Grundy and Jamieson, 2004) and consideration has been given as to why this is the case. General apathy, perceived inaccessibility of political struc-tures, a lack of confidence in political influence, and changes in the patterns of youth transitions have all been suggested as possible explanations (Kimberlee, 2002; Fahmy, 2003). Henn and colleagues describe young people as as 'engaged sceptics' who are 'are interested in political affairs, but distrustful of those who are elected to positions of power and charged with running the political system' (2002: 187).

So, is such political apathy and non-participation another symptom of an increasingly individualised society or are political structures and processes indeed inaccessible and irrelevant to young people today? An interest in environmental issues and participation in anti-war protests might suggest that young people's motivation around politics is specific and issue based, and is not about participation at a broader level, or necessarily about belonging. Denise, from the rural site, who we meet later in Chapter 10, is an environmentalist and was described in researcher case notes as 'too much of an individualist to have a strong sense of belonging'. Her interest and involvement in environmental projects and politics is a product of her family heritage and the eco-politics with which she was brought up (Henderson, 2005). Denise chose to identify with the politics and lifestyle of her parents to the point of choosing a career in this area. Her political interest is channelled and focused in much the same way as Khattab's investment in religion is. Both made biographical investments in identity politics as part of their transition to adulthood, and chose a lifestyle that reflected their convictions. The importance of place is also evident in the lives of both these young people. Just as her parents returned to the countryside to live out their green politics, Denise returned from her metropolitan life at university to invest in a rural lifestyle. As we see below, Khattab draws on Pakistan as his religious and cultural homeland and on places that hold particular religious significance. The interconnections between place and religion and politics are also very poignant for young people in Northern Ireland, as are the identities that accompany these (McGrellis, 2005a).

Ethnonational identities

Religious and political identities are enmeshed in young people's construction of self and influence their transitions to adulthood. If ethnicity is a social construction rather than a blood link (Baumann, 1999), and more to do with boundary maintenance and asserting difference than a celebration of cultural sameness (Fawcett, 2000), then it is easy to see how religion can become a marker of ethnicity.

Khattab

Questioned about identity in the early interviews Khattab noticeably drew a distinction between nationality and citizenship. Identifying as a British citizen, he aligned with an identity label that was perhaps important to him for its inclusive and pluralist association. This 'invisible' aspect of his identity gave him legitimacy within a potentially contested and fragmented multicultural space. By contrast, his construction of self as Pakistani was, something he 'let people know' about. His ethnic heritage contributed significantly to his identity at this stage. His dream to play football for Pakistan and thoughts about living there in the future all suggested an allegiance and identification with a society and culture that he was linked to by birth:

> In my identity I'm a British citizen, but I always let people know that I'm a Pakistani. Everyone I see I say, 'Yeah I'm a Pakistani mate'. That's the thing, I always let myself be known as, a Pakistani. (Khattab, 15, 1999)

The events of September 11th led to a new reality for Muslims, as they were subjected to increased racism and suspicion. This suspicion of Islam at a global level increased the trend for people, more usually identified as Asian, to identify first and foremost by their religion rather than ethnicity or race. This pattern is reflected in the way in which Khattab presented himself in the research. In our third meeting Khattab was invited to reflect again on the question of national identity. He had just returned from Pakistan and his response highlights the fluidity of identity:

> *INT*: Just going back briefly to kind of being from Pakistan, do you feel British as well as Pakistani or do these things sort of line up in any way or not?
>
> *Khattab*: I don't know, I mean. I'd say, when I'm back home in Pakistan people see me as, oh look, there's the British. No, because if my, if one of my parents was English, like they were proper English and my mum was Pakistani, then I'd say I've got a bit of a conflict because um, I'd say, alright am I English or am I Pakistani, but because both of my parents are Pakistani, my roots are from Pakistan. All it is is I'm a British citizen, I'm not English, so I class myself not English but British citizen but I'm Pakistani, that's what I say I am, so I don't think there's much conflict. I'm a Pakistani, I mean, if someone said to me, where you from? I always say I'm a British-born Pakistani.
>
> (Khattab, 17, 2000)

It is interesting that at no point did Khattab subscribe to being 'Asian'. This is in keeping with what is regarded as an ongoing disassociation from the Asian identity label by those formally described in Britain in this way (BBC Radio 4, 2005; Modood 2005).

By the time Khattab was 21 he had made his Umra pilgrimage to Mecca and another visit to Pakistan. He had also taken on a strict Muslim lifestyle and grown a beard. In his last interview he explained how his religious identity had become a resource that he sought to communicate outwardly against the backdrop of negative publicity following the events of September 11th:

> The one reason that I grew my beard was so that, you know, people think Islam is bad and I thought, let me grow my beard, let me look like a Muslim, and when they see this Muslim who has got a degree, who is gonna have an MSc, who is educated, who has got a good job, who plays his football, they're gonna think, 'No this Muslim's alright. The guy – the people with the beard, they're alright, they're not bad people.' It's one of the reasons why I did it, was to portray the image that we're not bad. (Khattab, 21, 2004)

Over time Khattab's religion provided him with increased certainties, and with teachings that he applied to his personal, social, moral, economic, and political lives. He became more conservative with regard to relationships and friendships, severing contact with female friends and subscribing to the practice of arranged marriage, adamant that his future 'Miss Right' would be Muslim. Our most recent contact with Khattab revealed that he had indeed married a young woman to whom he had been introduced in Pakistan. His belief in fate and a preordained pathway was something that both influenced his thinking around arranged marriage, and also acted as a way of dealing with the twists and turns of life. For example, such a philosophy helped him to come to terms with the realisation that he was not going to succeed as a professional footballer, which he described as 'my fate basically'.

Khattab increasingly embraced the teachings and practice of Islam over time. At one point his mother expressed concern that he was becoming too religious and was, as she saw it, at risk of losing sight of the more earthly and practical demands of life (such as getting a job and earning money). Khattab became more and more channelled. Indeed, without a range of different interests and potential sources of return and recognition, Khattab had become more and more channelled on a pathway that drew almost exclusively on his religious beliefs and identity. The concern his mother expressed possibly reflected an awareness of how such an investment could close down opportunities and options, contributing to forms of inequality associated with the emergence of new forms of racialised identity.

Khattab's case study illustrates how religious and political identities can be interlinked and influenced by events and debates that take place on a global level. It can be productively counterposed by the accounts of young people in Northern Ireland, a place where religious identity and faith-based belonging is less to do with ritual practice and more with ethnic boundaries and denominational politics. The intricate way in which religion, politics and ethnicity intertwine in the 'local' can be seen in young people's accounts of how religion is acted out in the streets, through the use of flags, boundary markers, parades and so on. It is a context in which religion has a more secular feel and perhaps falls into what has been referred to as 'civil religion' a term coined by Bellah (1966) to account for the symbols of national and collective consciousness.

Religion and politics in the lives of young people in Northern Ireland

Statistics from the Northern Ireland Young Life and Times survey, 2004, suggest a continuing close link between religious and national identity among young people in Northern Ireland, in that those who identify as Catholic are also likely to identify as Irish, and those who identify as Protestant also likely to identify as 'British' or with 'Ulster' (www.ark.ac.uk/ylt). The survey also indicates how religious affiliation, identity and practice continue to be an important aspect of many young lives, with, for example, over half saying that religious identity was either quite or very important to them and just under half reporting attendance at church once a week or more. As already noted, the findings from our own survey in 1998 (McGrellis et al., 2000) suggest higher levels of religious affiliation and religiosity among young people in Northern Ireland compared to those in the English sites within our sample.

Religion is a vital marker of community and political identity for young people in Northern Ireland. Historical events act as collective reference points, but it is everyday families' practices that provide the medium through which the historical is transformed into the intimate lives and imaginations of young people. Questions on religion were frequently assigned political meaning by young people. When Glen was asked if religion had any place in his life he immediately made the jump to sectarianism and community politics, and in so doing highlighted how divisions along religious lines can create chasms of exclusion for some young people:

> Religion, it's just been the same as fucking always. Like you can't – you never can win in this town. The town is divided with fucking religion like. You know what I mean – hatred. Like I'm a Protestant, me Mum lives in [nationalist area], and so I'm either a dirty hun or a fenian – you can't win really like, can you? And people from over there find out that you're going over there, and people over here find out that your parents live over here – then you're fucked, you know what I mean, and you just get called. So I just keep me head down like and walk on most of the time like. (Glen, 23, 2004)

Cynthia's experience as a young girl brought to Northern Ireland from Scotland further highlights the active work young people engage in to locate and affirm their sense of identity, place and belonging. Although she had family connections in Northern Ireland, Cynthia felt very much an outsider when she moved there. Up until her move from Scotland at age 11 she had lived a life where space, identity and culture was, in her experience, uncontested, and her sense of belonging was overwhelmingly confirmed. Although she was brought up as a Protestant it was not, she argued, a significant part of her identity, and church attendance was not obligatory. However, in her new living environment, religion became a more defining element and Cynthia found herself having to defend aspects of her identity that had previously gone unquestioned. In Northern Ireland she was forced to unpack the significance and interrelationship between religion, politics, nationality and culture in her own life and to understand how these were mediated in the lives of those she was now a part of:

> … if anybody asks me 'what do you think of this, that and the next thing', 'what are you? Are you a nationalist or are you a loyalist?'. But I would say 'I'm a Scottish nationalist' and automatically I think people at work think I'm a Catholic. And I goes 'no I'm not' and they go 'Oh of course you are', and I goes 'but no I'm not, you could be a nationalist but that's nothing to do with me and nothing to do with religion'. For me that's nothing to do with religion, it's kind of naïve of them and they automatically think that's you. They've even put it into a group whereas I wouldn't do that with people. Like I said before, the minute I arrived here [in Northern Ireland] it was such a culture shock. I had never seen anybody as like a Protestant or anything like that. I just seen everybody as my friends who I walked to school with, who ever you are they've a name not the religion. (Cynthia, 19, 2004)

Unable to find a foothold in her new place of residence Cynthia also found, to her dismay, that she was simultaneously losing her connection in her Scottish homeland. While she was comforted to learn that her name was still, mistakenly, included in the class roll call, she was annoyed when she returned for holidays to be excluded by her one time friendship group who taunted her as 'Irish'. Like Khattab who found he was regarded as British on his return to Pakistan, Cynthia's reflections highlight how much belonging is linked with place and locality and, as we shall see in the next chapter, how it is central to young people's experience of home. Physical mobility in this instance, shook the foundation of Cynthia's experience of home, it undermined her sense of belonging, and placed her in a situation where she was constantly defending her identity.

Conclusion: Believing and belonging

Religious identity is central to many, defining as it does community and ethnic belonging. It does not necessarily imply ritual practice, as many of the young people in the study attest. Several young people in our study subscribed to their religion as an identity marker; they believe in God; they pray, but rarely attend services; and feel no obligation to live by the teachings of their church. They come from families where parents continue to practise their faith but no longer have an influence over them.

This kind of pattern of belief and practice fits with studies that repeatedly find that people continue to express a belief in God or a higher order, and often give religion as an identifying marker in census and survey forms, but do not practice their faith or accept many of the teachings within it. This phenomenon has been named 'believing but not belonging' (Davie, 1990). Declining church attendance figures in the UK (Brierley, 2000) seem to support Davie's argument that 'more and more people in British society are, it appears, wanting to believe but without putting this belief into practice' (Davie, 1990: 463). However, Voss and Crockett (2005) take a critical look at the conclusions drawn by Davie and many others in this field. They question the emphasis and interpretations drawn by these studies as an indicator of declining religiosity, and suggest that it may merely reflect that a growing number of people 'believe that belonging doesn't matter' (p. 18).

Belief statements and patterns of church attendance among the young people in this study seem to support the theory of believing but not belonging. However, in considering the narratives of the young people from a biographical perspective, it is evident that a sense of 'religious' belonging is not just achieved by church attendance, and belonging in itself is a fluid concept. An investment in a religious identity for many young people brings with it membership of an institution that not only defines their cultural and ethnic heritage in the present, but constitutes a down payment that potentially allows them, or their children, to capitalise on in the future. This applies to Karin, for example, who although disillusioned with the Catholic church at present, suspects she will return to it in the future as a guardian and transmitter of the faith. Despite her 'crisis of faith' she remains a Catholic, willing to defend her church or perhaps more so, her identity as a Catholic. It also fits with many like Emer, also from Northern Ireland, who express a desire to find a partner who would share her concern that children are christened so that they too can belong and capitalise on religious affiliation in the future, and use their religious identity as a resource:

I think as I get older I probably would, I don't know if I would be into someone that goes to mass every day but maybe I think if I had children or something I would probably bring them you know and I think if I get into teaching you have to make it in a Catholic school you have to make an effort to go to mass because you're teaching children about God you have to know what you're talking about. (Emer, 21, 2004)

Serendipity and critical moments can play a part in when and how young people choose to invest in or withdraw from religion. Birth, death, illness, new relationships, new places, all act as triggers for both investment and withdrawal. Khattab's investment, at this point in his life, is all encompassing. Such commitment might be regarded as a biographical solution, a pathway to adulthood chosen by him when other options narrowed. His changing narrative provides rich insight into the processes that contribute to identity formation in the transition to adulthood, providing an account of the solid links between religion and community and how a connection between the two cements a sense of belonging. His story and that of others featured in this chapter helps us understand how religion becomes, or ceases to be, an active force in the young people's lives, potentially operating as a biographical strategy or solution. The family and the household are central to young people's narratives of belonging, though in diverse ways. In the following chapter we will focus more closely on the importance of 'home' in young people's accounts of the transition to adulthood.

Chapter 10
Home

Introduction

Home means comfort and happiness and love – you know, everything that you love and everything that makes you happy is at your home, is here where you live, where you know. And I think, another thing, when you're in your home you feel safe, you feel like nothing can touch you because you are here and, you know, this is where you live, this is where you like to be. You know, this is your home, this is your safety, this is where all your memories are. (Estelle, 19, 2002)

Home – I don't really have a meaning for it because I don't really have – I have a home, like a house where I live – but I don't really. To me, I would love my home to be with my Mum and with my Dad and with my brother, with my grandparents round the corner, and my auntie just up the road – who is, but – and my other grandparents just in the next village and um like me – or like my Mum and Dad living here and then me living a few streets over with my kids and my husband, so I'm able to come in here for a cup of coffee and a chat. But that'll never happen, so … (Beth, 17, 2002)

These young women each evoke emotions associated with the ideal of 'home'. Both live in reconstituted families, but Beth has lost her traditional dream of home. In Chapter 11, 'Intimacy', however, we will see how she builds her own home with those she loves, to provide her own security. Recurrent themes on the meaning of home emerge in the literature across a range of disciplines, as a projection and realisation of self identity and social and cultural status; a centre for family life; a place of retreat, safety, relaxation and freedom; a space of privacy; a social support mechanism; and as a place of familiarity and continuity (Kenyon, 2003). In a review of the literature across disciplines Mallet (2004) discusses different physical, social, cultural, and psychological meanings of home, from a physical structure, a place where space and time are controlled, to an imagined or aspirational ideal place bounded by memories and linked with identity. The term home has great moral and symbolic density, and carries considerable emotional and psychological investment and anxiety. Home also refers to a physical space that includes material and physical aspects of life experience, and it can be a pivot, relating the individual to broader social structural forces, and linking them into community. In this chapter we examine the meaning of home for the young people, transitions from home, actual housing possibilities in the different sites of the study, and look at home and family in the biographical contexts of their lives.

In the Inventing Adulthoods study, home was of great importance and bore many of the meanings discussed here for the young people, carrying great weight at emotional and psychological levels. It is at these levels, as well as the physical and social that we first examine their responses. To unravel the rich, layered meanings young people attach to home we have conceptualised three broad domains: the emotional/psychological; material/physical; and the social/structural (Somerville, 1997; Lahelma and Gordon, 2003). Time, space, memory, movement, identity, and belonging all cut across the conceptualisation of home at these levels and are affected by factors such as gender, class, ethnicity, location, mobility/health and age. The meaning of home is continually in flux as young people experience, construct and revise housing pathways in response to the changing realities of their home circumstances and the turning tides of life. The salience of past experiences and memory runs through young people's understanding of home, and this lies at the heart of their lives.

The meaning of home at the emotional/psychological level

It's like a sanctuary ... I think always it's a sanctuary, somewhere you feel at peace, somewhere you don't have to – you can just be yourself – where you feel welcome. (Shannon, 19, 2003)

The literature is rich with evidence of home construed as a private haven, somewhere to escape from the public, outside world, a place where we can be content and be ourselves. In contrast the outside world is seen as public, open to scrutiny associated with work, surveillance, strangers and danger. Mallett (2004) suggests that this dichotomy has been criticised as over simplistic and often inaccurate (Sibley, 1995; Wardhaugh, 1999). The home has been a site of work for many, both historically and today, and for women housework and caring work have always taken place in the home. Jones (2000b) and others have also highlighted that the home is often a place of isolation, conflict, violence or abuse.

The association with home as a place of retreat was in fact made by many of the young people in this study. Home was linked to 'safety', 'security', 'comfort', 'contentment', 'privacy' and 'stability', it was described as a 'chill out zone', a 'comfort zone', as somewhere with 'ridiculously familiar surroundings', and where 'nothing can touch you,' 'a place where you can sleep, eat and come back to'. These associations illustrate the basic nurturing needs and expectations of home. While these associations were made across the data a closer look suggests that they were more likely to be made by young women, and particularly by young women from families headed by a single mother or by a biological mother and stepfather. The importance of home as an emotional resource comes through strongly in these descriptions and associations, but it is the family, coterminous with home, that produces this sense of safety, security and contentment. Home is where the family is:

It means home, family, my brothers and sisters, my ma and da like. Like when we're over in London or wherever we are, going back to the digs you don't say back to the house like or home like you never call, it's digs or B&B or whatever. (Adrian, 21, 2003)

Those who drew attention to the nurturing and emotional aspect of home by virtue of its absence had all experienced a 'broken home'. Sandy, living with her mother, stepfather and stepsiblings did not feel 'at home' in her new family:

> *Sandy:*   No I've never felt 100 percent comfortable in my house anyway. So ... they're all a complete family, you know dad, [list of stepsiblings] and there's me ... I know I'm part of the family but you know I'm just not quite in there properly ... Know what I mean?
>
> *INT:*   I do, it's a bit like they've made a bit of a new family but you're still part of the old family.
>
> *Sandy:*   Yeah.
>
> (Sandy, 20, 2002)

Yet some did report getting on well with parents' new partners or suggested that their parents' happiness was more important than their own feelings about the new home situation. Having two homes to move between, with resources doubled, could for some be seen as a positive outcome of parental separation, as for example Maureen did in Chapter 3.

For the young people, then, home was invariably connected to the family of origin, and an associated physical space. Those whose family was fragmented through parental divorce, separation, or death and who also experienced the loss of the physical family space, found themselves reconfiguring the meaning of home. For some this involved investing in the idealised creation of a future home, while for others it meant dealing with the practical realities of their current home status.

When Nat's parents divorced and moved to new and separate locations, he cut his emotional investment with the family home (that was no more) and shifted his attention to his practical housing needs (see also Chapter 4, 'Well-being', for the effects of the family break up on Nat). His university home and city became his new home – the place that provided his bed and shelter. For him, practical housing needs defined the meaning of home:

> *INT:*   So thinking of your family, do you feel your family is sort of a bit fragmented now – like home life, do you feel you've got any sort of home life?
>
> *Nat:*   Not really. I live here now – that's the way I see it, I've moved out now, full-stop. I'm just visiting when I come back down.
>
> (Nat, 21, 2004)

Nat's experience is shared by Glen (again see Chapter 6), whose parents also separated and moved to new and different locations with new partners. He moved from short-term social housing projects to short-lived, private rented accommodation, and temporary arrangements with girlfriends and friends. In the aftermath of his parents' split, he too concentrated on his physical needs and emphasised the well-stocked fridge, the TV and the bed as the important ingredients of his new home.

Timing, age, gender, class and ethnicity can also affect the meaning of home, as can tenure and other practical housing needs (Madigan et al., 1990). As Shannon says:

> 'Cos you want different things in different times of your life.' (Shannon, 19, 2003)

Home as a physical/practical resource

Home can also be a physical and practical resource for young people – with this meaning changing over time and across groups as we saw above in Nat's case. At a basic level it means a bed, food and shelter, and practical comforts:

> I mean um home – just a place to chill out really now. It's just, it's just a chill out zone, it's really cool – no stress or anything, nothing to worry about. Just lay back listening to music, go on the net, watch telly, go out with my friends, come back, have dinner, go to sleep. (Jade, 18, 2002)

For Luu home has practical and emotional value, and she draws attention to the power of memories associated with a physical space. But home for her is really her family and their relationships, and she recognises how hard it would be to leave:

> *Luu*:   Home is decent bed (laughs) to sleep in and then, I dunno, have comfort with your family and being happy, that's – yeah that's what I call home.
> *INT*:   And do you think you could make your home anywhere?
> *Luu*:   You could but I don't think I could – I dunno – I will miss the house that I live right now 'cos I have so much memories there. And it's kinda sad to sort of move out. So I dunno.
>
> (Luu, 18, 2002)

The practical and physical resources provided by home vary by social class and location. The socio-economically disadvantaged estate provides a physically stressful and unsafe location in general, with high levels of crime and drug taking. With this background the physical space of homes can be put under pressure through changing social circumstances. With changing family formations different combinations of relatives move into and out of limited spaces in overcrowded homes. In other sites and for others in the sample, a comfortable home with their own room and facilities was taken for granted.

Many of the young people themselves provided home comforts, and took responsibility for household chores and childcare, largely gendered activities. Corinne accepted housework as 'normal' duty for a girl but was reconciled to the fact that she would never meet her mother's high standards:

> You just do your own stuff but that's normal to us like, never up to my mammy's expectations like, but it's normal do you know what I mean, it's I mean you're a girl you sort of you're expected to sort of do it, but that's what I'm saying because your mother always has these expectations of a house. (Corinne, 21, 2003)

Shannon felt an obligation or moral duty to carry out the household tasks as her mother worked full time:

> And I sort of feel it's my duty, you know, to do it. And I mean I don't mind – at the end of the day you have to sort of help. She is at work … (Shannon, 21, 2003)

Jean complained about the expectations of her as a woman to take on the household tasks, and of the sexist attitudes of her brother and father. Housework and caring for siblings or nieces or nephews is part of young people's experiences of home and some, particularly in the working class, offset these responsibilities as a form of payment or repayment to parents or to siblings for their keep. For example, Jimmy lived with his sister and baby-sat for her on a regular basis as he could not afford to make a financial contribution towards the rent.

Home in social/structural and community context

A number of the young people enlarged the meaning of home to include their extended family and the community in which they live. The importance of the extended family to the meaning of home was most commonly mentioned in the Northern Ireland and the inner city site. Having relatives living nearby provided resources at all three levels, physical, social and emotional, in the form of accommodation, protection, a sense of belonging and ownership of place, and a social outlet within the community:

> Anna: I think I'll always end up back here because I am too close to my family to to leave them forever.
> INT: So that would be your immediate family, your mum?
> Anna: No my entire family because we're all really close.
>
> (Anna, 19, 2003)

For young people in both these locations, the extended family also included relatives and connections in other countries. It was also evident from their narratives that immigration, emigration and a global dispora had an effect on the concept of home (see too Chapter 8, 'Mobility').

The cycle of exchange and movement influences young people's construct of what home is, and how it might be shaped according to links with other places and other times. Memories, history and emotion, (personal, familial and community), all come to play a significant role in the meaning of a home – aspirationally elsewhere (as in a desired return to the homeland), or as a passport to a variety of other locations (through diasporic family connections).

From the beginning of the project young people in Northern Ireland made significantly more references to other places than did young people in any of the other sites. It is perhaps no surprise that they have been the most mobile over the course of the project. Having relatives or friends in England, Scotland, Ireland, America, and Australia has made the idea or the practice of journeying to other places possible for many. Leaving home to study, travel or work, forces or allows young people to regard home in a different light. When Maeve (aged 18) moved to a city in Ireland her family home was no longer central to her community, social space or sense of identity. Her new university home and location fulfilled these needs. The emphasis of the meaning of home shifts in these processes. Take for example returning university students who have established strong social networks independently of their homes but live in busy shared accommodation and enjoy few home comforts. The meaning of home as a nurturing and private space rises in importance. This is emphasised by those who talk about home as a place where they can relax and just be with their family:

> Where I suppose it's because you're familiar with everything around you, and the people around you, and the people just do their thing every day and it's grand. You know, you can slide in there and nobody'll change anything, you know. (Emer, 20, 2003)

As we can see from the examples given at both the emotional/psychological and material/ physical levels, these are entwined and the social/structural cuts across both, with class, gender, culture and ethnicity bringing their own effects to bear on meanings, conceptions, and ideals of home.

Home and transitions

For young people, feelings, desires and expectations associated with home can relate to the family home (as we have seen, home and family are often elided for them) or to their 'own' home in the future. Most at some stage wish for home, partner and children (Jones 1995; Thomson and Holland, 2002), they wish to avoid loneliness and uncertainty (Kenyon, 2003) but this expectation is cast into the future, and the route towards it is varied and complex. In youth studies, as in life, leaving home is seen as a key stage of transition and as a rite of passage from youth to adulthood, a first step towards economic and residential independence (Jones, 1995). As we have seen, in recent decades, changing social pressures and processes have rendered this, as with other transitions to adulthood, lengthy, complex and subject to contingent effects (for example of government policies in education and welfare), and structural and historical changes (e.g. in family relations and formations, in employment and pay, and in housing markets) (Irwin, 1995; Jones, 1995; Morrow and Richards, 1996; Catan, 2004).

Youth transitions to adulthood in general are subject to structural constraints of class, gender, and ethnicity, but within this framework of socio-structural factors and the impact of the macro social environment here is space for individual agency. Proactivity, independence and autonomy can be facilitated or restricted by social, cultural and institutional factors (Thomson et al., 2002; Catan, 2004). Theorists of late or postmodernity argue that processes of individualisation and disembedding are typical of this historical phase, seeing traditional supports for transitions to adulthood, and for adulthood itself as eroding, leaving individuals responsible for creating their own biographies and projects of self (Giddens, 1992). But others see this as an insufficient explanation for current processes of change, particularly in relation to demographic and economic processes, intimacy and young people's lives (Irwin, 1995; Furlong and Cartmel, 1997; Jamieson, 1998).

Irwin (1999) argues more generally that patterns of autonomy emerging for different groups that are argued to be signs of individualisation in fact reflect 'a shifting pattern of social claims, obligations and patterns of mutuality in social reproduction' (p. 38). With Wendy Bottero she argues that the decline of familiar social patterns should not be seen as the decline of social structuring itself, but a move to new forms of social structuring (Irwin and Bottero, 2000: 263). Using the concept of a 'moral economy' these authors emphasise the social assumptions, evaluations and norms that structure claims to resources, in order to draw attention to relational aspects of both family and social life. Their analysis is counterposed to emphases on individualisation. An immense field of literature and research supports the position that families are crucial sites through which inequalities are produced and reproduced. We have seen in Chapter 3, 'Education', how critical family background and experience is for educational and employment opportunities. In Chapter 4, 'Work', we have noted recent arguments from theorists suggesting, as do Irwin and Bottero, that inequalities are being reworked and reformulated more generally in social, economic, and cultural arenas in late modernity (Devine and Savage, 2000; Skeggs, 2004; Adkins, 2005b).

In this context of shifting social norms, structuring claims to resources and the reworking of inequalities, many empirical studies attest to the importance of families, family relationships and support for young people, some highlighting that its absence can have dire consequences in terms of life experiences, including homelessness and exclusion (Jones and Wallace, 1992; Morrow and Richards, 1996; Gillies et al., 2001). In our own study we found two models of adulthood between which young people moved, one stressing independence and autonomy and the other relationship, interdependence and care (Thomson et al., 2004). These models play out through the changing meaning of home for young people over time.

Housing possibilities for young people

Our sites differ in the actual possibilities for young people to move to a home of their own. In Northern Ireland as a whole 72 percent of homes are owner-occupied and a further 26 percent are rented, and the most common reasons given for homelessness are a breakdown in sharing arrangements/family dispute, or marital/relationship breakdown (Department of Social Development Northern Ireland, 2005). These figures are reflected in the research site where single people are the highest group on the Housing Executive waiting list, but young people in the sample were often able to find flats in the area. The pressure for housing is more acute in nationalist areas. In the rural site, second-home ownership, downsizing and retirement to the countryside have contributed to a growing lack of affordable housing. Most young people considered the price of property in the area well beyond their reach, and there are few supported housing schemes for young people aged 16 to 24. Considerable change has taken place on the large, disadvantaged public housing estate, with the balance of public to private housing shifting dramatically through changing government policies, right-to-buy, regeneration projects, the affordability of property in the area, and the transfer of a considerable proportion of the estate to a housing association. Ironically, the young people here talked about the ready availability of flats in their local area and this was borne out by the experiences of some who either spent much of their time at a peer's flat or obtained a flat of their own (by declaring themselves homeless).

The inner city and commuter belt sites present the most contrasting pictures in our study. In the inner city 53 percent of properties are owner-occupied compared with a national average of 68 percent, 10 percent privately rented, and 24 percent owned by the local council. The council stock has experienced an annual 3 percent reduction over the past few years due mainly to right-to-buy sales and regeneration schemes, and this trend is expected to continue. The young people in this area were predominantly from working-class families and would wish to stay in the city, probably having to enter rented accommodation when they left home permanently. The commuter belt site is in contrast located in one of the most expensive areas of England in which to buy a house. In 2002, for example, 88 percent of the housing stock was in private sector ownership. The young people here would find it hard to get a foot on the housing ladder, unless given considerable help by their parents (a possibility for some) and there is relatively little rented housing in the area. Many of the young people do aspire to remain or return to the area and lifestyle of their parents, but will clearly have difficulties in finding somewhere comparable to live.

At the fourth round of interviews in 2003, slightly more than half of the young people were still living with their parents, or with either mother or father. Whilst there were no strong relationships between location, social class and housing situation, reflecting how difficult it is for young people to have access to and be able to afford a home of their own in the UK early in the 21st century, there was a slight tendency for middle-class young people to be in university halls or sharing flats, and for working-class young people in Northern Ireland to share a flat or have a place of their own. Young people in the rural area were most likely to be living with their parents at that stage.

Home and family in biographical context

The cases briefly discussed earlier highlighted not only the importance of family, home and belonging for many of the young people in the study, but also how the meaning of home changes as the young people's lives and experiences change. While the family home might remain a comfort zone for some, the need for independence and autonomy can create home as a fluid, imagined future space. Relationships can often be the spur for moving into this space.

The following case studies illustrate diversity and contingency amongst the young people in the sample in relation to home and housing experiences, and the importance of family relationships and support. They also suggest ways in which new forms of inequality can arise and indicate some different ways of desiring and achieving independence. We look at two young mothers in Northern Ireland, one young woman from the disadvantaged estate and another from the rural area, and contrasting experiences of a gay young man and lesbian young woman.

Cheryl

Cheryl's transitions to date appear to represent a straightforward traditional working-class order, stressing the importance of family and community. Interviewed four times between 16 and 20, she continued to live in the same close-knit community in Northern Ireland, moving out of the family home at 17 for 3 months, returning for a while and then buying and settling in her own home with her fiancé, around the corner from her parents, by the time she was 19. At 20, she had a new baby. There was considerable continuity in her story over time but there were currents that ran counter to this.

At 17 Cheryl left school:

> I've just got wile claustrophobic you know with the school sort of treating us really
> like children. We're not allowed to go out of school on our own and we're not allowed
> to do this and we're not allowed to do that … So I seen jobs and I just started
> applying and went for interview and half an hour later I got the job. (Cheryl, 18, 2000)

With the job came a more diverse social life. Tired of staying in and saving with her then
boyfriend, Cheryl left him, left home and began a full-time job. Based in a Catholic area, the
job opened up geographical space for Cheryl and exposed her to other lifestyles and
options. She swapped her more traditionally 'adult' aspirations and pastimes for socialising,
partying and notions of extended 'youth' – which involved a return to an earlier desire to
leave Northern Ireland:

> I don't think I'd like to stay here for the rest of my life … Maybe in a couple years
> time after I do get a couple years' experience I might go over to England and work, I
> definitely wouldn't rule it out … I'd love to travel around the world. (Cheryl, 18, 2000)

But the withdrawal from her parental emotional and material resources began to take a toll
and, after 3 months of renting a room in an older friend's home, Cheryl returned home:

> I thought I was the big woman, I didn't realise how much my parents did for me.
> Being independent really scared me … And em, when I moved back home I had a
> far better relationship with me Mum and Dad, far better. (Cheryl, 20, 2003)

It was at this point that she fell in love with a fellow party person and work mate in her new
place of work, and seized this opportunity to revert to her more traditional aspirations. Within
6 months, they had bought a house together and Cheryl had become pregnant (by mistake).
Leaving home this time involved a consolidation of family, community and previous
aspirations for a particular version of heterosexual adulthood. It was also fortunate for Cheryl
that house prices in her area were affordable, whereas in some of our sites they certainly
were not.

In many ways Cheryl has returned to the version of adulthood that she had previously
created and predicted for herself, and she also secured much of what she had been looking
for in the various domains in her life over the course of the research. Consumption had
always been an important aspect of her sense of herself as competent and free. As a
homeowner she has, with her partner, invested significant amounts of time, finance and
energy into creating a designed interior environment. Through the security of both a couple
and a parenting relationship, she has achieved independence from her family and created
her own home. Although both sets of parents were a major source of practical and material
help and advice in this. The experience of experimenting with a more cosmopolitan life also
enabled her to imagine a future where it might be possible to return to education or to
progress within the work field. Time will tell.

Sheila

Sheila, also living in Northern Ireland, experienced a much more rocky road through relationships and pregnancy to her own home. Despite low self-esteem Sheila had always been very independent and had worked for what she had from an early age, never expecting or demanding anything from her parents (who split up when she was 8) since their financial position was precarious. She had a love–hate relationship with her housing estate – declaring that she wanted to leave at the first opportunity, but at the same time valuing the community feeling and support that she saw as there for her. Her aspirations to have a professional career and move from the restrictive working-class environment fell by the wayside when she dithered about her educational route. It suffered a further blow when she became pregnant, fell out with her boyfriend, and became a single mother living in her own house in her local community. While her mother and sister provided emotional and practical support, being a single teen mum was a struggle for her. Having a child made Sheila think of the future, plan and consider the implications of her life for her son. She did not want a life on benefit and hoped to return to education, encouraged by a new affirming relationship that boosted her confidence and became a huge source of material, emotional, social and cultural capital for her.

Rebecca

The pull of home and community also remained strong for Rebecca, who at our last meeting in 2000 was 18. She was preparing to move out of the three-bedroom family home on the disadvantaged estate that she shared with her mother and four sisters. Rebecca felt that she had no option but to move out – her sister, a university student was not in a position to do so and her other sisters were too young:

> Well like I've got four sisters and the youngest one sleeps in the box room. So there's me and my older sister and one the year below me as well, so it's like three adults in one room. And there's no room at all. She's always at her boyfriend's, I'm always at my nanny's so we can get a bit of space. So she can't survive 'cos she's at university, so I said right, well it's got to be me moving isn't it? (Rebecca, 18, 2000)

Rebecca applied to the council for a flat citing overcrowding and domestic conflict. They provided her with a one-bedroom flat fitted with a new kitchen, newly decorated and carpeted. A follow-up call a few months later confirmed that she had indeed moved into her council flat but was spending most of her time at the family home.

Although she was in a long-term relationship, unlike Cheryl, Rebecca did not want to share the flat with her boyfriend. The flat fulfilled a physical and practical need for her, it gave her the option of space and independence, but the fact that she continued to spend most her time in the family home suggested that the emotional and social links were stronger than those she was in a position or willing to build from her new flat.

Fay

Fay is similarly linked to her family and community. She comes from a more middle-class background in the rural site. Fay's parents did not approve of her boyfriend and banned him from the family house. In partial response to this and in the quest for a more independent life Fay moved in with him. She made a contribution towards the running cost of the flat she shared with him but moved freely between it and her family home. She returned to her parent's home daily, and continued to draw heavily on family resources there (food, animal care), but made no contribution to the household.

While she had not officially moved out of home, she lived a significant part of the time with her boyfriend and the financial contribution she made to the flat they shared gave her a sense of independence and control. This sense of independence was boosted significantly when she acquired her own car, a practical necessity as she moved between her two distinct experiences of home and living. While she had not realised full independent living and remained emotionally and practically connected to her parental home, Fay had established a version of adulthood that was both familiar to her and available locally. She took up a career option that her parents and grandparents shared before her, and became part of a community network in which she shared friendships with her mother. Her choice of boyfriend did not however fit into this localised version of adulthood, and as such triggered a family fall-out. Whilst this relationship resulted in family conflict, it also gave her access to an alternative and more cosmopolitan lifestyle beyond the local. At last contact she was still struggling to negotiate both worlds, clearly wanting to hold on to both, although the strong ties she has with her family and community may make leaving home and the community it is part of difficult for her.

Lesbian and gay young people tend to leave home and school earlier than their peers. The additional problems of the process of coming out and living a gay/lesbian lifestyle can create difficulties in separating from the family and family home and constructing their own independent space. Mal who comes from a working-class background in Northern Ireland and Denise whose background is more middle class had very different routes at this point.

Mal

Mal's parents accepted his sexuality, although he did not get on so well with his father. He had a series of short-term jobs, but nothing permanent, and unlike his siblings, had not pursued university or a career. His social life was located in the gay scene, and he had a lot of friends. At 24 he left his rural family home to move into a flat to be close to the gay scene in a nearby town. But he was lonely living by himself:

> I'd rather share a house or flat with someone because I tried living on my own once and the first few weeks are great bloody lonely then because I remember living on edge and I used to drag my parents up to stay with me and they used to get bored after a while when I said stay I don't want to stay here on my own. (Mal, 23, 2004)

Ultimately Mal found it difficult to cope financially and practically. He was reluctant to turn to his parents for help as he did not 'want to make it look like I'm not coping'. But his experience of independent living came to an end when he fell behind with his rent. He slept rough for a short time after losing his flat then returned to his parents' home. At last contact he was reliant on his father for lifts to and from town and feared growing old as a gay man in rural isolation.

Denise

Denise too returned to the family home in the rural site. When appropriate work was not immediately or easily available after completing university she returned home as an instrumental choice with a negotiated financial arrangement with her parents. She has remained in the rural setting, and thinks of building her own home when her financial situation improves – her parents will take out a mortgage on her behalf. She came out whilst at university, living in her own bedsit, and at that time, as throughout the research period, generated wide and far reaching networks of friends and contacts. She has also benefited from her professional parents' social and cultural capital. Originally scathing about the narrow mindedness and limitations of the rural locality in which she grew up, Denise has come to value the resources of her rural childhood. The countryside has also been a key aspect of her environmentalist career aspirations and now she can imagine settling in somewhere like (rather than her actual) her home village with a lesbian partner – which she could not imagine in the past.

Conclusion

The story of this chapter has been of the changing meaning of home for young people as they move through the transitions to adulthood, reflecting the intersecting models of adulthood with which they operate, one stressing independence and autonomy and the other relationship, interdependence and care. Our brief examples from their lives indicate some of the structural constraints of class, gender, and culture that impinge on their trajectories and experiences of home. They show too the importance of the moral economy of family relationships, obligations, and expectations, and of the emotional, material, and social space of the family home to their security.

For some of these young people, as we have seen here, a couple relationship can play an important part in moving them into another home space. In the next chapter we examine the types of intimate relationships that the young people formed.

Chapter 11

Intimacy

It may be a cliché to say that home is where the heart is, but intimacy and home are indeed closely connected. In the last chapter we explored how home and leaving home fits into young people's transitions to adulthood, and here we look at the place of the couple relationship in this, and patterns of relationship formation.

Having a couple relationship took increasing prominence in the young people's narratives over time, often representing critical moments and providing motivation in their lives. As mentioned in Chapter 3 on education, when asked to predict their relationship status at the age of 25, many young people in the Inventing Adulthoods study thought they might have a steady relationship, and by 35, almost all assumed marriage and children. It was clear from the earliest stage of the study that young people still crave commitment in relationships (Sharpe, 2001). Finding the right relationship (or any relationship) can be a strong motivating factor, encouraging young people to take pathways that they may not otherwise consider. It can affect the point at which they leave home and the sort of home in which they then live. For young women, finding 'Mr Right' has traditionally been important, and often a crucial factor in whether or not to have a sexual relationship (Sharpe and Thomson, 2005), while for some young men, finding 'Ms Right' and becoming a father can also be a critical motivating factor in leaving criminal and other misbehaviour and irresponsibility behind (Laub and Sampson, 2003; Webster et al., 2004; MacDonald and Marsh, 2005).

For the young people in the study, the haziness of their imagined lives in 20 or so years' time contained an assumption that they would be 'settled down' with a family of their own. Yet Bauman (2003) suggests that relationships are 'troublesome incarnations of ambivalence' like many other aspects of late modernity and in our study we found that in practice young people had varied approaches towards relationships. Some opted for long-term committed relationships whilst others preferred singledom, short-term or casual relationships. At this stage in their lives, most young people did not appear to enter and sustain relationships simply for the sake of getting married and having children. The majority described various benefits, both psychological, such as having a social or sexual partner, someone to talk to, and to provide security, trust and stability, as well as practical, such as helping with transport and money. As we saw in Chapter 7, relationships could also be an asset to emotional well-being, and good health. So although young people's aspirations for relationships were relatively conventional, in practice their relationships seemed to last 'as long as they were good' and in this case 'good' was applied to the purpose relationships were chosen for.

Trends in relationships and marriage

Over the last century social attitudes and expectations around relationships and marriage have changed considerably, those of women having altered more than those of men. After the Second World War ideas began to shift, particularly among young middle-class women who were being encouraged to take advantage of educational possibilities. By the 1960s and 1970s, women aspired to a job or career for themselves as well as marriage. Research in the 1980s and 1990s (Lees, 1986, 1999; Sharpe, 1994, 2001; Oakley, 1996; O'Donnell and Sharpe, 2000) suggested that marriage was losing its appeal for young people, particularly young women, many of whom wanted to delay or even reject marriage. Living together, as a prelude or alternative to marriage, had become much more acceptable and popular. Today, with women's increased potential for economic independence, marriage is no longer necessarily a source of financial security. This is especially so for the working class, where a lack of good job opportunities and unemployment make men appear less attractive as prospective husbands and fathers. Analysis of the attitudes and expectations of the young people in the first stage of the study also confirmed this. They valued and desired relationships and commitment, but marriage was less important (Sharpe, 2001). Many viewed the first stage of a serious relationship as involving cohabitation, which might or might not lead to marriage. Clearly culture and religion also play a part, and marriage is part of our popular culture. It has become more a matter of identity than social structure or survival, another aspect of consumption and lifestyle choice.

Figures illustrate how the popularity of marriage in England and Wales has declined dramatically over the last few decades as the trend towards cohabitation has increased, although there has been a small rise (4.7% from 2002 to 2003) since an all-time low in 2001 (National Statistics Online, 2005). In 2003, the number of first marriages registered was less than half those registered in 1970; in the same year remarriages accounted for just over two-fifths of all marriages. The average marriage age has also risen for both sexes, and for both middle-class and working-class people (partly due to cohabitation before marriage): from 26 for men and 23 for women in 1963, to 31 and 29 respectively in 2003 (National Statistics Online, 2005).

An increase in the number of young people, especially women, pursuing higher education over the last 60 years has also affected their life paths, including relationships and marriage. Research suggests that young people who choose to take higher education are less likely to marry, and those married by the age of 26 tend to have fewer qualifications (Blackwell and Bynner, 2002). There is a strong link between higher education and household formation, and women obtaining a higher level of education, are less likely to marry; while men with less education are least likely to marry or cohabit. Pursuing higher education and its related socio-cultural milieu can open up young people's opportunities to increase economic prospects and experience independent living arrangements (Heath and Cleaver, 2003). Those not doing so tend to have more 'accelerated transitions' (Bynner and Pan, 2002), which involve early partnership formation and parenthood, often leaving home to move in with a partner rather than living with peers or independently.

Location and class factors

Relationships took on different styles and sometimes different meanings in the various localities of the study, and there seemed to be some evidence of local cultures of intimacy, or 'local moral economies' (Thomson, 2000), which affect young people over time. In the more working-class environments, relationships were often embarked on earlier, and there tended to be more concern with settling down and making a home with someone than pursuing individual aspirations. This was illustrated by the disadvantaged northern site in comparison with the affluent (middle-class) suburban area. In the former, status could be gained for young men by cultivating a sexual reputation, and for young women through accessing the experience and authority of motherhood, which was valued highly. The mainly middle-class young people in the latter tended towards more androgynous and desexualised identities, characterising early sexual activity as a sign of 'immaturity'. The heterosexual couple was seen as something for the future, when major examinations were in the bag (Thomson, 2000). In Northern Ireland, proportionally more young people were in long-term relationships than in the English sites and these relationships were complicated by the enduring Northern Irish dilemma of staying local or moving away. Those who entered relationships near home would probably perpetuate their own family structure and dynamics. Having a more middle-class background, or higher educational aspirations, often led to the pursuit of dreams away from home, and relationships put on hold. In the ethnically mixed inner city site, those whose families who were not originally from England tended to pursue a higher level of education and careers than their parents' generation, although they did not wish to go far away but chose colleges or universities close to their family homes, and usually lived at home. Relationships often ran in parallel with education and family activities.

Who's in a relationship?

Our longitudinal perspective has allowed us to explore how young people approached intimate couple relationships over time. We have looked across our data set in order to discover the variety of relationships that young people were in at the fourth round of interviews, and we have looked at the data over time in order to see patterns for individuals. From this we have identified several tendencies, or general approaches to relationships demonstrated by the young people in the study. These are explained and illustrated using three case studies.

Of the young people participating in the round of biographical interviews that took place in 1999, just over half (59) were single, 17 were in short-term and 19 in long-term relationships (including three in serial monogamy), and 10 were dating. By the fourth round of biographical interviews in 2002 and 2003, 70 young people – aged between 17 and 26 – continued to participate in the study. Of these 29 (42%) were single, three were dating, seven were in short-term relationships, and 30 (43%) were in long-term relationships. Only one (a young woman) was married, but there was some movement towards living together (eight young people including a young mother and an expectant father), and four young people were engaged. Proportionally more of the young women were in relationships (short-term and long-term) than young men at both the first and fourth interviews but our data did not show much variation in relationship status according to class and age. In terms of the young people's sexual orientation, 62 identified as heterosexual and eight as non-heterosexual (five gay men, one bisexual man, one bisexual woman and one lesbian). It has been argued that detraditionalising forces are reshaping heterosexual life, bringing the heterosexual and non-heterosexual world closer together (Bech, 1997; Weeks et al., 2001) and in our analyses we include data from both heterosexual and non-heterosexual people together. Some aspects of lesbian and gay young people's transitions to adulthood are distinctive, and we have commented on these throughout the book as they arise. However, in the context of intimate relationships we have been able to integrate heterosexual, lesbian, gay and bisexual accounts.

In the intermediate period between the first and fourth interviews, clearly the young people have become older and more inclined to develop relationships, but the data also shows many young people who have reached the same status through different routes. For example, Su was single at round one, and also at round four, but had short-term relationships in between while Allen went from a short-term to a long-term relationship with an intermediate period of singledom, and Sam went from being single to an active dating period after he 'came out', after which he settled into a long-term relationship.

Tendencies in young people's approaches to relationships

Young people's patterns of relationship changed over time. After the fourth round of interviews we attempted to reflect on patterns of relationship, and in doing so identified what we are calling three different 'tendencies' among the young people in the study. These tendencies are 'fuzzy' categories created in order to facilitate our conceptualisation of the general trends in the data. As we go on to suggest, such tendencies in relationship patterns map onto other patterns relating to educational trajectory, level of parental support and access to material resources.

Fusion

Many of the young people appeared to value the intimate qualities associated with couple relationships. Some who were already in long-term relationships valued the emotional support and security that these kinds of relationships could offer, while some single young people desired a close relationship for the same reason. Beck and Beck-Gernsheim (1995) have suggested that individualisation can have a positive impact upon relationships, placing the couple as the stable primary bond in a world where traditions become diluted. The biographical narratives of the young people demonstrated that trusting and intimate relationships enabled some of them to cope with the uncertainties of the 'risk' society through providing them with a significant other who was understanding and accepting.

Partners were often described as friends or soul mates, illustrating the importance of an open, trusting and understanding relationship. We met Hazel in Chapter 6, a young woman from a middle-class background who got married (against the trend) at 19, having emerged from a period of drug taking and 'living for the weekend'. Significantly she had met her husband whilst clubbing, and as such the relationship was a shared project in changing lifestyle. In some way, her previous 'fusion' with drugs had been replaced by fusion with her relationship:

> ... the fact that I wouldn't want to live without him, I couldn't live without him, I just couldn't, it's like I could never remember him not being in my life and ... the fact that he's just like, he's not just a husband, and lover he's the bestest friend I've ever had, completely made for each other. And it's always having someone there, when you need them. (Hazel, 19, 2003)

Beck and Beck-Gernsheim (1995) have pointed to the narcissistic elements of contemporary couple relationships, suggesting that couples may 'mirror' each other. This mirror allows a young person's identity to be reflected, further processed and understood. So, as Hazel felt safe to discuss her innermost thoughts and feelings, she was also able to explore and change her identity. Mary Holmes (2004) has argued that self-actualisation and fusion are not in conflict, as individual identity is developed in relation to others. If human life and personal identity become meaningful and of worth through sharing one's biography with a significant other, then the couple relationship may offer some kind of existential salvation to those individuals who feel alienated from their own self and others. This interpretation of what takes place in the couple relationship is consistent with Anthony Giddens' (1992) idea of the 'pure relationship', characterised by confluent love, trust, mutual self-disclosure and emotional and sexual equality, where individuals can produce a reflexive narrative of self consistent with their social world view.

For some young men, this kind of couple relationship could be seen as offering a sanctuary where they could create and share their reflective narratives of self without feeling exposed to societal expectations of masculinity and power. Glen (also someone with a history of drug taking) trusted his girlfriend with his most personal feelings:

> I don't know why I find it while hard when I'm really pissed off, just like you know, parents problems or whatever, I just feel stupid and foolish talking to a friend or something, but my girlfriend like I could talk to her about anything and she'd just sit and she'd be listening, I can talk to her about it. (Glen, 21, 2003)

We saw in the previous chapter that home is seen to be where the family is, and that young people who had experienced a disrupted home life tended to define 'home' in terms of security and nurturing, which in some cases is something that 'fusion' in a long-term relationship can provide. As well as stability, acceptance and understanding, a couple relationship may also appear to be a solution to the existential concern of loneliness:

> Um I suppose you always have someone there to talk to, to, you know, rely on or, you know, if you're lonely there's someone there to – just that you know that there's someone there for you, and that they choose to be with you, it's not that they're related to you or something. (Carol, 22, 2003)

It may be that where individuals are unable to access the support and influence of religion, class and neighbours, a stable primary bond may become increasingly important in providing them with a sense of identity. In this sense 'individualisation may drive men and women apart but paradoxically it also pushes them back into one another's arms' (Beck and Beck Gernsheim, 1995: 32). But investing in a committed relationship may also involve compromise or sacrifice in other domains of young people's lives, especially within educational and professional arenas. For example, Shannon (see also Chapter 7) was aware of the consequences of prioritising her relationship over her university choice:

> I went to this university which was a polytechnic, which I really – I was a bit gutted that I chose it, but I chose it because my partner ... – inside I knew that I was doing the wrong thing. Because I mean yes it is a good university for certain subjects, but for (mine) you need to go to a recommended one ... because if not, you're not gonna get taken seriously. (Shannon, 19, 2003)

Autonomy

The second 'tendency' we identified in relationship formation, relates to those who appeared to prefer autonomy to fusion. These young people adopted a more instrumental approach to living, facing the uncertainties of the labour market as an individual, unhindered by a close couple relationship that might require time and effort. They were generally single or in casual relationships and their accounts prioritised self-fulfillment and academic or professional achievement. However, this category could also include young people in long-term relationships who were unwilling to allow their relationship arrangements to influence their professional or educational routes. They were shaping their biographies and love life through decision-making, appearing to prioritise rationality over emotion. Here, Karin, (who we met in Chapter 8), talks in highly instrumental terms about how to manage her boyfriend's expectations and her educational ambitions:

> I'm definitely, definitely going. I have offered him he can come with me if he wants, I've even offered since we've broken up he can come with me as a friend as I would love to have him come with me, but he's not going to hold me back because if he held me back I would hate him, it might take a while because I might be happy to stay with him now but come a year's time or come 15 years time I would hate him for taking away my chance like, because I wouldn't see it as me giving up my chance for him I would see it as him taking away my chance, I know I would. (Karin, 19, 2003)

Unlike Shannon (above), Karin can be seen as attempting to prioritise her academic achievement over her previously committed relationship. Becoming an educated and successful woman stands in tension with being a committed and 'local' girlfriend. The instrumental character of her words no doubt belie the difficult emotions and choices involved, including as we saw in Chapter 8 the obligations that she also felt towards her mother as the last child to be leaving home and leaving town. Karin was in a position to make a decision, but without her resources or the potential to further her education she could be left with little choice but to invest in her relationship as Beth did (illustrated below).

Uncommitted

The third tendency in young people's patterns of relationships includes those who wanted to live an extended independent and fun-filled youth, and who tended to see relationships as a threat to this. Most of them were either single or in casual relationships. Some of them spoke about the downside of relationships and pointed to things like emotional vulnerability, tensions with family or friends, loss of freedom and independence, and compromised plans:

> You don't have your own time any more, you can't do what you want to do, you always have to consider someone else now, just not me. (Malcolm, 18, 2002)

These young people tended to place special value on friendships and socialising with friends without having to explain themselves to partners. Some of those who had strong views regarding independence had emerged from oppressive relationships themselves or had learnt that relationships were oppressive through the experiences of their parents and friends. Naz, who we met in Chapter 6 is typical in seeing a relationship as impinging on his freedom to have fun:

> I suppose you're always together stuck to each other like most of my friends and their girlfriends are, like they never do anything without each other, they always have to ask permission can I go here, can I do this, whereas I don't need to ask I just go and do … so I don't have to worry about any of that so I'm happy. (Naz, 21, 2003)

Bauman (2003) argues that although individuals may say they wish to form intimate relationships, they are also concerned with preventing a relationship from 'curdling and clotting'. Hence they replace committed relationships with 'virtual relations' which are seen as 'romantic possibilities' that do not require emotional investment. This option seemed to be a good solution for those young people who feared the 'negative consequences' of fusion:

> After being with someone I just – it's just nice to be able to just go out when you want, where you want and you don't have to ring up someone and say, 'I'm just going here', or, 'can't see you 'cos I'm doing this', which is so nice to be able to do what you like. (Tamsin, 19, 2002)

Bauman suggests that this form of relating does not make individuals any happier as numerous virtual relations cannot replace the quality of the committed relationship. Nevertheless, there were some young people involved in intense couple relationships who expressed nostalgia for an uncommitted lifestyle.

> Um I don't know, sometimes it's just like I think I'd like to just go out there and have fun again or, you know, maybe like to meet somebody else and see what it's like being with somebody else. (Estelle, 19, 2002)

Those young people in our study who followed this approach did not appear to miss the rewards of the committed relationship and viewed its costs as outweighing the benefits in this particular period in their lives.

Linked to this last tendency is what Bauman describes as the 'semi-detached' couple. Such couples reject the idea of living together, they keep separate circles of friends and finances and spend time together when they feel like it. Similarly, Bawin-Legros (2004) describes the emergence of long-distance relationships, which, she notes, seem to be tailored to the postmodern individual's needs as they permit them to be free but not alone.

These three tendencies are neither permanent nor mutually exclusive. Rather they can be viewed as a kind of continuum, where at one end young people are as free as they can be, and at the other, they are obligated to having and maintaining a partnered relationship. The extent to which individuals 'choose' the kinds of relationships that they enter is also interesting. Parents may intervene in relationships for a range of reasons: to protect their education, their well-being, to ensure that they keep within cultural or religious norms.

Even where young people were from traditional backgrounds, family expectations varied. Su and Luu were both second generation Vietnamese but experienced relatively little pressure from their families to make traditional marriages, despite some complaints about the gendered division of labour in the home. Naz, from a Sikh background, had opted out of his religious community, and was in no hurry to settle down. He worked in the family business and would soon run one of his own, but in the meantime was enjoying an active social life including drink, drugs, and casual girlfriends.

Where young people embraced religion this could make a difference. Khattab was keen to fall in with traditional practice and to marry a young woman he met when he went to visit relatives in Pakistan. Having finished his degree, he has taken a job that will earn the money to support her when she joins him. Yasmin was also Muslim, although from a Turkish family. Her parents expected her to marry a suitable Muslim man and were not happy about her having boyfriends. Unlike Khattab, Yasmin resisted these expectations and managed to have one or two clandestine (but non-sexual) relationships. She had a responsible job, and while she accepted that her future marriage relationship would be arranged, she trusted that her sympathetic relationship with her mother would mean that she has an important role in deciding whom she eventually married. Morris provides a good example of how it is possible to choose tradition. Although brought up in a non-religious family and having had girlfriends and sexual relationships, on converting to Christianity he decided to live a chaste life, saving sex for marriage. It is clearly the case that certain cultures exert stricter controls on young women than men, but the picture is far from simple.

We cannot generalise from our study as to wider patterns in relationship formation among young people. But drawing on a rich longitudinal data set we can suggest the particular characteristics and dynamics of the three tendencies that have emerged from our data. These tendencies do not have clear boundaries, and people can move between them over time, but we have chosen three young people – Beth, Denise, and Richard, to illustrate each of these tendencies, as they have remained fairly consistent throughout the study.

Beth (fusion)

Beth was in a long-term relationship from the age of 15 to 19. She lived with her father in a council house in an affluent area near a commuter belt town since her parents divorced when she was 5. From an early age, she became aware of differences between herself and many of her peers at school, who came from well-off middle-class and intact families. Lacking emotional and material resources, she was often left feeling vulnerable and insecure.

Beth's life changed when she met her first serious boyfriend Vic, who was 3 years older (18) and worked in the motor industry. She saw him every evening, which caused tensions with her father and friends. Her schoolwork suffered and she reduced visits to her mother. Her father was often out, so in many ways she became very dependent on her boyfriend. They contemplated having sex but delayed it until they both felt ready. When it finally happened it proved something of a disappointment rather than a critical moment, but was something they would work on in the context of trust and mutual affection. As her relationship became stronger Beth started to feel more empowered, and by the age of 16 she had turned from a shy schoolgirl into an attractive and confident young woman. Her emotional and social resources came from Vic, who had become increasingly important in her life. She still talked to her mother but did not see her often, and did not discuss certain subjects with her father.

Over a year later and at art college, Beth's relationship was still strong, she had matured both physically and emotionally and become more assertive. She was low on material resources and behind at college, but had in her life the two people she loved, her father and Vic. She wanted a career in fashion design and planned to go to university, but this would have been somewhere local: 'I couldn't just get up and leave Vic here. I mean I trust him with my life and I hope he trusts me as well, 'cos I would never, ever jeopardise our relationship.' It perhaps reflects some of the less secure aspects of Beth's upbringing and early family breakdown that she did not want to jeopardise a stable and secure relationship that offered her a sense of identity and purpose in life. This was confirmed when there was a crisis in the relationship and she contemplated breaking up with Vic. It was a critical moment for Beth as the thought of losing him made her realise that she could not live without him. From that point on, investing in her relationship became of primary importance.

When we last saw Beth, aged 19, she had abandoned her career plans. She decided that she lacked the ability to do a degree, that competition for jobs was too tough, and had taken a full-time job in a shop. She now redefined herself as 'a stay at home person' who wished to get married and have children with Vic:

> I've got a really strong feeling that I'm not meant to be, have a career, I'm meant to be a mother you know and I don't know why but I just think that I'm meant to be like your typical stay at home housewife, look after the kids, have a part-time job and I think that's 'cos I don't know, I really haven't got a clue what I want to do. And I think that's the only thing that I really want to do. (Beth, 19, 2004)

At this time, Beth was more concerned with caring for and preserving her home and her relationships with her father and her partner than pursuing anything separate for herself. Making a home and becoming a mother are markers of adulthood that Beth can achieve and in this sense she is conforming to a traditional gender and class pattern. Her dream of home and family life expressed at the beginning of the previous chapter can never come true, but she is making the best home she can for herself and those she loves.

Denise (autonomy)

Denise falls into the second tendency, as she has consistently prioritised education and work over committed relationships. A well-resourced, white middle-class young woman, she aspired to a career in ecology but also actively pursued different kinds of social opportunities. Denise's strong drive to succeed in her career seemed to be a family value, as her mother's family expected and encouraged women to become successful in their field.

During the study, Denise followed a smooth linear trajectory from her first year of final school examinations and through 3 years of university, always certain that education was her route to the future and success in her preferred career. Her personal strategy involved self-belief, positive motivation and an avoidance of being fixed to a relationship or place:

> I just want to be able to sort of change my mind and do what I want when I want to at the moment, rather than sort of finding the opportunity to do something and don't want to leave someone behind. If someone turns up then who I really get on with it'd be nice but I'm really not that bothered, quite happy being single. (Denise, 20, 2001)

Denise's individualistic approach seems to demonstrate Beck's theory (1992) of 'choice biographies' being dependent on decision-making and individual initiative:

> ... I got so used to just deciding what I was doing regardless of anybody else, and um sort of just seeing who fancied fitting in with it ... And that is pretty much the way I treat most things now. I tend to make my own decisions on what I want to do and then just see whether or not anybody else fancies sort of ... (Denise, 22, 2003)

Denise also presents her sexual identity as a matter of decision-making, with questioning and experimentation enabling her eventually to come out as a lesbian. However, while her future aspirations – apart from achieving the career she pursued – were to settle down in the countryside with a female partner and have children, she currently felt that a relationship would hinder her life plans. In general, Denise saw relationships as feasible only to the extent that her partner could conform to her lifestyle and support her professional career moves. Consequently, over the last 5 years she had only a couple of short relationships and a few flings, generally describing herself as 'single as ever'.

By comparing Beth and Denise's case studies we could demonstrate, as discussed earlier in the chapter, the influence of location and class upon young people's relationship choices. For example, Beth prioritised her relationship over her academic or professional achievement partly because Vic could provide her with the emotional resources she needed in order to overcome the insecurities caused by the early breakdown of her family and limited financial resources. For Denise, on the other hand, relationships appeared to be less important as her short-term plans entailed a successful career in her preferred domain. Having received consistent emotional support from her family throughout, she aspired to a trajectory that could enable her to produce a reflexive project of self appropriate for a middle-class woman. As much as it seems that Denise's choices were a product of her own decision-making, we should recognise that she chose a traditional middle-class path followed by many with similar socio-economic characteristics.

Richard (uncommitted)

Richard falls into the third tendency. He is someone who has moved between disinterest in relationships to having a fairly stable but casual relationship for a while, before moving as befitted his changing life circumstances, into a single existence again. He comes from a reasonably well-off middle-class family living in the leafy suburb.

When interviewed at 16, Richard's social life tended to revolve around a mixed but mainly male group of friends, and he had not had any girlfriends. He adopted a cool, laid back approach to school and life in general:

> I'm just too lazy I reckon … to be bothered, to be like um, always like around someone … it's better just to be just hanging around with loads of people in our group … had a girlfriend at college but didn't last very long, dunno why, I'm too much of a, like go out with my mates and have a good time. (Richard, 16, 1999)

Nevertheless, he met Sienna, almost by accident and they stayed together for a year. It was a sexual relationship, and he saw their main role to have fun and sex, rather than love and romance:

> We just kind of have a laugh together, … it's not like a, oh you didn't call me here and then and you didn't do this, there's no hassles, just go out and have fun … I'm not up for clingy loving relationships at all. (Richard, 17, 2000)

This relationship ended when Sienna moved abroad. Richard said he was 'not bothered about finding someone', and 'if something came along that was fine'. His plans now were to take a trip to New Zealand with a friend, to work and travel there.

At the fourth interview, Richard was 21 years old, and had matured from his travels. However, he still retained the same cool, laid back, easy-going persona. While away he had a 'not serious' relationship with a young woman for a while, but did not bother to maintain contact with her after he returned home.

Now he was earning some money in a part-time job, Richard thought he might seek a girlfriend again, although he was at pains to say that he did not really need one:

> I prefer – I don't wanna say a typical bloke thing and say I just prefer a purely sexual relationship but without the, you know, relationship bit … – yeah sometimes it's good to have a girlfriend, but I'm not one of those people like who needs a girlfriend to like

feel, you know, wanted (laughs) or something ... But sometimes, when you haven't had a girlfriend for a while, you just sort of miss – I dunno – just a hug, you know what I mean, here and there, just that sort of little thing that you just don't get from a normal friend, you know what I mean. (Richard, 21, 2003)

Clearly these accounts of young people's relationships are filtered through discourses of appropriate masculinity and femininity. It may be that it is easier for Richard to express this 'bored' attitude towards relationships than to talk about feelings of rejection and loneliness. Yet Richard did seem to enjoy being single and doing his own thing, only having a relationship provided that it was not too serious and would not tie him down. He wanted equality and enjoyed some intimacy, but not the 'clingy' sort. He seemed to respond more to circumstances, rather than taking the initiative himself in starting a relationship. His main girlfriends so far have been found in situations that he has 'fallen into', and he continues with the relationship as long as it remains good and enjoyable. In some ways he is similar to Denise but lacks her self-motivation, and contrasts with Beth, who needs the security of a relationship and home life.

What is particularly interesting about these young people's accounts of their relationships is the way in which they do not simply conform to traditional gendered scripts in which 'women want love and men want what they can get' (Holland et al., 1998/2004). Although strongly gendered patterns continue to exist, making it difficult for young people to transgress gendered discourses of appropriately feminine and masculine behaviour, we found evidence that the three tendencies were neither simply gendered, nor necessarily circumscribed by sexual identity. We found uncommitted heterosexual women, and fused gay couples, as well as the stereotypical figures of the macho man (gay and straight) and the emotionally committed woman. How and why young people moved between tendencies could usually be explained by other aspects of their biography – the kinds of resources that they had to draw on, their investments in other fields and the opportunities that they could access.

Sexuality and young parenthood

Research into sexual relationships has questioned whether there has been movement from traditionally gendered to more detraditionalised attitudes and practices in heterosexual negotiation and activities. In earlier research we explored the sexual negotiation of young people during the 1990s, suggesting the existence of a kind of 'male in the head' that regulated young women's sexual expectations and behaviour, and undermined their own potential sexual agency (Holland et al., 1998/2004). Subsequent studies have tentatively pointed to changes, whereby women may be developing greater sexual confidence and assertiveness, and young men may be becoming more emotionally connected (Stewart, 1999; Allen, 2003). Sexuality was not an area that we pursued in detail in our interviews for this study. However, it was often an important aspect in their narratives, and has a role in their transition to adulthoods. By the fourth interview, 62 out of the 83 remaining participants (75%) had been or were sexually active.

Some young people spoke of their parents knowing they were sexually active, but not discussing this, while others had parents who accepted their children's sexual relationships. Some parents allowed the young couple to sleep together in their house, usually because they approved of the relationship or also saw this as a 'safer' way for their children to have sex. It was with their friends that young people talked most about sex, often in intimate detail. Young people of all classes have to rely on parental resources in many ways, and increasingly for financial support. In this context, Jones et al. (2005) explored parenting beliefs and practices in relation to young people and suggested a tension between the increasing autonomy of young people, who are forming partnerships while still remaining somewhat dependent, and the power of the parent in this situation. Hence, despite some democratisation of parent–child relationships, parents are still actively involved in, and can influence the partnership formation of their children.

We do not have a lot of information about the use or non-use of safe sex, apart from finding that any awareness and action was around preventing pregnancy rather than sexually transmitted infections. It was clear from the young people's accounts that there were many variations in timing and style of sexual relationships. Some had been quite carefully planned, while others had been more spontaneous and risky. Many of the young people believed that sex had a positive effect on their relationship, bringing them closer together, with young women in particular asserting that love and trust were prerequisites for sex (Sharpe and Thomson, 2005). Some who had lacked a secure relationship before having sex, or were pressured, found this a cause for regret, or saw their relationship break up. For some individuals, more young women than young men, losing their virginity was symbolically important and another step on the path to adulthood. Where sex resulted in a pregnancy the significance was more than symbolic. Some young women had experienced pregnancy scares, and this usually precipitated the use of safe sex. A few had become pregnant, mainly, but not all, unplanned.

At our last contact with the young people we knew of eight young mothers, and one father. This precipitated them into young parenthood, and as case studies in the previous chapter illustrate, the precise way that this plays out is affected by timing and the levels of material, social and emotional resources available to them. Being a young mother can be rewarding, but may also involve psychological stress, and material hardship. Parental support, especially from their own mothers, can be crucial (Elliott and Sharpe, 2003; McDermott and Graham, 2005). Lorraine was typical of the young parents in the study who came from disadvantaged areas (in her case the inner city site). She had moved out of home to live briefly with her boyfriend until she became pregnant at 19, at which point she then chose to return to live with her mother and siblings. In their study of the experiences of young people growing up in the poorest parts of Britain, MacDonald and Marsh (2005) challenge the notion of a young 'underclass' motivated by benefits to get pregnant, describing instead the 'sense' that early motherhood can make to those living in an environment shaped by experiences of poverty and lack of choice. This combines with the specific 'logic of sexual practice' operating in the local community (Thomson, 2000). In the more working-class communities young people tended to value parenthood, reject abortion, and were invested in the values and responsibilities of good motherhood (Turner, 2004). In our study Monique is an example of this. From our first meeting she imagined her future largely through parenthood (see Chapter 2). She became pregnant while at university and postponed finishing her degree for a few years. In the meantime she lived between her own flat (with the baby's father), and her mother's home. From Monique's perspective becoming a mother was as important a measure of 'success' as was gaining a degree and securing well-paid work. Despite the difficulties of managing these competing demands, she did not see them as being mutually exclusive.

Conclusion

In this chapter we have examined the style of, and approach to, relationships demonstrated by the young people in the Inventing Adulthoods study. Relationships no longer follow a linear trajectory on a continuum starting with being single, meeting someone significant, developing a relationship, getting engaged and finally getting married and having children. On the contrary, the biographical accounts of the young people in our study show them moving in both directions of the 'relationship continuum', although some are static either through choice or through their life circumstances. There are also some young people who have moved through several 'long-term' relationships, following a pattern of serial mono-gamy. In general, it appears that today, transitional points in life are no longer prescribed by age, living situation or financial circumstances, and relationships can be embarked on at any stage. We developed the tendencies – fusion, autonomy and uncommitted – in order to explore the qualitative differences characterising approaches to relationships. But while there can be different outcomes, it is apparent that young people might arrive at the same relationship stage for different reasons. Denise and Richard, for example, had different reasons for preferring singledom to coupledom: Denise did not want a relationship in case it complicated her life plans; Richard did not particularly look for a girlfriend in case she restricted his freedom and alienated him from his friends. It is the longitudinal nature of the study that enables us to map the paths of these young people's relationships over time.

Both young men and women expressed a fear of losing independence. Most young people appeared to aspire to an equal relationship and young women were no longer will-ing to give up power on entering a relationship. Despite the common assumption that great changes have taken place in the area of gender equality, especially for women, in reality, many of the 'old' inequalities still exist in both personal and more formal relationships. In common with other research findings (O'Donnell and Sharpe, 2000), some young men in the Inventing Adulthoods study expected women to fulfil more 'traditional' roles or to combine these with new ones, thus both perpetuating and remaking inequalities. While the fluidity of the tendencies we describe allows for movement in gender identities at differ-ent times, according to the strength of personal rather than material resources, and appears to express greater equality, the old gender inequalities may be reconfigured in new ways. Levels of personal agency and parental support are central resources in negotiating out-comes, and inequalities in the resources available in and for relationships can crucially affect young people's own resourcefulness.

Despite statistics demonstrating marriage and family breakdown, relationships were of great importance to these young people, who placed a high value on love and commitment whilst simultaneously seeking freedom and fulfillment for themselves as individuals, goals that would not always prove compatible. Those young people in relationships were greatly motivated by being loved, cared for, and having security, and this punctuated their biogra-phical accounts of themselves. Those expressing ambivalence did so mainly in relation to their short-term plans, and the majority envisaged a partnered future.

Young people's relationships are affected by the many other aspects of their lives described in earlier chapters, such as education and work, home life and well-being, mobility, and living in a culture of violence. They are also facilitated today by the technological revolution that has brought them instant social communication through Information and Communication Technologies (ICTs). Email and the internet can provide young people with access and privacy for social and sexual communication and to meet new people. Mobile phones can provide a medium for romance and a way to make or break relationships. It is the impact on sociality of this new ICT age that is discussed in the next chapter.

Chapter 12
Sociality

Introduction

In writing this book, we have struggled to find ways of doing justice to a rich data set that provides a unique window onto the ways that lives, identities and stories unfold over a 10-year period. Keen to avoid mirroring the dominant ways of viewing young people's lives in disparate, disconnected terms, we nonetheless found it impossible to avoid a topic-based approach to structuring this rich historical as well as biographical material. Inevitably, this involved breaking up powerful, holistic stories and, in so doing, sacrificing elements of a biographical and historical perspective to one geared to areas of policy concern (Part 2) and biographical salience (Part 3).

Time and history were, nonetheless, crucial dimensions of the study, not least since it documents the teenage and early adult years of a particular generation growing up at the turn of the 21st century. These young people have been living through interesting times and, in generational terms, may well have faced unprecedented uncertainties as to how to achieve status and recognition as adults, as well as new forms of opportunity. At the same time, they have also carried with them powerful continuities in terms of the material, emotional and cultural resources they have drawn and continue to draw on. One of the aims of the book has been to show how enduring elements of the transition from childhood to adulthood are mediated by historically specific cultural and material processes. In Part 2, we saw how the erosion of the youth labour market, removal of welfare benefits for 16 year olds, the introduction of student loans and tuition fees, urban regeneration policy, leisure markets and consumer marketing to young people are shaping school-to-work transitions, patterns of youthful drug taking, violence and well-being. Similarly, in Part 3, we have seen some of the ways that, despite the growing rhetoric of choice and opportunity, new forms of exclusion associated with mobility, belonging, home and intimacy can overlay and compound more traditional understandings of inequality.

Another aim of the book has been to explore differences in how young people navigated these common terrains and illustrate the unevenness of the impact of processes of individualisation (described in Chapter 2) on individual young lives. While the contradictory dimensions of disembedding, disenchantment and liberation (Beck, 1992) have been hallmarks of these historical processes, young people's responses depended in large part on: the particular situations they were located in; the historical and familial legacies that they carried with them; the resources they were able to draw on, such as material support from family and friends; and the kinds of social and cultural capital that made particular pathways 'make sense'.

As a means of beginning to pull the threads of the book together, we want now to turn our attention to that most basic and seemingly timeless 'glue' of everyday life – communication as a social practice. Our particular interest is to consider the impact on social practices of a historical process that is specific to this generation of young people – and nothing marks them out more clearly as different from those before them, than the 'digital revolution'. During a period that saw ICTs such as computers, the internet and mobile telephones become a part of everyday life, just what was the effect of these innovations on young lives? The impact on their health and moral well-being has been cause for considerable public concern. At the same time, ICTs are obviously very important to young people. Clearly a broad topic, we focus largely on certain aspects of the impact of mobile phones. And, continuing the theme of the remaking of inequalities, we also pay attention to differences in the significance and currency of the new technologies in young people's lives.

The digital revolution

When the Inventing Adulthoods study began in 1996, over 5 million people in the UK owned a mobile phone and while this figure rose to almost 7 million in 1997 (Crabtree et al., 2003), the youth market had yet to take off. By early 2005, the Mobile Data Association suggested that for the first time there were more mobile phones in Britain than people (60 million, up from 55 million in autumn 2004) (Thomson, 2005). Eight out of 10 adults owned mobiles, as did 90 percent of secondary school children, and as many as one in four under-10s. Household mobile phone ownership was highest in the South East (77%) and lowest in Northern Ireland (51%) (EFSFS, 2004). Internet access was also on the rise, in 1998, 9 percent (2.2 million) of UK households could access the internet from home. This rose to 55 percent (13.4 million) by the end of 2004 (ONS, 2004, 2006). An initial 'digital divide', involving lower access to the internet and other new technologies among low-income households, narrowed as the century turned.

We first began asking about ICT use in general in May–October 1999. Coincidentally, this turned out to encompass a transitional moment in the history of UK mobile phone culture. Ownership doubled between January 1999 and the end of 2000 (Stoble, 2000), leaping from nearly 15 million, to over 30 million. By November 2000, 54 percent of UK adults and 75 percent of 15–24 year olds owned their own mobile phone. This was followed by a 'text message explosion' in early 2002 and by the summer of 2003, 'six million text-crazy children' formed part of a British market involving over 50 million mobile phones (MDA, 2003). Ninety-six percent of 15–24 year olds owned a mobile by this stage, with many preferring to text rather than speak, feeling isolated/deprived if they were unable to use their mobile phones or access the internet, and regarding making and receiving calls as a sign of popularity.

Mobile phone ownership among young people in the study tended to reflect these trends. Very few young people had access to either mobile phones or the internet in 1999 but, two interview rounds later in 2001, ownership had increased significantly. Christmas

1999 and 2000 both saw particular surges in mobile phone ownership and SMS (short message service) 'texting' became an established part of the young people's everyday cultures at this point. Access to the internet at home also increased at this stage (often as a consequence of the cheap internet access provided by cable companies) but took much longer to become widespread.

At first, these developments appeared to have positive implications for the research process, providing the research team with a 'direct line' to the young people. However, the impermanence of contact details and the unreliability of new communication technologies became evident as young people swapped, lost or updated their mobiles, and land line numbers changed frequently with the proliferation of new phone networks. Ironically, keeping in touch and arranging interviews with young people was not always easy in this new technological age. Researcher fieldnotes describe 'long and laborious' hours of arranging meetings, of 'communicating via mobile phone, calling and sending numerous texts', of being 'stood up' at arranged venues and then phoning mobiles to discover them 'switched off' – an indicator of 'no intention to show'. However, dogged persistence often paid off:

> Kept calling but his moby went straight to voicemail, mum's number unobtainable and dad's always went to answerphone. Continued in this way until, at the beginning of October, I left messages on both his step-dad's old mobile number I dug up and his dad's voicemail. I received responses from them both within five minutes of one another! (Researcher Notes, 2003)

This rapid development of mobile phone culture was uneven, with notable variation according to locality. Ownership in the inner city and Northern Irish sites was proportionately higher in 1999 but, by 2000, mobiles were just as popular amongst the young people in the disadvantaged estate. By 2001, a majority of young people in these three sites owned a mobile phone. In contrast, things developed more slowly outside the city and 2001 still saw ownership at only half of young people in the more middle-class commuter belt town and the rural village (notably our more affluent research sites on the whole). By 2005, almost all of the young people in the study had mobile phones, most had email accounts and several had their own web pages. The digital generation had arrived.

Mobiles, emails and telephones: Doing sociality

Keeping in touch with friends, family and colleagues has grown in significance in an increasingly individualised late modern life, where a progressive freeing of individual agency from social structure demands that individuals must be active and creative in securing class and gender privileges (Bauman, 2000; Hey, 2005). In this context, commentators have viewed such activities as practices of 'sociality'. These involve the choice, rather than assignment, of social ties and networks that need to be 'established, maintained and constantly renewed by individuals' (Beck, 1992: 97). They also help to secure social capital, that is, resources based on connections and group membership (Bourdieu, 1986). However, as we set out in Chapter 1, different forms of social capital have different outcomes: bonding social capital ties young people into closed social networks, and bridging social capital enables them to move beyond existing networks, accessing new people and opportunities (Putnam, 1993, 2000). As earlier chapters have shown, negotiating tensions between these can rely, in part, on the different types of reputations that can arise in young people's relationships and networks. Reputations tend to form within localities, and can be positive, negative and most often contradictory. For example, coming from a 'hard family', or being a 'tough guy' or 'bad girl' may offer young people rewards in the short term in the form of respect and safety. In the longer term such reputations may become a burden, tying young people into places, patterns of behaviour and obligation that constrain their choices of who to be and how to act (see also Hey 2005; MacDonald and Marsh, 2005). Aspects of young people's reputations and social capital are beyond their control, attributed by others on the basis of wider community dynamics and popular discourses. Here we are interested in young people's ongoing active engagement in practices of 'sociality', particularly in exploring how the acquisition and use of ICTs provides a window into this work and the 'emergent accomplishments' that it secures (Bauman, 2000).

By virtue of their place in the life course and as part of the digital generation, the young people in our study were arguably in the vanguard of these changes and, as such, acutely aware of the need to realise opportunities for personal improvement and development (Catan et al., 1996). For them, keeping 'in touch' was part of a dynamic process of constructing a social identity as they grew up. On a day-to-day level, friendships and membership of social groups required varying degrees of emotional, social and even cultural labour. Of course, much of this work took place in school, the college cafeteria and the street, without any help from communication technologies. This was particularly the case for those living in physically bounded communities with friends in close proximity: hanging out on the street and 'popping round' was still the most common and cheapest method of keeping in touch outside school. In Northern Ireland, Ruth's description of organising a night out at the pub without the aid of mobile phones was equal in complexity to any involving a series of calls. She and her friends met 'in each other's houses really … one friend goes out gets another one and then another one'. Belinda from London's inner city had a mobile, and although its use was dictated by her financial situation this had little effect on her friendships as she explains here: 'When I've got money I ring up loads of people, but when I ain't, I just go round to their house or something.' However, the mobile phone also had an obvious and immediate impact. Luu pinpointed this when she described how, in the past, she would call her little sisters in from play by going out on the street and looking for them, 'which took ages … Whereas ringing them now and saying, "Oh it's time to come home, yeah", they'll come home, automatically come home.' (Luu, 18, 2002).

Early in the study, two key ways in which mobile telephones were embedded in local social practices became clear: as *commodities* within a material economy; and as a *medium* for the generation and exchange of social capital. As time and the technologies progressed, we began to see how these initial patterns changed and to understand the different ways in which the mobile phone operated: as a technology for managing social groups and networks when young people left school; for conducting their intimate relationships; and for parenting.

Fashions and fads: ICTs and material culture

Differences in the currency and meaning of mobile phones were stark in the early part of the study and these were linked to locality, class and, to a lesser extent, gender. In Northern Ireland and the deprived estate – both predominantly working-class landscapes with relatively high levels of social deprivation, unemployment and a discernible culture of violence, where youthful 'hanging around' on the streets and extended family networks were the norm – they were largely discussed in terms of material culture. At this time, the increased visibility and audible presence of telephones was forcing schools to create regulations about their appropriate use, and young people reported rules such as no phones in school, or the classroom. Just like other items of material worth, telephones became a target for intimidation and petty crime. It was usually young men who placed their phones conspicuously on the table in front of them during interviews, keeping half an eye on incoming messages during the course of the discussion. As a result of this, having the latest mobile also became important currency in the research relationship, for our male researcher here:

INT:	See you've got a phone as well?
Graham:	Yeah.
INT:	All you guys have got phones, amazing.
Graham:	Where's yours?
INT:	In there.
Graham:	Let me see it. Brian said you've got a wicked one. How much is that?
INT:	It's not that much different to the others.
Graham:	Wicked.
INT:	Do you use the phone a lot Graham?
Graham:	Yeah.
INT:	Who do you ring?
Graham:	Anyone, like with this one go on free phone number.
INT:	So all your calls to it are … who are you with?
Graham:	BT Cellnet.

(Graham, 15, 2000)

In the northern England estate, mobile phones were largely taken up as another 'label' in a context of conspicuous consumption where not wearing the 'right' type of sportswear, bag or coat was punishable by being 'called' – a form of public humiliation that involved acquiring a reputation for the particular transgression, for example, being poor, being sexually promiscuous. Thus phones constituted one more aspect of material one-upmanship that characterised both private and public young life. Changing phones was a frequent occurrence here and young men, in particular, displayed detailed knowledge of, and interest in the various deals available for financing the phones as well as the latest technological and design developments:

> When you go to the shop you just say, 'I don't want airtime on it' cause once the airtime runs out you've still got credit that just goes. If you've not got credit by the time your airtime runs out, you've got to think of it as back on line again … I'm changing this one on Saturday as well cause I want an Ericsson flip, that bit just flips down. (Alf, 15, 2000)

Whilst mobile phones were still predominantly viewed as a transitory fashion accessory among young people from more deprived communities in Northern Ireland, the currency of designer labels was less extreme in a landscape where consumer culture and a lively nightlife vied with sectarianism in the shaping of competitive peer social relations. Here, mobile phones were largely seen as being for 'rich kids'. Young men were more engaged in this process of social change: whilst Lucy reported that, 'They're really in at the minute' and Corinne apologised for not 'being up to date', young men were more likely to be proud owners. Patrick, for example, explained that, 'You wouldn't get phoning in school, you'd just bring them in for show, sit them on your belts or something.' Luke admitted that he bought his to show off to his friends:

> I seen the phone for 70 pounds, pay as you talk, and I went, 'That there's good', just for show like. I walked around and showed all my friends ... then we started going mad with them and then they ran out of ... and there's only two of us now that have phones. (Luke, 16, 1999)

As the study progressed, the ownership of mobile phones became normalised and their role of status symbol slipped out of young people's discussions. Even maintaining the 'advantage' of having an up-to-date telephone became more complex, as suggested by Luu's discussion of how she used her international family contacts to keep up to date:

> My Mum's friend goes to America and he sort of every month and he gets new stock from there and sort of sends it back, changes the chip, and then sells it. [...] Otherwise people can't keep up – people like me can't keep up with people changing their mobiles all the time, it's quite hard sometimes. (Luu, 18, 2002)

Phones as a medium for social capital

In the affluent, 'media rich' commuter belt, mobile phones arrived slightly later and meant something very different from the start. Here, moving into further education at 16 years was mediated by the parallel emergence of a pub culture and a lifestyle where 'mobility and flexible scheduling are central' (Gillard et al., 1996). Young people were more likely to have access to a computer and to email in their own or a friend's home. They were also far more self-conscious and anxious about making the right friends and contacts at school. This, combined with their greater economic and cultural capital, gave rise to a particular mobile phone culture involving the 'micro organisation' of social activities (Ling, 2000) and a 'bulimic' use of the telephone (Manceron, 1997: 80). Valerie Hey characterises the information-rich new middle class as having an 'offensive' form of sociality, taking an instrumental approach to networking and communication (Hey, 2005).

For these young people, dotted across a landscape of commuter villages, mobile phones, like the car before them, transcended the boundaries of geographical distance and facilitated the maintenance of social capital. Not having a mobile phone rapidly became a means of exclusion from the new forms of sociality it facilitated. However, there was a period when one phone among friends serviced a social network. While Richard did not have a mobile himself, many of his friends did:

> … enough people so that when people are out, there's at least one person in, give even space between words like, a group of four with a mobile, which is quite good so you can contact people. (Richard, 16, 1999)

Stan described the chain of phone calls that took place within his group of friends in relation to a trip to the pub:

> Normally what'll happen is if someone's going out we'll make one phone call and someone phones someone else and by the time you get down the pub, they'll all be waiting for you. (Stan, 17, 1999)

Leaving school and university: A critical moment in sociality

The transition from school to further/higher education or work represents a critical moment in the maintenance or transformation of young people's social networks. Other (less universal) critical moments occur when young people leave home for university, and when they leave university itself. Although some young people had phones while still at school during the research period, leaving school was a key moment for acquiring one. Ownership in all sites increased as young people became more independent and mobile and, as a result, it became more difficult for their families and friends to contact them.

Previous differences in the place and meaning of mobile phones in young people's lives continued at this time. In Northern Ireland and the disadvantaged northern England estate, friendship groups fragmented as the majority got jobs or went on to further education colleges. Una from Northern Ireland echoed other young people in these locations when she said of her school friends: 'I've lost all touch with them and they only live beside me.' Although they recognised that it was necessary to adopt positive strategies for keeping in touch by making an effort to phone, in practice this rarely happened:

> At the start and all we would be like, you know, trying to whatever, call for each other, go out at the weekends or whatever, but then I would be working and then when I'm off work she would be working. (Una, 17, 1999)

In the northern estate, Justin went to college and lost touch with many of his friends from school who did not. Some of them joined the army or moved away:

> The brunt of 'em live round Stokehill area and it's like a bit of a hike to go down so I've lost contact with a lot of 'em. (Justin, 17, 1999)

This break-up of old networks was rarely defined as traumatic. Indeed many of these young people welcomed the opportunity to make more mature or relevant friendships with the people they met at college or work. Una, for example, made a new group of friends at college and several of them had jobs in the same bar. Significantly they 'all got [ourselves] mobile phones so we send each other messages'. For her, friends had been shed and owning a mobile was a symbol of the process of transition to a new form of sociality and identity. However, there was a great sense of loss for others. Karin, for example, from Northern Ireland, was very sad when she was unable to keep a relationship alive with her best school friend Anna:

> I was sending 'Happy Halloween' messages to everyone. And I sent one to her and she phoned me and goes, 'Who's this? Oh it's Karin. Happy Halloween.' And she goes, 'Oh right, I didn't know it was you, cause I've taken your phone number off my phone.' And I cried that night. (Karin, 17, 2001)

Karin might have been happier in the leafy suburb of the commuter belt, where keeping in touch with friends from school was so important that Suzanne, for example, talked about a friend who found a job instead of going into the sixth form and now phoned her up 'every other night' in an attempt to maintain contact with his old friendship groups:

> You kinda get the feeling that he's quite insecure and scared of losing touch with everyone because, you know, we're sort of the only friends he's got cause he's you know working all the time so, if he loses contact with us then it's gonna be hard for him to meet people his age. (Suzanne, 17, 1999)

The currency of educational networks and of using ICTs to maintain them was so strong that Edward and his friends from middle school continued to keep in contact by phone and email and, in the days before 'Friends Reunited' became a popular website, planned to set up a website for everyone to keep in touch. This currency continued into and beyond the university years, as young people from the commuter belt site maintained contact with new friends as well as old friends attending universities elsewhere. Even if this was not acted upon, the ability to get in touch with old friends if necessary appeared to provide a sense of security for young people like Reuben stepping into the unknown environment of university and a new 'home':

> I think we will keep in touch, or at least try to, 'cos it's quite easy with email, etc. Um, a lot of my friends are computer literate as well, so it's not a difficulty to keep in touch by email. And they will all be taking their computers with them, most likely. Um, but yeah I mean I don't know whether they'll be coming back or not. (Reuben, 18, 2002)

ICTs were an important way of keeping in touch with family for several of the more middle-class young people as they left home and moved into university halls of residence. Paul's parents had set up a chat room 'so that we can meet at a certain time each day, or whenever'. Things were more complicated for Donal and his rather less media literate parents:

> I would talk to them by text so I text my sister as well but my mum hasn't worked out how to read texts yet so she phoned me up and says, 'Are you at the bus station?' I said 'No that was about three weeks ago.' (Donal, 26, 2002)

Sociality can be understood as reflecting class and cultural practices. Valerie Hey's distinction between the 'offensive' sociality of the privileged and the 'defensive' sociality of the disadvantaged can be discerned within the accounts of ICT use described above (Hey 2005: 868). Yet individual biographies suggest that it is also possible to see ICTs as being deployed actively as mechanisms in the construction of identities, often against the grain of existing tradition and local or family expectation. In the next section, we explore how the gendered boundaries between private and public domains are negotiated in the communicative practices made possible by mobile telephones.

Mediating the gendered boundaries between the public and the private

A computer can open a bedroom to the public and media can make the public sphere more private. (Reimer, 1995: 64).

Traditionally, the public/private divide has played a structural role in the mediation of youth and adult identities (Habermas, 1989; Fornas and Bolin, 1995). Adult status has been defined by entry into public institutions and roles – such as worker, marriage and political citizenship. With the extension and fragmentation of the different strands of the transition there is no longer a clear sense of movement from the private to the public in the process of becoming an adult (Jones and Bell, 2000). ICTs have had a role to play in this increasing uncoupling of physical and social spheres in providing a situation where you 'create your own private and public spheres'. Bedrooms can no longer be understood as the epitome of the private, being wired to global networks (Miller, 1992) and constructed as 'chill out zones' (Lincoln, 2000). Meanwhile, whilst young women may be moving out of the bedroom, technologies such as the internet and mixing decks have drawn young men back in (Henderson, 1997; MacNamee, 1998).

We found a number of instances where the mobile phone or the internet helped those who felt 'trapped' in private space to extend their social worlds. For example, Graham and Neville's physical impairments limited their ability to be 'out and about' but they were able to keep in touch with the world in ways that would not have previously been possible. In Yasmin's case, the mobile phone played a crucial role in enabling her to escape the heavy surveillance of the domestic sphere and, in so doing, to subvert the operation of a particular set of gendered power relations. Although considered 'private' in the adult world, this sphere offered her little privacy. As the only daughter of a British/Turkish family, she had suffered the protective surveillance of brother, father and mother and, when we first met her aged 16 years, was relatively restricted in her ability to socialise in comparison with her friends. Despite his previous role as guardian, it was her brother who gave her the mobile phone that transformed her social life by allowing her to talk privately with girlfriends and boyfriends, away from the watchful eyes of her parents. She received her own telephone calls from her newly acquired boyfriend: 'well because he can't ring my house that's one of the reasons why I've got to have one', and opted for a pay-as-you-go phone for obvious reasons: 'I don't get like the bills. No numbers or anything.'

ICTs as technologies of intimacy

Yasmin's case was just one of many examples of how ICTs secured some privacy in young people's intimate relationships and provided a space for forging a sexual identity. It was the internet for example that facilitated the 'coming out' process for young lesbians, gay men and bisexuals in the study. When he was 17, for example, Mal's first 'secret' boyfriend moved away from his neighbourhood, leaving him feeling isolated and depressed. Initially, he described retreating to his bedroom and avoiding phone calls from his local friends but in time this isolation eventually led him to look beyond the limits of his local community to the possibility of finding more meaningful friendships at a global level. He discovered a whole new set of relationships by going to an internet café and visiting online gay chat rooms. Ironically, Mal met someone in a chat room who happened to be sitting next to him in the internet cafe. They became friends and a short while later both came out on the gay scene in their city.

The relationship between cyberspace and offline social and sexual practices was described in detail by other young gay men. Donal, for example, became 'addicted' to the dating website 'Gaydar' after a long term relationship broke up:

> You meet anyone now, like the first question they ask you, 'What's your Gaydar profile?' [...] Like um 'cos you – on the Gaydar you have a – you get a profile and you put on your picture, and all your likes and dislikes, and what you're into and what you're not into, and your age, and that carry on you know. [...] Everyone's got them like, do you know what I mean, you have to have a Gaydar profile [laughs] and actually my friend just broke up with a boyfriend there, and he come round to my er place during the week, and um we set him up a Gaydar profile, you know, he didn't have one. And like it was so weird, [laughs] you know, it was like, 'Ooh this is what you do when you're single', like [laughs] go on Gaydar. (Donal, 28, 2004)

In reworking the boundaries between the public and the private, these social networking technologies created opportunities not only for new kinds of intimacy, but also for new kinds of transgression and risk. This first became obvious from young gay men's accounts. These constructed a form of erotic sociality that appeared to be a key 'gay skill' to be acquired in the process of 'coming out', one in which the sexualised and potentially dangerous nature of the contact intertwined. Newly single, Donal, for example, found in Gaydar a way of meeting others with complementary sexual preferences outside his locality, even flying to the USA to meet an online contact:

> People were going, 'Oh my God, you're gonna be chopped up and blah, blah, blah', and I was like, 'Hmm well maybe I want to be on the wanted person's list'. [laughs] No but er it was fine, you know, I knew – I chatted to him loads. I chatted to him a couple of months ago, and then I'd stopped chatting to him, and then I started to talk to him again. And then he'd phone me and I mean I knew I wasn't gonna go into, into anything dangerous, you know, I knew he wasn't going to and I mean I left all his contact details here and stuff, and I was phoning my friend and stuff when I got there. You know, so I was safe like, I wasn't, I knew I would be safe. I was too safe [laughs]. No it was grand like. It was grand, but it was just kinda sad, it was kinda, Ooh flying back, you know, it's just all like hmm, hmm. You know, 'cos we were both kinda lonely people. (Donal, 28, 2004)

If the internet was an important resource for forging gay sexualities and communities early on in the study, the mobile phone increasingly had a role to play in mediating a much wider range of intimate relationships. By the interview rounds in 2000 and 2001, mobile phones and 'texting' were an integral part of youth culture and of romantic and friendship cultures. Mal, for example, went on to 'meet' a boyfriend in another city via the internet and maintained this relationship by mobile phone. For young people not yet engaging in sexual relationships, the phone and text messaging offered a medium for flirting. At her first interview, Monique described 'chatting' as a central part of her social life and relationships, a practice with its own unwritten rules of engagement. Giving one's landline telephone number to a boy, for example, was a relatively serious gesture. For this to be given away by another could be seen as a betrayal.

> I ain't gonna give out somebody's phone number, if it ain't – if I don't even talk to them, to be giving it. She's giving out my phone number, even though it's Ryan's, I mean me and Ryan's tight. It ain't a big thing for Ryan to have my number, but I'd rather give it to him myself. (Monique, 17, 1999)

At her second interview Monique talked about the exchange of voice and text messages as a medium for making and breaking relationships. When asked in the interview if she was still seeing her boyfriend she demonstrated the breakdown of the relationship by phoning him there and then, 'watch if I don't phone him and he don't answer', 'he'll put me to voice mail'. He did. By her fourth interview Monique had become highly proficient at dating online:

Monique: Some boy just emailed me his picture. Yeah I can work with that, yes, yes. And there's another guy that I met on the internet the other day like, I was meant to meet him, but he's 21 – no is he 21? – I don't know how old this one is, I haven't bothered – I haven't spoken to this one on the phone yet.

INT: Is he an internet kind of friend, or someone you know anyway?

Monique: No all these people are just people that I've met off the internet.

INT: [laughs] Oh right.

Monique: Save – I'm going to save this picture. He won't tell me his name.

(Monique, 20, 2002)

Text messaging could also become an erotic practice in its own right and research on young people's use of text messaging in Finland confirms that the medium lends itself to the development of transgressive and explicit language (Kasesniemi and Rautiainen, 2000). At her second interview, Sandy read out a 'database' of saved X-rated text exchanges with her boyfriend. An initial flurry of erotic banter had been facilitated by the free messaging that formed part of their phone 'deals'. When this ended, she explained, 'we condensed our messages down a bit. So the occasional dirty text every now and again'.

There has been relentless media coverage of new forms of bullying that have grown up around the use of mobile telephones by young people, including the practice of 'happy slapping' where the humiliation of a physical attack is sealed by a photograph that is taken and then circulated by telephone. More mundanely Karin told us about how she was excluded from a friendship group as a result of a series of slanderous email messages and texts, that appeared to have come from her telephone and which had been sent to numbers in her own address book. In externalising the intimate in the form of a mobile phone address book or an email account, ICTs also pose the danger of losing control of the intimate and of the social invading the personal.

The telephone as a technology of parenting

In an exploration of the 'coining of new forms of social interaction' arising from the use of mobile telephones among Norwegian youth, Rich Ling observes that the telephone, like all symbolic relics is open to multiple interpretations. 'While some see it as a way to mark their departure from the home, others use it symbolically to integrate themselves further with their parents' (2000: 108). Moreover, parents themselves play an active role in inventing these new forms of interaction, 'trying to reassert their control'.

In our study, we found a number of examples of how the ownership of a mobile phone gave parents access to arenas of young people's lives that would formerly not have been available to them. Una provided a graphic example of how the mobile phone enables a transcendence of social and physical space, when she described her mother calling her at her new job as a podium dancer in a local bar. If she was late home, her mother phoned to find out if she was all right and she answered: 'but sure you knew I was all right because I answered the phone!' Safety was an enduring theme among young women. In the following extract Monica distinguishes between what she sees as 'practical' and more shallow reasons for having a phone by comparing herself with her sister:

> I only got it when I was 18. So I didn't – I haven't had it – I mean like everyone got theirs like when they were 16/17. I mean like even my younger sister who is 13, all her friends seem to have got one, but I don't see the need of having one then. The reason why I've got one now is 'cos obviously I need it when I'm driving, in case I break down. (Monica, 20, 2002)

Resistance to having a mobile phone could be related to anti-consumerism (as suggested by Monica's comments on 'need') but we also found a variety of ways in which mobile phones were implicated in strategies for resisting parental control.

One obvious advantage of taking responsibility for the cost of a mobile phone involved by-passing parental restrictions on the use of landlines. Landline bills were one of the focal points of conflict with parents reported in the study. Their itemisation was a parental tool not only for making young people accountable for the cost of their calls but also for scrutinising who they called. For example, Su's parents took the step of switching their landline contract to incoming calls only, while Heather reported her father's rule of '10 minutes per day, per person'. Ruth, meanwhile, was banned from using the family landline when the bill was inflated by the cost of her calls to friends' mobiles.

The role of the mobile phone in liberating young people from the hierarchy of the domestic sphere extended well beyond this area of parental control. It was, for example, useful in helping them to negotiate the complications of a reconstituted family, allowing them to bypass parental authority and gain control over contact and access. Market research has found that young people whose parents have split up were much more likely to own a mobile phone (Duff, 2000). At her second interview, Monique, for example, talked about her father making contact with her again after a period of estrangement linked to his reluctance to come to the house (as he and her mother were not on speaking terms). Her acquisition of a mobile was central to facilitating this contact. Once he had her mobile number, he would 'ring my phone, "Monique, I'm outside, come"'.

Accounts of liberating oneself from the new forms of parental surveillance that mobile phones facilitated were limited to young men. At 16, Luke explained that having a phone was 'a bit of a curse with my mother and father – they can always get you wherever you are'. By the next interview, Luke had got rid of his phone, explaining that 'people can get to you too easily'. Sixteen-year-old Paul had learned to screen his calls. He explained that his mother only phoned him on his mobile if he had done something wrong. So, when he saw she was calling him he simply turned his phone to voicemail, then listened to her message.

By the fourth round of interviewing (2002–03) we still found young men resisting the demand to be 'reached' by friends and family. Although middle-class Edward had a mobile phone he did not like people to think that they could rely on reaching him on it:

Edward: About this time last year, in fact almost exactly this time last year – the contract's just being renewed, it was a one-year contract – my father decided that I should have a mobile phone. And he got me one and I will admit that it is useful, but I don't like it.

INT: Right so do you use it?

Edward: Yes I do but people generally know that they can't rely on contacting me on it. They try my land line first, first of all because it's cheaper if I do answer [laughs], and secondly because I'm fairly unreliable about having my mobile switched on.

(Edward, 20, 2002)

Working-class young men such as Luke, Paul and others came to rely again on their phones when they made the transition from school to work. One strategy for resisting surveillance was to juggle different phones. Allan reported having loads of different phones for a range of different reasons – different people different numbers, different deals. Luke overcame his resistance to owning a mobile when he started working in the building trade. His phone became the key to his working life, a means of receiving information about jobs and for storing work-related contacts (his accumulated social capital). When we last spoke to him he was planning on giving the mobile and all the contacts stored on it to his brother when he travelled abroad.

The individual as the centre of communicative practice

In this chapter, we have dipped in and out of the lives of the emerging digital generation via our young people. Whilst they were initially able to drop the mobile phone from their social worlds and to employ alternative practices of sociability, we have seen how they gradually became more dependent on this personal technology over time. By the fourth round (2002–03), Amanda described herself as having 'an unhealthy obsession with text messaging'; Donal feared he was 'addicted to the internet'; and, Judy felt she would 'die without my mobile' having stored all her friends' contact details there and there alone.

As they emerged, ICT cultures were associated with particular forms of sociality, transitional moments and communities. The changes they facilitated were mediated by the particularities of localities and practices of sociality that were embedded in local cultures, shaped by class, geography and time. The specific conditions of these young people's lives led them to realise the potential of ICTs in particular ways: as a means of 'buying' forms of privacy and independence from parental control; accessing new social networks; and positioning themselves within social hierarchies. Viewing the use of ICTs in the context of particular projects of self, allows us to see how the mobile phone, messaging and the internet together facilitate a reworking of public and private boundaries, as the individual becomes the centre of a network of communicative practices, easily accessed and able to access others. For some young women, this offered a range of new possibilities to move beyond the confines of the domestic sphere. In different ways and for different reasons, Yasmin, Monique and Sandy all exploited the potential of their mobile telephones to claim greater personal and sexual freedom in a movement from the domestic to more public spheres. Similarly, Mal, Donal and others used the internet to expand their social worlds and forge a gay sexuality and identity. The sense of reassurance that parents gained from being able to contact their daughters out and about at work and play may also have enhanced this freedom. In sharp contrast, young men like Luke and Paul initially utilised their mobiles to protect themselves from the reciprocal responsibilities to their parents that were opened up by the technology, later realising their potential as a medium for storing and trading the information that is the key to the working life of a modern skilled manual worker. While the phone may provide one with the freedom to contact others it also makes others free to contact you, for some this may be experienced as a loss (Zadvorny and Bond, 2005).

Conclusion

The relationship between changing technologies and social practices is iterative. Individuals and families use ICTs in order to fulfil the demands of existing relationships and obligations. In that sense they are simply tools for existing practices. Yet in facilitating new forms of communication they also make new things possible, whether that is 'elastic parenting', 'happy slapping' or the shorthand logic of 'Gaydar profiling'. In focusing on this particularly dynamic aspect of the Inventing Adulthoods study we hope to have shown some of the ways that different temporalities intersect: the fast changes of ICT development and emergence of different forms of 'mobile manners' (Crabtree et al., 2003); how a particular generation progress through their teens and into their 20s and make these technologies their own; and slower historical changes that take place over generations that are described by the late modern theories of 'individualisation' and 'detraditionalisation'. Mobile technologies have been recognised as a means to contact young people and are being exploited by commercial companies and the public sector alike. Certainly, the lens of ICTs provides a way of seeing young people at the centre of networks of information, in which public and private boundaries are fluid and in which intimacy, eroticism and the potential for transgression abound.

Chapter 13

Conclusion: Looking to the future

Interview 1: Felt that she genuinely wanted to do the things she talked about and that she had a great deal of determination – but that she also didn't have the resources to draw on. Also, with ill-health and teen pregnancy hanging around her in the ether, that it was going to take a lot to pursue her dreams. Hoping she would, fearing she would not be able to.

Interview 2: Showing determination, hanging on in college and no signs of further pregnancies. The sense of agency that came across in the interview felt limited – by her poverty (underlies much of what she says and does, it feels), her health, her compliance with her boyfriend. I felt I was wrong and hoped so.

Interview 3: I'm seriously in awe of this determined young woman who seems to achieve against all the odds. Although she is not finding university exactly easy. Holds down two jobs and funds and runs her family home and cares for her ailing mother and siblings. It all feels so shaky but she just seems quietly determined to make it happen. Definitely got it wrong on the agency front – this girl is made of steel!

Interview 4: Interim contact had left me seriously concerned. Did not feel that there was sufficient support to see her through. However, she has, with the support of uni staff and her friends, turned things around, it seems, at the moment. She is more confident that she will complete this time around. I so hope she does and feel confident that if there is a way, she will – such is her fortitude. However, there are so many chaotic factors to consider and, although she is desperate to get away from the locality, she also clearly feels a strong sense of duty towards her family.

(Researcher Notes 1999–2005)

One of the challenges of studying young people over time is that it cautions us against 'explaining' how and why young people's lives shape up as they do. As we draw this book to a close we are very aware of the provisional nature of the analysis that we have offered. Although we can gain a good sense of the resources that young people can draw on and the opportunities that they have access to, we can never know exactly how the future will unfold. Their lives will change in ways that neither we, nor they, have anticipated, yet in ways that will no doubt make sense retrospectively. There have been many surprises for us in the study so far. For example, the undersized 12 year old living in the northern

England estate who told us he wanted to be a jockey, and who against our predictions did become a jockey. Anything is possible, yet some outcomes are more likely than others – and of the many boys in the study who had dreams of being professional footballers, only one succeeded.

We began this study by exploring the world of teenagers. As a result much of the material that we generated focused on schooling, friendship, relationships with siblings and parents. As time went on, we heard more about young people's worries about examinations, about choosing the right subject, the fraught transition from school to college and the growing significance of a social life and of romantic and intimate relationships. Increasingly we hear about the development of working identities, the desire for a home of their own, setting up home and experiences of parenthood. It may be that the most valuable material collected in this study has been accidental, such as the accounts of experiences such as bereavement, drug taking, mental health and ICT – issues that we did not seek, but which have emerged as part of a documentary approach. This data makes an important contribution to more specialist data sets, documenting some of the less spectacular and more ordinary experiences of young people, showing the very different ways in which these phenomena play out over the long term (Ribbens McCarthy, 2006).

In writing this book we have made some unexpected connections between lives as apparently different as those of Hazel (Chapter 5) and Khattab (Chapter 9), who both embrace tradition as a response to the experience of uncertainty. We have also found that different groups of young people appear to 'star' in different chapters. For example it was middle-class young men who appeared to be leading the 'story' in our chapter on chemical cultures and working-class young women who lead the story in our chapters on work and education. Both are involved in social class journeys, and grappling with associated biographical problems. The working-class young women seeking to negotiate between ties of belonging and social mobility, the middle-class young men investing in forms of masculinity that facilitate a reworking of 'success'.

We are often asked about the kind of impact that the study has had on the young people who have taken part. It is something that we regularly check out with the participants, and take seriously ourselves. Taking part in the project has meant different things to different young people at different points in time. Initially getting out of class at school was perhaps a good enough reason to take part and gave some a little bit of status and set them apart from their classmates. But over time, the interviews became an opportunity for some to reflect more on their lives and the direction they were travelling, with an interested but detached adult. Obviously, being part of a study that invites you to regularly reflect on your past and to predict your future will have an effect, what kind of effect is dependent on many other factors. Young people's decisions to stay in the study, to drop out (and sometimes to drop back in) are inevitably influenced by the way in which they experience this incitement to reflection (for a full discussion see Thomson and Holland, 2003). Here Cynthia, a young woman growing up in Northern Ireland, reflects eloquently on her involvement:

> *Cynthia*:   Aye, I thought it was like. I just thought it was something about children and to see how their lives was and how they were getting on in different things like that. You know and seeing if they were okay or if they were like taking drugs and things like that just to … like a kind of study on the youth of today.

INT: Yep. That's exactly what it was! [both laugh]. And do you think um …
             I mean your first impressions then were that you were happy enough to
             do that and take part in that.
Cynthia: Hmm. Aye, I thought it was like a cool idea.
INT: A cool idea right. And did that change over time as you kind of got more
             into it and …
Cynthia: No I think it's just (…) I think it's a really good thing to do because like, I
             mean like it is keeping a track of the people and like how they've changed.
             And as you've done their *Lifeline* like how ideas change and like how like
             maybe at the start, as you said like, I'd never smoke and then in years to
             come, are they smoking? Have they tried smoking and different things.
             And I think that's good and it shows like the troubles and different things
             that people today have you know. So it's showing like an outline in how
             we feel you know and not how people think we feel.
INT: Hmm right. And how do you feel being a part of it?
Cynthia: I'm glad to be a part of it you know because like it's (…) it's like as if
             somebody wants to hear about my life you know. It's like 'Hmm I'd be
             not boring as I thought I was' you know 'cos like. I mean like it's doing
             good you know. Like I mean if somebody wants to listen to me sitting and
             talking, you know? [laughs]
INT: Absolutely. And do you feel that it's had any affect on you at all? You
             know sort of like coming to talk about what's happening in your life or
             not?
Cynthia: I think it just gives me a wee break you know. Instead of talking to my
             friends and all about everything, it just gives you a wee break to talk tae
             just (…) not a stranger but just somebody that really doesnae necessarily
             know you on a day to day basis and things like. And I mean like kind of
             really isnae kind of judging you in a way. You know? That kind of way
             so I think it's really good, so it is.
INT: Right so it's kinda some value for you?
Cynthia: Hmm.
INT: Right. Has it influenced you in any way or had any impact on your life
             do you think?
Cynthia: I just think it's made me look at my life really. Just made me sit and go
             'Oh like okay' like, 'You're looking into my life – is my life like the way
             I want it to be?' and different things like that. Like I mean is it a good
             life? Just things like that you know. Just reflecting on my life to make it
             better for myself and seeing what I could've done differently and
             different things you know – that kind of way.
INT: Alright. And do you think you've reflected more on your life as a result
             of being part of this project or do you think you would've done that
             anyway?
Cynthia: I think I've done it more you know because like (…) 'cos like you're talk-
             ing back on what's happened and everything and I mean like you're look-
             ing over it and you're thinking about it and I think it's (…) it helps you
             deal with it in a way because like if I wasn't sitting here talking away,
             maybe I'd put it back at the back of my mind and try not to think about

it and it could like affect me in the long term whereas like I'm sitting here talking about it and different things so it makes (…) it brings it to a head and makes you think about it anyway and it's like 'Oh it's over now, it doesn't matter' and it makes you feel better, so it does, 'cos like you are talking about it instead of just kind of hiding it away.

INT: Right. Well, that's good. I like the idea that you kind of get that out of it as well.

We have no immediate plans to interview the young people in the Inventing Adulthoods study again, but we are working out ways in which this huge and rich data set can be shared with others who are interested in such a unique document. In writing this book at this moment we have attempted to capture some of the ways that we have made sense of this material, in a form that is useful to those working with young people or interested in developing policies and practices to enhance young people's lives. There are other ways in which we plan to further realise the potential of this data set for more specialist audiences. As with all of the writing that we do from the Inventing Adulthoods project, an overriding and enduring concern is that we do justice to the contribution that the participants made to this endeavour, and that we represent them in ways that are just and respectful. This desire can sit uneasily with the demand to speak to different policy agendas, and to focus on problems as well as possibility. From this perspective it is possible to rethink life experiences that are currently framed in terms of social exclusion, as the consequences of young people's labours to be socially included and recognised as competent adults. This is a perspective that is urgently needed in a policy and practice environment driven by the desire to find effective and replicable interventions that will change a range of what are increasingly seen as 'antisocial behaviours': teenage parenthood, dropping out of education, and involvement in criminal and drug sub-cultures. Our approach seeks to avoid problematising young people, 'recognising' the social actors at the centre of these policy problems by making sense of their choices through an understanding of their investments. More importantly, it provides a way of seeing the totality of young lives (including the limited character of their 'choices', and the critical role of timing in their biographies), in a way that generates insights that could inform practice with young people.

Appendix 1: Methods

Inventing Adulthoods: A study of young lives in England and Northern Ireland 1996–2006

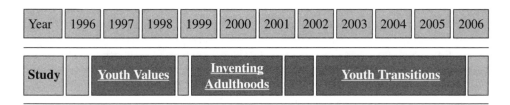

Year	1996	1997	1998	1999	2000	2001	2002	2003	2004	2005	2006
Study		Youth Values		Inventing Adulthoods				Youth Transitions			

Inventing Adulthoods is a qualitative longitudinal study of young people growing up in England and Northern Ireland at the turn of the 21st century. It provides a unique window on most aspects of growing up during an important period of social change in the decade 1996–2006. The project combines three consecutive studies funded by the Economic and Social Research Council through three different programmes (*Children 5–16: Growing up in the 21st century*; *Youth Citizenship and Social Change*; and the *Families & Social Capital ESRC Research Group* http://www.lsbu.ac.uk/families respectively) and based at London South Bank University: *Youth Values* (L129251020); *Inventing Adulthoods* (L134251008); and *Youth Transitions* (M570255001). An in-depth account of the study is available at http://www.lsbu.ac.uk/inventingadulthoods. The dataset is also in the process of being prepared and archived for use. The study took a participatory approach, involving young people in the development of innovative research methods. It also involved the considerable achievement of maintaining a core research team of five (the authors of this book) throughout the research period.

Youth Values (September 1996–February 1999) explored sources of moral authority among young people; how young people understand the processes of their own moral development and how this contributes to adult identity; how they respond to moral diversity and perceive generational changes in values; and how their values relate to expectations and experiences of social inclusion/exclusion. A questionnaire was completed by 1800 young people aged 11–17 years from eight schools and specialist services in five UK research sites. Three hundred and fifty-six of these young people took part in focus groups and 57 were interviewed individually; 272 also completed Research Assignments that involved interviewing an adult about life when they were the same age as the young interviewer.

Inventing Adulthoods (April 1999–October 2001) built on the sample and methods of the previous study and explored young people's stories of growing up; the impact on their life trajectories of local differences in the material, social and cultural resources available to them and of broader social processes of individualisation and globalisation; and the role of 'critical moments' in the construction of adulthood and in processes of social inclusion and exclusion. Aged 14–23 at the outset of this study, young people from the previous study were interviewed three times during this period (initially 121, 98 at the next round and 83 at the next). They also kept memory books and completed lifelines (in which they predicted their future situations – in terms of home/housing, education, work, relationships, travel and values – in 3 years' time, at 25 and at 35). Four focus groups (two in London and two in Northern Ireland) brought a few young people together from different research sites towards the end of the study.

Youth Transitions (July 2002–June 2006) built on the sample and methods of the two previous studies, incorporating a focus on the relationship between family and social change, the types of social capital deployed by the young people, and their experiences of education, employment and intimate life, related to age, social class, family form, gender, ethnicity and religious affiliation. Aged 17–26 at the outset of this study, young people from the previous study were interviewed twice more during this period ($N = 70$ and 64 respectively).

The following table shows the age range of the sample at each of three stages of the study, and the sample size for each method.

Table 1   Sample: age and numbers

Inventing Adulthoods	Age	Questionnaire	Focus group	Interview	Lifeline	Memory book	Research Assignment
Youth Values 1996–99	11–17	1800	356 62 grps	Int. 1 57			272
Inventing Adulthoods 1999–2001	14–23			Int. 2 121	104	49	
				Int. 3 98			
				Int. 4 83	Revisited at this round		
			4 groups				
Youth Transitions 2002–06	17–28			Int. 5 70			
				Int. 6 64			

The following table shows how the sample changed over time according to gender, ethnicity, class and locality.

Table 2 Sample: gender, ethnicity, class and locality

Inventing Adulthoods	Total sample	Age	M	F	Ethnicity	Working class	Middle class	NI	Disadvantaged estate	Inner city	Leafy suburb	Rural area	Extra Grps
Youth Values 1996–1999	Int. 1 54	11–17	25	32	4[1]	44	13	22	8	7	9	6	7
Inventing Adulthoods 1999–2001	Int. 2 121	14–23	58	63	19[2]	85	36	42*	21	14	20	18	6
	Int. 3 98	14–24	40	58	12[3]	66	32	34	17	12	19	15	1
	Int. 4 83	15–25	38	45	11[4]	53	30	28	11	12	18	14	–
Youth Transitions 2002–2006	Int. 5 70	17–26	28	42	9[5]	43	27	27	5	9	17	11	1
	Int. 6 64	19–28	26	38	9[6]	39	25	27	7	8	14	8	–

Notes:

*After *Youth Values* those recruited outside the schools in NI (extra group people) are included in the overall NI figures. This includes three at interview 5 and two at interview 4; three at interview 2 and 3; two at interview 4; three at interview 5 and two at interview 6.

[1] 1 African Caribbean, 1 Vietnamese, 1 Mixed Race, 1 Black British

[2] 3 African Caribbean, 3 Vietnamese, 2 Mixed Race, 2 Black British, 1 African, 6 South Asian, 1 Southern European, 1 Mauritian

[3] 2 African Caribbean, 3 Vietnamese, 2 Mixed Race, 1 Black British, 1 African, 2 South Asian, 1 Southern European

[4] 2 African Caribbean, 3 Vietnamese, 2 Mixed Race, 1 African, 2 South Asian, 1 Southern European

[5] 2 African Caribbean, 3 Vietnamese, 1 Mixed Race, 1 African, 2 South Asian

[6] 2 African Caribbean, 3 Vietnamese, 1 Mixed Race, 1 African, 2 South Asian

Bibliography

6, P., Jupp, B., Parry, H. and Lasky, K. (1997) *The substance of youth: the place of drugs in young people's lives today*, London: Joseph Rowntree Foundation.

Adkins, L. (2002) *Revisions: gender and sexuality in late modernity*, Buckingham: Open University Press.

Adkins, L. (2005a) 'Social capital: the anatomy of a troubled concept', *Feminist Theory*, 2 (2): 195–211.

Adkins, L. (2005b) 'The new economy property and personhood', *Theory, Culture & Society*, 22 (1): 111–30.

Aldridge, J., Parker, H. and Measham, F. (1999) *Drug trying and drug use across adolescence. A longitudinal study of young people's drug taking in two regions of Northern England*, Home Office, Paper 1, London: Home Office.

Alexander, C. (2000) *The Asian gang*, Oxford: Berg.

Allen, L. (2003) 'Girls want sex, boys want love: resisting dominant discourses of (hetero)sexuality', *Sexualities*, 6 (2): 215–36.

Anderson, C. (1999) *Codes of the streets: decency, violence, and the moral life of the inner city*, New York: W.W. Norton.

Ashton, D. and Field, D. (1976) *Young workers*, London: Hutchinson.

Ashton, M. (1998) *Between two stools: children in trouble with drugs*, Drugs Forum Focus: Spring, London: Local Government Drugs Forum.

AUCC Advisory Service to Institutions (1998) *Guidelines for university and college counselling services*, Rugby: BACP.

Ball, S. (2003) *Class strategies and the education market: the middle class and social advantage*, London: RoutledgeFalmer.

Ball, S.J., Maguire, M. and Macrae, S. (2000) *Choice, pathways and transitions post-16: new youth, new economies in the global city*, London and New York: RoutledgeFalmer.

Bauman, Z. (1992) *Intimations of postmodernity*, London: Routledge.

Bauman, Z. (1996) 'From pilgrim to tourist – or a short history of identity' in S. Hall and P. du Gay, *Questions of cultural identity*, pp. 18–36, London: Sage.

Bauman, Z. (1999) *The multicultural riddle: rethinking national, ethnic, and religious identities*, London: Routledge.

Bauman, Z. (2000) *The individualised society*, Cambridge: Polity.

Bauman, Z. (2003) *Liquid love*, Cambridge: Polity.

Bawin-Legros, B. (2004) 'Intimacy and the new sentimental order', *Current Sociology*, 52 (2): 241–50.

BBC Radio 4 (2005) 'Don't call me Asian', 11 January.

Bech, H. (1997) *When men meet: homosexuality and modernity*, Oxford: Polity.

Beck, U. (1992) *Risk society: towards a new modernity*, London: Sage.

Beck, U. and Beck-Gernsheim, E. (1995) *The normal chaos of love*, Cambridge: Polity.

Bell, C. (1968) *Middle class families*, London: Routledge and Kegan Paul.

Bellah, R. (1966) 'Civil religion in America', *Daedalus, Journal of the American Academy of Arts and Sciences*, 95: 1–21.

Bertaux, D. and Thompson, P. (eds) (1997) *Pathways to social class: a qualitative approach to social mobility*, Oxford: Clarendon Press.

Beynon, J. (2002) *Masculinities and culture*, Buckingham: Open University Press.

Bird, L. and Faulkner, A. (2000) *Suicide and self-harm*, London: The Mental Health Foundation.

Bjerrum Nielsen, H. and Rudberg, M. (1994) *Psychological gender and modernity*, Oslo: Scandinavian University Press.

Blackman, S. (2005) *Chilling out: the cultural politics of substance consumption, youth and drug policy*, Maidenhead: Open University Press.

Blackwell, L. and Bynner, J. (2002) *Learning, family formation and dissolution*, DfES Research Brief RCB08, London: DfEs Centre for Research on the Benefits of Learning.

Blanden, J. and Machin, S. (2004) 'Educational inequality and the expansion of UK Higher Education', *Scottish Journal of Political Economy*, 51: 230–49.

Blanden, J., Gregg, P., and Machin, S. (2005) *Intergenerational mobility in Europe and North America: a report submitted by the Sutton Trust*, London: London School of Economics.

Bolton, A., Pole, C. and Mizen, P. (2001) 'Picture this: researching child workers', *Sociology*, 35 (2): 501–18.

Bourdieu, P. (1977) *Outline of a theory of practice*, Cambridge: Cambridge University Press.

Bourdieu, P. (1986) 'The forms of capital', in J.E. Richardson (ed.), *Handbook of theory of research for the sociology of education*, pp. 241–58. New York: Greenwood Press.

Bourdieu, P. and Wacquant, L. (1992) *An invitation to reflexive sociology*, Cambridge: Polity.

Bradley, H. and Hickman, P. (2004) 'In and out of work? The changing fortunes of young people in contemporary labour markets', in J. Roche, S. Tucker, R. Thomson and R. Flynn (eds), *Youth in society*, pp. 120–30. London: Sage.

Brannen, J. and Nilsen, A. (2002) 'Young people's time perspectives: from youth to adulthood', *Sociology*, 36 (3): 513–37.

Brannen, J., Moss, P. and Mooney, A. (2003) *Working and caring over the twentieth century: change and continuity in four-generation families*, Basingstoke: Palgrave.

Brierley, P. (2000) *The tide is running out*, London: Christian Research.

Briggs, S. (2002) *Working with adolescents: a contemporary psychodynamic approach*, New York: Palgrave Macmillan.

Brown, S. (2002) *Understanding youth and crime: listening to youth?* Buckingham: Open University Press.

Bruce, S. (1996) *Religion in the modern world: from cathedrals to cults*, Oxford: Oxford University Press.

Bunting, M. (2004) 'Our teenage canaries', *The Guardian*, 13 September, p. 17.

Bynner, J. (2001) 'British youth transitions in comparative perspective', *Journal of Youth Studies*, 4 (1): 5–23.

Bynner, J. and Pan, H. (2002) 'Changes in pathways to employment and adult life', in J. Bynner, P. Elias, A. McKnight, H. Pan and G. Pierre (eds), *Young people's changing routes to independence*, pp. 13–26. York: Joseph Rowntree Foundation/York Publishing Services.

Bynner, J., Elias, P., McKnight, A., Pan, H. and Pierre, G. (2002) *Changing pathways to employment and independence*, York: YPS for the Joseph Rowntree Foundation.

Calcutt, A. (1998) *Arrested development: pop culture and the erosion of adulthood*, London: Cassell.

Callender, C. and Jackson, J. (2004) *Fear of debt and higher education participation*, Families and Social Capital ESRC Research Group. Working Paper No. 9, London: London South Bank University.

Callender, C. and Kemp, M. (2000) *Changing student finances: income expenditure and the take up of student loans among full and part time higher education students in 1998/9*, DfEE Research Report 213, Nottingham: DfEE.

Callender, C. and Wilkinson, D. (2003) *2002/03 Student income and expenditure survey*, Research Report 487, Nottingham: DfES.

Casanova, J. (1994) *Public religions in the modern world*, Chicago: University of Chicago Press.

Castells, M. (1996) *The rise of the network society*, Oxford: Blackwell.

Castells, M. (2000) 'The institutions of the new economy', address to the Delivering the Virtual Promise? Conference, London, June, available: http://virtualsociety.sbs.ox.ac.uk/text/events/castells.htm, (accessed October 2005).

Catan, L. (2004) *Becoming adult: changing youth transitions in the 21st century. A synthesis of findings from the ESRC research programme, Youth, Citizenship and Social Change 1998–2003*, Brighton: Trust for the Study of Adolesence.

Catan, L., Dennison, C. and Coleman, J. (1996) *Getting through: effective communication in the teenage years*, Brighton: BT Forum/Trust for the Study of Adolescence.

Census (2001) National Statistics, available: www.statistics.gov.uk/census/ (accessed December 2005).

Chamberlayne, P., Bornat, J. and Apitizsch, U. (eds) (2004) *Biographical methods and professional practice: an international perspective*, Bristol: Policy Press.

Chitty, C. (2004) *Education policy in Britain*, Houndsmill: Palgrave.

Cohen, P. and Ainley, P. (2000) 'In the country of the blind? Youth studies and cultural studies in Britain', *Journal of Youth Studies*, 3 (1): 79–95.

Cohen, S. (1972) *Folk devils and moral panics: the creation of Mods and Rockers,* London: MacGibbon and Kee.

Coleman, J. and Schofield, J. (2005) *Key data on adolescence* (5th edn), Brighton: Trust for the Study of Adolescence.

Coles, B. (1995) *Youth and social policy: youth citizenship and young careers*, London: UCL Press.

Coles, B. (2000) *Joined up youth research, policy and practice: an agenda for change?* Leicester: Youth Work Press.

Collier, R. (1998) *Masculinities, crime and criminology*, London: Sage.

Collin, M. (1997) *Altered state: the story of ecstasy culture and acid house*, London: Serpent's Tail.

Countryside Agency (2003) *The state of the countryside 2020*, West Yorkshire: Countryside Agency Publications.

Crabtree, J., Nathan, M. and Roberts, S. (2003) *MobileUK: Mobile Phones & Everyday Life*, available: http://www.theworkfoundation.com/research/isociety/MobileUK_main.jsp (The Work Foundation – Society; accessed 15 March 2006).

Crozier, M. (2001) Y*oung men and violence: from theory to practice,* Young Men and Violence Project, Belfast: Youth Action Northern Ireland.

Davie, G. (1990) 'Believing without belonging: is this the future of religion in Britain?' *Social Compass*, 37 (4): 455–69.

Denzin, N.K. (1989) *Interpretative biography*, Qualitative research methods series, No. 17, London: Sage.

Department of Social Development Northern Ireland (2005) *Northern Ireland housing statistics 2004–2005*, A National Statistics Publication, available: http://www.dsdni.gov.uk (accessed 10 October 2005).

Devine, F. and Savage, M. (2000) 'Conclusion: renewing class analysis', in R. Crompton, F. Devine, M. Savage and J. Scott (eds), *Renewing class analysis*, pp. 184–99. Oxford: Blackwell.

Devine, F., Britton, N., Halfpenny, P. and Mellor, R. (2003) 'Family and community ties in space and time' in G. Allan and G. Jones (eds), *Social relations and the lifecourse*, pp. 172–86, Basingstoke: Palgrave.

(DfES) (Department for Education and Skills) (2003) *The future of higher education*, Cmnd 5735, London: HMSO.

Dodd, T., Nicholas, S., Povey, D. and Walker, A. (2004) *Crime in England and Wales*, London: Home Office.

DOH (Department of Health), DfES (Department for Education and Skills) (2004) *National service framework for children young people and maternity services: the mental health and psychological well-being of children and young people: standard 9*, London: HMSO.

Drugscope (2000a) *Vulnerable young people and drugs: opportunities to tackle inequalities*, London: Drugscope.

Drugscope (2000b) *Homelessness and drugs: managing incidents,* London: Drugscope.

Du Bois-Reymond, M. (1998) '"I don't want to commit myself yet": young people's life concepts', *Journal of Youth Studies,* 1 (1): 63–79.

Du Bois-Reymond, M. and Lopez Blasco, A. (2003) 'Yo-yo transitions and misleading trajectories: towards integrated transition policies for young adults in Europe', in A. Lopez Blasco, W. McNeish and A. Walther, *Young people and contradictions of inclusion: towards integrated transition policies in Europe,* pp. 19–41. Bristol: Policy Press.

Duff, R. (2000) 'Teens and new technology – Latest data on mobile phones', *Insights,* available: http://www.childwise.co.uk (accessed 11 May 2006).

Dwyer, P. and Wyn, J. (2003) *Youth, education and risk: facing the future,* London: Routledge.

EC (European Commission) (2001) *A new impetus for European youth,* White Paper, available: http://www.europa.int/comm/dgs/education/youth (accessed March 2006).

Edwards, R., Franklin, J. and Holland, J. (2003) *Families and social capital: exploring the issues,* Families and Social Capital ESRC Research Group. Working Paper No. 1, London: London South Bank University.

EFSFS (Expenditure and Food Survey, Family Spending) (2004) 'Consumer durables' report, available: http://www.statistics.gov.uk/cci/nugget.asp?id=868 (accessed January 2006).

Egerton, M. and Halsey, A.H. (1993) 'Trends in social class and gender in access to higher education in Britain', *Oxford Review of Education,* 19: 183–96.

Elliot, H. and Sharpe, S. (2003) *'Sometimes you feel your life just stops': a report of the findings from research about young mothers and their therapeutic needs,* London: The Maya Centre.

Erikson, E. (1968) *Identity, youth and crisis,* New York: W.W. Norton.

Evans, J., Rich, E. and Holroyd, R. (2004) 'Disordered eating and disordered schooling: what schools do to middle class girls', *British Journal of Sociology of Education,* 25 (2): 123–42.

Everitt, P. (1986) *'You'll never be 16 again.' An illustrated history of the teenager,* London: BBC Publications.

Fahmy, E. (2003) 'Disconnected generation? Encouraging young people's political participation in the UK', *Youth and Policy,* 81, Autumn: 1–20.

Fawcett, L. (2000) *Religion, ethnicity and social change,* Basingstoke: Macmillan.

Fenton, S., Bradley, H., West, J., Guy, W., and Devadason, R. (2002) *Winners and losers in changing labour markets,* Report to ESRC, Swindon: Economic and Social Research Council.

Flood-Page, C., Campbell, S., Harrington, V. and Miller, J. (2000) *Youth crime: findings from the 1998/99 youth lifestyles survey,* London: Home Office Research, Development and Statistics Directorate, Crime and Criminal Justice Unit.

Fornas, J. and Bolin, G. (eds) (1995) *Youth culture and late modernity,* London: Sage.

Franklin, J. and Thomson, R. (2005) '(Re)claiming the social: a conversation between feminist, late modern and social capital theories', *Feminist Theory,* 6 (2): 161–72.

Fukuyama, F. (1995) *Trust: the social virtues and the creation of prosperity,* New York: Free Press.

Furlong, A., and Cartmel, F. (1997) *Young people and social change: individualization and risk in late modernity,* Buckingham: Open University Press.

Furlong, A. and Spearman, M. (1989) 'Psychological well-being and the transition from school', *British Journal of Education and Work,* 3 (1) pp. 49–55.

Furr, S.R., Westfield, J.S., McConnell, G.N. and Jenkins, J.M. (2001) 'Suicide and depression among college students: a decade later', *Professional Psychology: Research and Practice,* 32 (1): 97–100.

Galindo-Rueda, F., Marcenaro-Gutierrez, O. and Vignoles, A. (2004) *The widening socio-economic gap in UK higher education,* London: Centre for the Economics of Education, LSE.

Garratt, S. (1998) *Adventures in wonderland: a decade of club culture,* London: Headline.

Gauthier, M. (2003) 'The inadequacy of concepts: the rise of youth interest in civic participation in Quebec', *Journal of Youth Studies,* 6 (3): 265–76.

Giddens, A. (1991) *Modernity and self identity: self and society in the late modern age,* Cambridge: Polity.

Giddens, A. (1992) *The transformation of intimacy: sexuality, love and eroticism in modern societies*, Cambridge: Polity.

Gillard, P., Bow, A. and Wale, K. (1996) *Ladies and gentlemen, boys and girls: gender and telecommunications services*, Melbourne: Telecommunications Needs Service.

Gillies, V. (2005) 'Raising the 'meritocracy': parenting and the individualization of social class', *Sociology*, 39 (5): 835–54.

Gillies, V., Ribbens McCarthy, J., and Holland, J. (2001) *Pulling together, pulling apart: the family lives of young people*, London: Families Policy Studies Centre/Joseph Rowntree Foundation.

Glucksmann, M. (2003) 'Shifting boundaries and interconnections: extending the "Total Social Organisation of Labour", paper presented at The New Sociology of Work Workshop, Policy Studies Institute, 4 Sept.

Goddard, C. (2004) *Media image of young people*, MORI in Young People Now, available: http://www.mori.com/polls/2004/young-people-now.shtml (accessed May 2006).

Goldthorpe, J., Lockwood, D., Bechofer, F. and Platt, J. (1969) *The affluent worker in the class structure*, Cambridge: Cambridge University Press.

Goodwin, J. and O'Connor, H. (2005) 'Exploring complex transitions: looking back at the 'golden age' of school to work', *Sociology*, 39 (2): 197–200.

Gordon, T. and Lahelma, E. (2004) 'Who wants to be a woman? Young women's reflections on their transition to adulthood', *Feminist Review*, 78: 80–88.

Grant, A. (2002). 'Identifying and responding to students' concerns: a whole institutional approach', in N. Stanley and J. Manthorpe (eds), *Students' mental health needs: problems and responses*, pp. 83–105. London: Jessica Kingsley.

Griffin, C. (1985) *Typical girls: young women from school to the job market*, London: Routledge and Kegan Paul.

Griffin, C. (1993). *Representations of youth: the study of youth and adolescence in Britain and America*, Cambridge: Polity.

Grundy, S. and Jamieson, L. (2004) 'Action, reaction, inaction? Young adults' citizenship in Britain', *Sociologia – Slovak Sociological Review*, 36 (3): 237–52.

Gunnell, D., Lopatatzidis, A., Dorling, D. Wehner, H. Southall, H. and Frankel, S. (1999) 'Suicide and unemployment in young people: analysis of trends in England and Wales, 1921–1995', *The British Journal of Psychiatry*, 175: 263–70.

Habermas, J. (1989) *The structural transformation of the public sphere: an enquiry into a category of bourgeois society*, trans. Thomas Burger, Cambridge: Polity.

Hall, S., Critcher, C., Jefferson, T., Clarke, J., and Roberts, B. (1978) *Policing the crisis: mugging, the state and law and order*, London: Macmillan.

Halsey, A.H., Heath, A.F., and Ridge, J.M. (1980) *Origins and destinations: family, class and education in Modern Britain*, London: Clarendon Press.

Hannerz, U. (1996) *Transnational connections: cultures, people, places*, London: Routledge.

Hardt, Michael (1999) 'Affective labour', *Boundary*, 26 (2): 89–100.

Harris, C., Roach, P., and Thiara, R. (2003) *Emergent citizens? African-Caribbean and Pakistani young people in Birmingham and Bradford: research briefing*, available: http://www.tsa.com (accessed July 2003).

Harrison, L. and Harrington, R. (2001) 'Adolescents' bereavement experiences: prevalence, association with depressive symptoms and use of services', *Journal of Adolescence*, 24 (2): 159–69.

Harrison, M. (1998) *High society: real voices of club culture*, London: Piatkus.

Hawton, K., Houston, K. and Shepperd, R. (1999). 'Suicide in young people: a study of 174 cases, aged under 25 years, based on coroners' and medical records', *The British Journal of Psychiatry*, 175: 271–76.

Hawton, K., Rodham, K., Evans, E. and Weatherall, R. (2002) 'Deliberate self-harm in adolescents: self report survey in schools in England', *BMJ*, 325: 1207–11.

Hawton, K., Simkin, S., Fagg, J. and Hawkins, M. (1995) 'Suicide in Oxford University students, 1976–1990'. *British Journal of Psychiatry*, 166 (1): 44–50.

HDA (Health Development Agency) (2001) *Boys' and young men's health: literature and practice review: an interim report*, London: Health Development Agency.

Heath, S. and Cleaver, E. (2003) *Young, free and single? Twenty somethings and household change*, Basingstoke: Palgrave Macmillan.

Hebdige, D. (1979) *Subculture and the meaning of style*, London: Methuen.

Heir, S.P. (2003) 'Risk and panic in late modernity: implications of the converging sites of social anxiety', *British Journal of Sociology*, 54 (1): 3–20.

Henderson, S. (1997) *Ecstasy: case unsolved*, London, Pandora.

Henderson, S. (2001) *'Protection' and 'It's a Fine Line': An evaluation of two multi-component interventions targeting drug use and sexual health in the context of nightlife in Merseyside and Ibiza*, Liverpool: HIT.

Henderson, S. (2005) 'Sticks and smoke: Growing up with a sense of the city in the countryside', *Young: Nordic Journal of Youth Research*, 13 (4): 363–79.

Henderson, S., Taylor, R., and Thomson, R. (2002) 'In touch: young people, communication and technologies', *Information, Communication and Society*, 5 (4): 494–512.

Henn, M., Weinstein, M. and Wring, D. (2002) 'A generation apart? Youth and political participation in Britain', *British Journal of Politics and International Relations*, 4 (2): 167–92.

Hey, V. (2005) 'Social logics of sociality and survival', *Sociology*, 39 (5): 855–72.

HM Government (1998) *Tackling drugs to build a better Britain: the government's 10-year strategy for tackling drugs misuse*, London: The Stationery Office.

Hobbs, D. (2005) 'Gluttony. 'Binge drinking' and the binge economy', in I. Stewart and R. Vaitilingam (eds), *Seven deadly sins*, pp. 24–7. Swindon: Economic and Social Research Council.

Hobbs, S., Lindsay, S. and McKechnie, J. (1996) 'The extent of child employment in Britain', *British Journal of Education and Work*, 9 (1): 5–18.

Hochschild, A.R. (1983) *The managed heart: commercialization of human feeling*, Berkeley, CA: University of California Press.

Holland, J., Ramazanoglu, C., Sharpe, S., and Thomson, R. (1998/2004) *The male in the head: young people, heterosexuality and power*, London: the Tufnell Press.

Holland, J., Thomson, R., Henderson, S., McGrellis, S. and Sharpe, S. (2000) 'Catching on, wising up and learning from your mistakes: young people's accounts of moral development', *The International Journal of Children's Rights*, 8: 271–94.

Holmes, M. (2004) 'The precariousness of choice in the new sentimental order: a response to Bawin Legros', *Current Sociology*, 52 (2): 251–57.

Honneth, A. (1995) *The struggle for recognition: the moral grammar of social conflicts*, Cambridge: Polity.

Humphrey, R. (1993) 'Life stories and social careers: ageing and social life in an ex-mining town', *Sociology*, 27 (1): 166–78.

Husain, S. (1995) *Cutting crime in rural areas: a practical guide for parish councils*, Swindon: Crime Concern.

Irwin, S. (1995) *Rights of passage: social change and the transition from youth to adulthood*, London: UCL Press.

Irwin, S. (1999) *Reproductive regimes: gender, generation and changing patterns of fertility*, Working Paper 16, Leeds: Centre for Research on Family, Kinship and Childhood.

Irwin, S. and Bottero, W. (2000) 'Market returns? Gender and theories of change in employment relations', *British Journal of Sociology*, 51 (2): 261–80.

James, A. and Prout, A. (eds) (1990) *Constructing and reconstructing childhood*, London: Falmer.

James, A., Jenks, C., and Prout, A. (1998) *Theorising childhood*, Cambridge: Polity.

Jamieson, L. (1998) *Intimacy: personal relationships in modern societies*, Cambridge: Polity.

Jamieson, L. (2000) 'Migration, place and class: youth in a rural area', *Sociological Review*, 48 (2): 203–23.

Jarman, N. (2005) 'Teenage kicks: young women and their involvement in violence and disorderly behaviour', *Child Care in Practice*, 11 (3): 341–56.

Johnston, L., MacDonald, R., Mason, P., Ridley, L. and Webster, C. (2000) *Snakes and ladders: young people, transitions and social exclusion*, Bristol: Policy Press.

Jones, G. (1995) *Leaving home*, Buckingham: Open University Press.

Jones, G. (2000a) 'Trail-blazers and path-followers: social reproduction and geographical mobility in youth', in S. Arber, and C. Attias-Donfut (eds), *The myth of generational conflict: family and state in ageing societies*, pp. 154–73. London: Routledge.

Jones, G. (2000b) 'Experimenting with households and inventing "home"', *International Social Science Journal*, 52 (2): 183–94.

Jones, G. (2002) *The youth divide: diverging paths to adulthood*, York: YPS for the Joseph Rowntree Foundation.

Jones, G. (2005) *Thinking and behaviour of young adults 16–25: a review*, Annex A, 'Young Adults with Complex Needs', London: Social Exclusion Unit, ODPM.

Jones, G. and Bell, R. (2000) *Balancing acts: youth, parenting and public policy*, York: York Publishing Services for Joseph Rowntree Foundation.

Jones, G., O'Sullivan, A. and Rouse, J. (2005) 'Young adults, partners and parents: individual agency and the problems of support'. Paper presented at Time, Space and Family Practices: A Dialogic Conference (British Sociological Association Families Study Group), Management Centre, Keele University, 14–15 January.

Jones, G. and Wallace, C. (1992) *Youth, family and citizenship*, Buckingham: Open University Press.

Kasesniemi, E. and Rautiainen, P. (2000) 'Mobile culture of Finnish teenagers'. Paper presented at Nordic Youth Research Symposium, University of Helsinki, June.

Kenyon, E. (2003) 'Young adults' household formation: individualization, identity and home', in G. Allan, and G. Jones (eds), *Social relations and the life course*, pp. 103–9. London: Palgrave.

Kimberlee, R. (2002) 'Why don't British young people vote at general elections?' *Journal of Youth Studies*, 5 (1): 85–98.

Kohn, M. (1997) 'The chemical generation and its ancestors: dance crazes and drug panics across eight decades', *International Journal of Drug Policy*, 8 (3): 137–42.

Kovalainen, A. (2004) 'Rethinking the revival of social capital and trust in social theory: possibilities for feminist analyses of social capital and trust', in B.L. Marshall and A.Witz (eds), *Engendering the social: feminist encounters with social theory*, pp. 155–70. Maidenhead and New York: Open University Press.

Kroger, J. (1996) *Identity in adolescence: the balance between self and other* (2nd edn), London: Routledge.

Lahelma, E. and Gordon, T. (2003) 'Home as a physical, social and mental space: young people's reflections on moving from home', *Journal of Youth Studies*, 6 (4): 377–90.

Laub, J. and Sampson, R. (2003) *Shared beginnings, divergent lives: delinquent boys to aged 70*, Cambridge, MA: Harvard University Press.

Lees, S. (1986) *Losing out: sexuality and adolescent girls*, London: Hutchinson.

Lees, S. (1999) 'Will boys be left on the shelf?', in G. Jagger and C. Wright (eds), *Changing family values*, pp. 59–76. London: Routledge.

Leichty, M. (1995) 'Media, markets and modernization: youth identities and the experience of modernity in Kathmandu, Nepal' in V. Amit-Talai and H. Wulff (eds), *Youth cultures: cross cultural perspectives*, pp. 166–201. London: Routledge.

Leonard, M. (2004) 'Bonding and bridging social capital: reflections from Belfast', *Sociology*, 38 (5): 927–44.

Levitt, M. (2003) 'Where are the men and the boys? The gender imbalance in the Church of England', *Journal of Contemporary Religion*, 18 (1): 61–75.

Levy, A. and Scott-Clark, C. (2004) 'Under the influence', *The Guardian*, 20 November, available: http://society.guardian.co.uk/drugsandalcohol/story/0,850,1354741,00.html (accessed May 2006).

Lincoln, S. (2000) 'Teenage girls 'bedroom culture' and the concept of zoning in socio-spatial configuration'. Paper presented at BSA youth study group conference Research Youth: Issues, Controversies and Dilemmas, University of Surrey, 12 July.

Ling, R. (2000) '"We will be reached": the use of mobile telephony among Norwegian youth', *Information Technology and People*, 13 (2): 102–20.

Lister, R., Middleton, S., Vincent, J. and Cox, L. (2003) *Negotiating transitions to citizenship: research briefing*, available: http://www.tsa.uk.com (accessed March 2006).

Lury, C. (2003) 'The game of loyalt(o)y: diversions and divisions in network society, *Sociological Review*, 51 (3): 301–20.

MacDonald, R. and Marsh, J. (2001) 'Disconnected youth?', *Journal of Youth Studies*, 4 (4): 373–91.

MacDonald, R. and Marsh, J. (2002) 'Crossing the rubicon: youth transitions, poverty, drugs and social exclusion', *International Journal of Drug Policy*, 13 (1): 27–38.

MacDonald, R. and Marsh, J. (2005) *Disconnected youth? Growing up in Britain's poor neighbourhoods*, Basingstoke: Palgrave.

MacDonald, R., Shildrick, T., Webster, C. and Simpson, D. (2005) 'Growing up in poor neighbourhoods: the significance of class and place in the extended transitions of 'socially excluded' young adults', *Sociology,* 39 (5): 873–91.

Machin, S. (2003) 'Unto them that hath', *CentrePiece*, 5–9, available from http://cep.lse.ac.uk/centrepiece/v08i1/machin.pdf (accessed March 2006).

Machin, S. and Blanden, J. (2004) 'Educational inequality and the expansion of UK higher education', *Scottish Journal of Political Economy*, 51: 230–49.

MacNamee, S. (1998) 'Youth, gender and video games: power and control in the home', in T. Skelton and G. Valentine (eds), *Cool places: geographies of youth culture*, pp. 195–206. London: Routledge.

MacNamee, S., Valentine, G., Skelton, T., and Butler, R. (2003) 'Negotiating difference: lesbian and gay transitions to adulthood', in G. Allan and G. Jones (eds), *Social relations and the lifecourse*, pp. 120–34. Basingstoke: Palgrave Macmillan.

Madigan, R., Munro, M. and Smith, S.J. (1990) 'Gender and the meaning of the home', *International Journal of Urban and Regional Research*, 14 (4): 625–47.

Mallett, S. (2004) 'Understanding home: a critical review of the literature', *Sociological Review*, 52 (1) 62–89.

Manceron, V. (1997) 'Get, connected! Social uses of the telephone and modes of interaction in a group of young Parisians', in A. Kant and E. Mate-Meijer (eds), *Blurring boundaries: when are information communication technologies coming home?* pp. 171–82. Stockholm: Nostedts.

Mandlebaum, D.G. (1973) 'The study of life history: Gandhi', *Current Anthropology,* 14 (3): 177–93.

Mason, J. (2004) 'Personal narratives, relational selves: residential histories in the living and telling', *The Sociological Review,* 52 (2): 162–79.

Massey, D. (1993) 'Power geometry and a progressive sense of place', in J. Bird, B. Curtis, T. Putnam, G. Robertson and L. Tickner (eds), *Mapping the futures: local cultures, global change*, pp. 50–69. London: Routledge.

Massey, Doreen. (1994) *Space, place and gender*, Cambridge: Polity.

McDermott, E. and Graham, H. (2005) 'Resilient young mothering: social inequalities, late modernity and the 'problem' of 'teenage' motherhood', *Journal of Youth Studies*, 8 (1): 59–60.

McGrellis, S. (2004) *Pushing the boundaries in Northern Ireland: young people, violence and sectarianism.* Families and Social Capital ESRC Research Group Working Paper No. 8, London: London South Bank University.

McGrellis, S. (2005a) 'Pure and bitter spaces: gender, identity and territory in Northern Irish youth transitions', *Gender and Education*, 17 (5): 515–29.

McGrellis, S. (2005b) 'Pushing the boundaries in Northern Ireland: young people, violence and sectarianism', *Contemporary Politics*, 11 (1): 53–71.

McGrellis, S., Henderson, S., Holland, J., Sharpe, S. and Thomson, R. (2000) *Through the moral maze: a quantitative study of young people's values*, London: the Tufnell Press.

McLeod, J and Yates, L. (2006) *Making modern lives: subjectivity, schooling and social change*, Albany, NY: SUNY Press.

McNiece, R., Bidgood, P., and Soan, P. (2004) 'An investigation into using national longitudinal studies to examine trends in educational attainment and development', *Educational Research*, 46 (2): 119–36.

McRobbie, A. (1980) 'Settling accounts with subcultures: a feminist critique', *Screen Education*, 34: 37–49.

McRobbie, A. (1991) *Feminism and youth culture: from 'Jackie' to 'Just Seventeen'*, Basingstoke, Macmillan Press.

McRobbie, A. (1994) *Postmodernism and popular culture*, London: Sage.

MDA (Mobile Data Association) (2003) report available from Media Centre: http://www.text.it/mediacentre/default.asp?intPageId=607 (accessed January 2006).

Measham, F. (1996) 'The 'big bang' approach to sessional drinking: changing patterns of alcohol consumption amongst young people in North West England', *Addiction Research*, 4 (3): 283–99.

Measham, F. (2002) '"Doing gender"– "doing drugs": conceptualising the gendering of drugs cultures', *Contemporary Drug Problems*, Summer: 335–73.

Measham, F. (2004a) 'Play space: historical and socio-cultural reflections on drugs, licensed leisure locations, commercialisation and control', *International Journal of Drug Policy*, 15: 337–45.

Measham, F. (2004b) 'The decline of ecstasy, the rise of 'binge' drinking and the persistence of pleasure', *The Journal of Community and Criminal Justice*, 51 (4): 309–26.

Measham, F., Parker, H. and Aldridge, J. (1998a) 'The teenage transition: from adolescent recreational drug use to the young adult dance culture in Britain in the mid-90s', *Journal of Drug Issues*, 22 (1): 9–32.

Measham, F., Parker, H. and Aldridge, J. (1998b) *Starting, switching, slowing and stopping*, Home Office Drugs Prevention Initiative Green Series Paper 21, London: Home Office.

Measham, F., Aldridge, J. and Parker, H. (2000) *Dancing with drugs: risk, health and hedonism in the British club scene*, London: Free Association Books.

Melrose, M. (2000) *Fixing it? Young people, drugs and disadvantage*, Lyme Regis: Russell House Publishing.

Meltzer, H. and Gatward, R. with Goodman, R. and Ford, T. (2000) *The mental health of children and adolescents in Great Britain: the report of a survey carried out in 1999 by the Social Survey Division of the Office for National Statistics on behalf of the Department of Health, the Scottish Health Executive and the National Assembly of Wales*, London: The Stationery Office.

Mental Health Foundation (1999) *Bright futures: promoting children and young people's mental health*, London: The Mental Health Foundation.

Mental Health Foundation (2003) http://www.mentalhealth.org.uk (accessed March 2006).

Mental Health Foundation (2005) *Child and adolescent mental health: understanding the lifetime impacts*, London: The Mental Health Foundation.

Metcalf, H. (1997) *Class and higher education: the participation of young people from lower social classes*, London: CIHE in conjunction with PSI.

Middleton, N., Gunnell, D., Frankel, S., Whitley, E. and Dorling, D. (2003) 'Urban-rural differences in suicide trends in young adults: England and Wales, 1981–1998', *Social Science and Medicine*, 57: 1183–94.

Miles, S., Cliff, D. and Burr, V. (1998) 'Fitting in and sticking out: consumption, consumer meanings and the construction of young people's identities', *Journal of Youth Studies*, 1 (1): 81–96.

Miller, D. (1992) 'The young and the restless in Trinidad: a case of the local and global in mass consumption', in R. Silverstone and E. Hirsch (eds), *Consuming technologies: media and information in domestic spaces*, pp. 163–82. London: Routledge.

Millham, S., Bullock, R. and Hosie, K. (1978) *Locking up children*, Farnborough: Saxon House.

Mizen, P. (2004) *The changing state of youth*, Houndmills: Palgrave.

Mizen, P., Pole, C. and Bolton, A. (1999) 'School age workers, the paid employment of children in Britain', *Work, Employment and Society*, 13 (3): 423–38.

Mizen, P., Pole, C. and Bolton, A. (2001) 'Why be a school age worker?', in P. Mizen, C. Pole and A. Bolton (eds), *Hidden hands: international perspectives on children's work and labour*, pp. 37–54. The Future of Childhood Series, London: RoutledgeFalmer.

Modood, T. (2005) 'A defence of multi-culturalism', *Soundings*, 29: 62–71.

Modood, T. and Acland, T. (1998) 'Conclusion', in T. Modood and T. Acland (eds), *Race and higher education*, pp. 158–73, London: Policy Studies Institute.

Moran, L. and Skeggs, B., with Tyrer, P. and Corteen, K. (2003) *Sexuality and the politics of violence and safety*, London: Routledge.

Morris, L. (1994) *Dangerous classes*, London: Routledge.

Morrow, V. and Richards, M. (1996) *Transitions to adulthood: a family matter?* York: Joseph Rowntree Foundation.

Murji, K. (1998) 'The agony and the ecstasy: drugs, media and morality', in R. Coomber (ed.), *The control of drugs and drug users: reason or reaction?*, pp. 69–86. Amsterdam: Harwood Academic Publishers.

Murtagh, B. (2003) 'Territoriality, research and policy making in Northern Ireland', in O. Hargie and D. Dickson (eds), *Researching the Troubles: social science perspectives on the Northern Ireland conflict*, pp. 209–25. Edinburgh and London: Mainstream Publishing.

National Statistics Census (2001), available: http://www.statistics.gov.uk/census/ (accessed December 2005).

National Statistics Online (2005) available: http://www.statistics.gov.uk (accessed January 2006).

Nayak, A. (2003) *Race, place and globalization: youth cultures in a changing world*, Oxford: Berg.

Newcombe, R. (1991) *Raving and dance drugs: house music, clubs and parties in the North West of England*, Liverpool: Rave Research Bureau.

Nicholas, S., Povey, D., Walker, A. and Kershaw, C. (2005) *Crime in England and Wales, Home Office Statistical Bulletin 2004/2005*, London: Research Development and Statistical Directorate.

Nilsen, A. (1999) 'Where is the future? Time and space as categories in young people's images of the future', *Innovation, European Journal of the Social Sciences*, 12 (2): 175–94.

Nilsen, A. and Brannen, J. (2002) 'Theorising the individual-structure dynamic', in J. Brannen, S. Lewis, A. Nilsen and J. Smithson (eds), *Young Europeans, work and family: futures in transition*, pp. 30–47. London: Routledge.

Norris, P. and Inglehart, R. (2004) *Sacred and secular: religion and politics worldwide*, Cambridge, Cambridge University Press.

Northern Ireland Young Life and Times Survey (2004) Queens University Belfast, available: http://www.ark.ac.uk/ylt (accessed October 2005).

Oakley, A. (1996) 'Gender matters: man the hunter', in H. Roberts and D. Sachdev (eds), *Young people's social attitudes: having their say, the views of 12–19 year olds*, pp. 23–43. London: Barnados.

O'Donnell, M. and Sharpe, S. (2000) *Uncertain masculinities: youth, ethnicity and class in contemporary Britain*, London: Routledge.

Olohan, S. (2004) 'Student mental health: a university challenge?', *The Psychologist*, 17 (4): 192–5.

ONS (Office for National Statistics) (2004) *National Statistics Omnibus Survey*, October 2004, available: http://statistics.gov.uk (accessed May 2005).

ONS (Office for National Statistics) (2006) *National Statistics Omnibus Survey*, January 2006, available: http://statistics.gov.uk (accessed May 2006).

Pahl, J. and Pahl, R. (1971) *Managers and their wives*, Harmondsworth: Penguin.

Pain, R. (1993) 'Women's fear of sexual violence: explaining the spatial paradox', in H. Jones (ed.), *Crime and the urban environment*, pp. 55–68. Avebury, Aldershot.

Pain, R. (1997) 'Social geographies of women's fear of crime', *Transactions of the Institute of British Geographers*, 22 (2): 231–44.

Parker, H., Aldridge, J. and Measham, F. (1998) *Illegal leisure: the normalization of adolescent recreational drug use*, London: Routledge.

Paterson, L. (2001) 'Education and inequality in Britain'. Paper prepared for the social policy section at the annual meeting of the British Association for the Advancement of Science, Glasgow, March.

Pavis, S., Cunningham-Burley, S. and Amos, A. (1998) 'Health related behavioural change in context: young people in transition', *Social Science and Medicine*, 47 (10): 1407–18.

Pearson, G. (1983) *Hooligan: a history of respectable fears*, Basingstoke: Macmillan.

Pettinger, L., Taylor, R., Parry, J. and Glucksmann, M. (eds) (2005) *A new sociology of work?* Oxford: Blackwell.

Pilkington, H. and Johnson. R. (2003) 'Peripheral youth: relations of identity and power in global/local context', *European Journal of Cultural Studies*, 6 (3): 259–83.

Pini, M. (2001) *Club culture and female sexuality,* London: Palgrave.

Platt, L. (2005) *Migration and social mobility the life chances of Britain's minority ethnic communities*, Bristol: Policy Press for JRF.

Plumridge, L. and Thomson, R. (2003) 'Longitudinal qualitative studies and the reflexive self', *International Journal of Social Research Methodology*, 6 (3): 213–22.

Presdee, M. (2000) *Cultural criminology and the carnival of crime*, London: Routledge.

Putnam, R.D. (1993) *Making democracy work: civic traditions in modern Italy*, Princeton, NJ: Princeton University Press.

Putnam, R.D. (1998) 'Foreword', *Housing Policy Debate*, 9 (1): v–viii.

Putnam, R.D. (2000) *Bowling alone: the collapse and revival of American community*, New York: Simon and Schuster.

Raffo, C. and Reeves, M. (2000) 'Youth transitions and social exclusion: developments in social capital theory', *Journal of Youth Studies*, 3 (2): 147–66.

Rana, R., Smith, E. and Walkling, J. (1999) *Degrees of disturbance: the new agenda. The impact of increasing levels of psychological disturbance amongst students in higher education*, Warwickshire: British Association for Counselling.

Raven, C. (2001) 'The safe and predictable world of drugs', *The Guardian,* 10 July: 5.

Reay, D. and Lucey, H. (2000) '"I don't really like it here but I don't want to be anywhere else": children and inner city council estates' *Antipode*, 34 (4): 410–28.

Reay, D., David, M.E., and Ball, S.J. (2005) *Degrees of choice: social class, race and gender in higher education*, Stoke on Trent: Trentham Books.

Reay, D., Davies, J., David, M. and Ball, S.J. (2001) 'Choices of degree or degrees of choice? Class, race and the higher education choice process', *Sociology,* 35 (4): 855–74.

Reilly, J., Byrne, C. and Muldoon, O.T. (2004) 'Young men as victims and perpetrators of violence in Northern Ireland: a qualitative analysis', *Journal of Social Issues*, 60: 469–85.

Reimer, B. (1995) 'The media in public and private spheres', in J. Fornas and G. Bolin (eds), *Youth culture in late modernity*, pp. 58–71. London: Sage.

Reynolds, T. (2004) *Families, social capital and Caribbean young people's diasporic identities*, Families & Social Capital ESRC Research Group, Working Paper No. 11, London: London South Bank University, available: http://www.lsbu.ac.uk/families (accessed March 2006).

Reynolds, T. (2005) *Caribbean mothers: identity and experience in the UK*, London: the Tufnell Press.

Ribbens McCarthy, J. (2006) *Young people's experiences of loss and bereavement: towards an interdisciplinary approach*, Buckingham: Open University Press.

Ribbens McCarthy, J. with Jessop, J. (2005) *Young people, bereavement and loss: disruptive transitions*, London: National Children's Bureau.

Robbins, Lord (Chairman) (1963) *Higher education: report of the committee appointed by the Prime Minister under the chairmanship of Lord Robbins 1961–1963*, Cmnd 2154, London: HMSO.

Roberts, K. (1995) *Youth and employment in modern Britain*, Oxford: Oxford University Press.

Roker, D. and Eden, K. (2003) *Young people's involvement in social action: research briefing*, available: http://www.tsa.uk.com (accessed June 2003).

Rutter, M. and Smith, D.J. (1995) *Psychosocial disorders in young people: time trends and their causes*, London: Wiley.

Sanders, B. (2005) *Youth crime and youth culture in the inner city*, London: Routledge.

Sansone, L. (1997) 'The new blacks from Bahia: local and global in Afro-Bahia', *Identities*, 3 (4): 457–93.

Savage, M. (2000) *Class analysis and social transformation*, Oxford: Oxford University Press.

Savage, M., Li, Y. and Tampubolon, G. (2007) 'Rethinking the politics of social capital: challenging Tocquevillian perspectives', in R. Edwards, J. Franklin and H. Holland (eds), *Assessing social capital: concepts, policy and practice*, Cambridge: Cambridge Scholars Press.

Schoon, I., McCulloch, A., Joshi, H., Wiggins, D. and Bynner, J. (2001) 'Transitions from school to work in a changing social context', *Young: Journal of Nordic Youth Research*, 9 (1): 4–22.

Schutz, A. (1982) *Life forms and meaning structure*, trans. H. Wagner, London: Routledge and Kegan Paul.

Seaman, P., Turner, K., Hill, M., Stafford, A. and Walker, M. (2006) *Parenting and children's resilience in disadvantaged communities*, London: NCB for JRF.

Sellars, A. (1998) 'The influence of dance music on the UK youth tourism market', *Tourist Management*, 19: 611–15.

Sharpe, S. (1994) *Just like a girl: how girls learn to be women*, London: Penguin.

Sharpe, S. (2001) *More than just a piece of paper? Young people's views on marriage and relationships*, London: National Children's Bureau.

Sharpe, S. (2004) *From fear to respect: young people's views on violence*, London: National Children's Bureau.

Sharpe, S. and Thomson, R. (2005) *All you need is love: the morality of sexual relationships through the eyes of young people*, London: National Children's Bureau.

Shiner, M. and Newburn, T. (1997) 'Definitely, maybe not: the normalisation of recreational drug use amongst young people', *Sociology*, 31 (30): 1–19.

Shore, H. (2000) 'The idea of juvenile crime in 19th century England', *History Today*, 50 (6): 21–7.

Sibley, D. (1995) *Geographies of exclusion: society and difference in the West*, London: Routledge.

Silcott, M. (2000) 'Superclubs and the mainstreaming of E culture', in Push and M. Silcott (eds), *The Book of E*, pp. 184–8. London: Omnibus.

Simpson, L. (2004) 'Statistics of racial segregation: measure, evidence and policy', *Urban Studies*, 41 (3): 661–81.

Skeggs, B. (1997) *Formations of class and gender: becoming respectable*, London: Sage.

Skeggs, B. (2004) *Class, self, culture*, London: Routledge.

Smith, D. (2004) *The links between victimisation and offending*, No. 5, Edinburgh Study of Youth Transitions and Crime, Centre for Law and Society, Edinburgh: University of Edinburgh, available: http://www.scotland.gov.uk (accessed February 2006).

Smyth, M. (1998) *Half the battle: understanding the impact of the troubles on children and young people*, Derry/Londonderry: INCORE, University of Ulster.

Somerville, P. (1997) 'The social construction of home', *Journal of Architectural and Planning Research*, 14 (3): 226–45.

South N. (1999) *Debating drugs and everyday life: normalisation, prohibition and 'otherness'*, in N. South (ed.), *Drugs: cultures, controls and everyday life*, pp. 1–16. London: Sage.

Spurling, L. (2004) *An Introduction to psychodynamic counselling*, New York: Palgrave Macmillan.

Stewart, F.J. (1999) 'Femininities in flux? Young women, heterosexuality and (safe) sex', *Sexualities*, 2 (3): 275–90.

Stoble, I. (2000) *Mobile phones come out on top*, available: http://www.vnunet.com (accessed 11 May 2006).

Sweeting, H., West, P. and Richard, M. (1998) 'Teenage family life, lifestyles and life chances: associations with family structure, conflict with parents, and joint family activity', *International Journal of Law, Policy and the Family*, 12 (1): 15–46.

Tempest, M. (2005) 'Blair pledges crackdown on yobs', *Guardian Unlimited*, 12 May, available: http://www.guardian.co.uk (accessed October 2005).

Thomson, I. (2005) 'The UK now has more mobiles than people', *IT week*, May, available: http://www.itweek.co.uk/vnunet/news/2127294/uk-mobiles-people (accessed December 2005).

Thomson, R. (2000) 'Dream on: the logic of sexual practice, *Journal of Youth Studies*, 4 (4): 407–27.

Thomson, R. (2004) 'Tradition and innovation: case histories of changing gender identities'. Unpublished PhD, London: London South Bank University.

Thomson, R. and Holland, J. (2002) 'Imagining adulthood: resources, plans and contradictions', *Gender and Education*, 14 (4): 337–50.

Thomson, R. and Holland, J. (2003) 'Hindsight, foresight and insight: the challenges of longitudinal qualitative research', *International Journal of Social Research Methodology, Theory and Practice*, 6 (3): 233–44.

Thomson, R., Bell, R., Henderson, S., Holland, S., McGrellis, S. and Sharpe, S. (2002) 'Critical moments: choice, chance and opportunity in young people's narratives of transition to adulthood', *Sociology*, 6 (2): 335–54.

Thomson, R., Holland, J., McGrellis, S., Bell, R., Henderson, S. and Sharpe, S. (2004) 'Inventing adulthoods: a biographical approach to understanding youth citizenship', *The Sociological Review*, 52 (2): 218–39.

Thornton, S. (1995) *Club cultures: music, media and subcultural capital*, Cambridge: Polity.

Thrift, N. (1998) 'Virtual capitalism: the globalization of reflexive business knowledge', in J. Carrier and D. Miller (eds), *Virtualism: a new political economy*, pp. 161–86. Oxford: Berg.

Tolonen, T. (2005) 'Locality and gendered capital of working-class youth', *Young: Nordic Journal of Youth Research*, 13 (4): 343–62.

Tully, C. (2002) 'Youth in motion: communicative and mobile. A commentary from the perspective of youth sociology', *Young: Nordic Journal of Youth Research*, 10 (2): 19–43.

Turner, B. (1999) *Ibiza*, London: Ebury Press.

Turner, K. (2004) 'Young women's views on teenage motherhood: a possible explanation for the relationship between socio-economic background and teenage pregnancy outcome?' *Journal of Youth Studies*, 7 (2): 221–38.

Urry, J. (2000) 'Mobile sociology', *British Journal of Sociology*, 51(1): 185–203.

Vickerstaff, S. (2003) 'Apprenticeship in the 'golden age': were youth transitions really smooth and unproblematic back then?' *Work, Employment and Society*, 17 (2): 269–87.

Voss, D. and Crockett, A. (2005) 'Religion in Britain: neither believing nor belonging', *Sociology*, 39 (1): 11–28.

Wadsworth, M.E.J. (1991) *The imprint of time, childhood, history and adult life*, Oxford: Clarendon Press.

Walkerdine, V., Lucey, H. and Melody, J. (2001) *Growing up girl: psychosocial explorations of gender and class*, Basingstoke: Palgrave.

Walkerdine, V., Lucey, H. and Melody, J. (2002) 'Subjectivity and qualitative method', in T. May (ed.), *Qualitative research in action*, pp. 179–96. London: Sage.

Wardhaugh, J. (1999) 'The unaccommodated woman: home, homelessness and identity', *Sociological Review*, 47 (1): 91–109.

Webster, C. (2003) 'Race, space and fear, imagined geographies of racism, crime, violence and disorder in North England', *Capital and Class*, 80, Summer: 95–122.

Webster, C., Simpson, D., MacDonald, R., Abbas, A., Cieslik, M., Shildrick, T. and Simpson, M. (2004) *Poor transitions: social exclusion and young adults*, Bristol: Policy Press.

Weeks, J., Donovan, C. and Heaphy, B. (2001) *Same sex intimacies: families of choice and other life experiments*, London: Routledge.

West, P. and Sweeting, H. (1996) 'Nae job, nae future: young people and health in a context of unemployment', *Health and Social Care in the Community*, 4 (1): 50–62.

Williams, R. (1976) *Keywords*, Oxford: Oxford University Press.

Willis, P. (1977) *Learning to labour: why working class kids get working class jobs*, Farnborough: Saxon House.

Young, J.E. (1999) *Cognitive therapy for personality disorders: a schema focused approach*, Sarasota: Professional Resource Press.

Young, M. and Willmott, P. (1957) *Family and kinship in East London*, London: Routledge and Kegan Paul.

Zadvorny, A. and Bond, K. (2005) *The western European mobile market: trends and forecasts 2005–2010* (6th edn), April, available: http://research,analysys.com/default.asp?mode=products. asp (accessed January 2005).

Zerubavel, E. (2003) *Time maps: collective memory and the social shape of the past*, Chicago: University of Chicago Press.

Index